Also by Molly O'Neill

The New York Cookbook
A Well-Seasoned Appetite
The Pleasure of Your Company

Mostly True

*A Memoir of Family, Food,
and Baseball*

Molly O'Neill

SCRIBNER

New York   London   Toronto   Sydney

SCRIBNER
1230 Avenue of the Americas
New York, NY 10020

SCRIBNER and design are trademarks of Macmillan Library Reference USA, Inc.,
used under license by Simon & Schuster, the publisher of this work.

For information about special discounts for bulk purchases,
please contact Simon & Schuster Special Sales:
1-800-456-6798 or business@simonandschuster.com

DESIGNED BY ERICH HOBBING

Text set in Adobe Garamond

Manufactured in the United States of America

1   3   5   7   9   10   8   6   4   2

Library of Congress Cataloging-in-Publication Data
O'Neill, Molly.
Mostly true : a memoir of family, food, and baseball / Molly O'Neill.
p. cm.
1. O'Neill, Molly. 2. Women food writers—United States—Biography.
I. Title.
TX649.O54A3 2006
641.3'092—dc22
[B]   2006042202

ISBN-13: 978-0-7432-3268-5
ISBN-10: 0-7432-3268-2

To my parents
with admiration, gratitude, and love

Strong hope is a much greater stimulant of life
than any realized joy could be.
—NIETZSCHE

Mostly True

We Would Be Heroes

Every one of my five brothers was bred to play ball. For a long time it wasn't clear which of the boys would make it to the major leagues, but we had no doubt that The One was among us. We were the chosen. I do not recall a single moment of my childhood in which I was not imagining my family's life—or my own—as an epic tale.

I kept a journal from the time I was seven years old. Across the thousands of pages, my handwriting changed—the wobbly print gave way first to a bloated cursive and then to a careful combination of print and script—but my purpose was unflagging. I was determined to redeem us, to save us not only from ourselves but also from the terrible possibility of being ordinary.

For their part, my family trusted me to write poignant and glowing accounts of its adventures and exploits. Knowing that our days would certainly be distilled into a heroic portrait of a certain America was a grave responsibility. My brothers, therefore, did not have time to worry about little things like social conventions or rules. They lived on an elevated plane, and their faith in future fame was absolute.

Before they were old enough to seriously practice the game, they spent hours in our backyard in Columbus, Ohio, tirelessly preparing themselves for the sound of the fans going wild. *"Ahhhhhhh!"* they'd gasp, bowing their heads, clenching their fists and stretching their arms straight up toward heaven. *"Aaaaaa haaaaaa haaaaaaaaaa."*

To create the sound of the fans going wild, they pushed hot air from their diaphragms up into the backs of their throats; then they added the sort of hacking that might signal the expulsion of a large blob of phlegm. Finally, they exhaled. The raspy, wheezing result approximated the distant roar of fans behind Red Barber's voice on the radio.

These public broadcasts contributed to our neighbors' ongoing exasperation. My brothers, however, were not concerned. Day after day, they created a piece of performance art in which they were, simultaneously, the fans going wild, the player being honored, and the announcer describing the scene.

With no apparent provocation, the sound of fans would erupt from various points in the backyard.

"Yeahhhhhhhhh," said the swing set.

"Haaaaaa aaaaa aaaa," said the whirligig.

"What could they be *doing* over there?" said the neighbor.

"Molly, can't you keep them quiet?" yelled our mother.

"Please, you guys," I pleaded.

But the fans could not be silenced by then, for the players had abandoned their positions and were stumbling toward the center of the yard. Their heads were down. Their mouths were open. Their eyes were squeezed shut. Their faces were wrinkled as if each were pushing a particularly challenging bowel movement. They collided, hugging and jumping on one another. They were falling together like ecstatic converts leveled by the spirit. They were a writhing pile of victory. And the fans were going wild.

"Aaaaaaaahhhhh!"

Bark-cloth curtains rattled on their plastic rings throughout the neighborhood: "Everything OK over there?" Screen doors screeched open—"Can you keep it down?"—and slammed shut. Babies awoke howling from their naps and the anguished voices of other people's mothers rose like thistles under our bare summer feet.

"Does anybody even keep an eye on those kids?"

But my brothers then rose from the pile of magnificent winners to become a team of commentators. They raced to the giant spruce in our front yard and scrambled up its branches. The tree was their radio tower. Each was determined to be the first to air the news. The spruce swayed precariously beneath the breathy wail of their broadcast. Boughs snapped. The trunk creaked. Dried needles showered down like ticker tape.

"Did you see that! I'm telling ya, that O'Neill! What a shot!"

"He had some wood on that one, O'Neill did! Heck, I don't think it's landed yet!"

"What a hitter! O'Neill won the ball game! He won the Series!"

It happened every afternoon. It was so embarrassing. They were so pathetic.

"My God, Molly, can you quiet them down?" My mother was inside nursing the baby but with each word—"All I'm asking for is a moment's *peace*!"—she was gathering a head of steam and getting closer to the window. "For-heaven's-sake-Molly-they're-breaking-the-pine-tree-what-in-the-name-of-God-is-the-matter-with-you-get-them-out-of-there-oh-my-God-one-of-them-is-falling-get-him-*Je*-sus-Chrrrr-*ist*-is-there-no-end-to-this?"

There *was* no end to it. And so, in the summer of 1962, I tried a different beginning. "I'm adopted," I told my friends. "You know Anastasia, the youngest daughter of the czar, remember, that story in *My Weekly Reader*? That's my real mother. But don't tell anybody," I would add solemnly. "Otherwise, people might think I'm a communist."

My real brothers were princes who rode white steeds through snowy forests and defended my honor with gleaming lances, not these small serfs wielding fat red plastic bats on the patch of grass behind a modest suburban house in the Midwest. No wonder I didn't care about baseball: I was Russian!

I cultivated the habit of checking for my crown—just to make sure that I wasn't wearing it in public by mistake and drawing attention to myself. Pat, pat, pat, pat. Using index and middle fingers, I would touch four spots in a circle around the top of my head.

"What in the name of God is the matter with you?" said my (supposed) mother. "Have you lost your mind?"

I took great comfort in my secret and superior station in life, but my royal status also had unforeseen consequences: the more I became Anastasia's daughter, the more keenly I suffered the pain of being deprived of a family who understood me. Then one evening Walter Cronkite mentioned Russia on the news. "What the heck?" said my (supposed) father as I rushed out the front door sobbing and trying to rend my garments.

As I came around the corner of the house, I saw that my mother had abandoned the dishes and was standing on the back stoop, waiting for my maniacal circuit to return me to our yard. I swerved to avoid her and headed for the maple tree. I flung my arms around its trunk and then, in what I hoped was heartbreaking desperation, began to wail.

"Now this is ab-so-*lute*-ly reee-*dic*-ulous," said my mother.

As she strode toward me, the low heels of her straw sandals creaking through the grass, I realized that it was time to tell my (supposed) mother who I really was. I braced myself to make the confession, but then, as she bent close to my ear, the smell of her lipstick—Firecracker by Revlon—erased my words.

"You are going to stop this right now and come in and help me dry the dishes. I mean it, Molly. Right now. Do you hear me?"

Meekly, I followed her back to the kitchen, took up a clammy linen tea towel embroidered with small chickens, and began drying the Boontonware plates. Somewhere between the salad plates and the dessert plates I realized that the daughter of the dead czarina didn't have the right stuff. Only the female offspring of my parents could survive being the only female offspring of my parents. And so I reluctantly parted with this fantasy and cast about for something else to explain my embarrassment, my scorn, and the lonely sense of separateness I harbored.

"My brothers are adopted," I told my friends.

In fact, my brothers and I were born to the same parents but we were raised by different people. Our parents changed, birth by birth, as their worries and consolations expanded and contracted like an accordion, usually in concert with their cash flow. We also grew up in different worlds.

An entire decade elapsed between my reign as tetherball champ at Indian Springs Elementary and 1972, when our youngest brother, Paul, began getting ejected from playground dodgeball due to poor sportsmanship. During that decade our hometown became a city, Ohio became Kent State, and the country became, however briefly, too cool for baseball.

My brothers and I therefore have differing accounts of the years we shared, but we all imagine the same beginning. There is the sound of a bat hitting a ball, steady and easy, like a metronome. We are in our backyard on Schreyer Place in Columbus. Our ballpark. The backstop is the chipped white clapboard on the back of the garage and home plate is an agreement, a general vicinity. First base is a honeysuckle that climbs the chain-link fence that separates our yard from the one next door, second is the redbud tree, and third a massive climbing rose. It is not exactly a diamond. It's more like an isosceles triangle, with third base about halfway along the hypotenuse. But it works for games as well as for fielding practice.

Our father is hitting fly balls—*thuk, thuk*—and four of my brothers are standing like very small chess pieces in the high grass just in front of the over-grown privet hedge that marks the end of our backyard. They are spanking the new leather baseball gloves. They are saying, "Hey batta batta batta." Our father's black hair rises in stiff Elvis waves that glisten with Brylcreem. Dusk is claiming the backyard and, as he watches the flight of the balls he hits, his slightly crooked smile is incandescent.

I am standing behind home plate, just out of reach of the bat, close enough to see how the hula girls on his Hawaiian shirt twitch whenever our father steps into his long, sweeping swing. Our youngest brother is balanced against my hip, facing out toward the field. He is eighteen months old and he is writhing against my forearm, kicking my thighs. He wants to run the bases.

Thunk! The Wiffle ball sails from our father's bat. "Lookie there!" he hollers. There is wonder and delight in his voice, as if a comet were arching through the humid Ohio air over his own backyard.

"Eye on the ball," he purrs. "Eye on the ball." His voice is initially soft as he directs his sons and then, as the ball wobbles at the crest of its rise, he explodes—"Go! Go! Go!"—like a commanding officer pushing his men out the open door of a plane.

Four of my brothers race through the grass, their gloves stretched toward heaven, their faces wrinkled fiercely, the tips of their tongues emerging like so many fat red nipples from between their teeth. I put the baby down and he begins stumbling along the baseline toward first. He is so pigeon-toed that he trips over his feet, falling and picking himself up, again and again.

I used to imagine that our cheers—my clapping and cooing as the baby toddled the baselines, my other brothers' shouts—would continue to grow as we did until they finally merged with the sound of real fans going wild.

It always comes back to that.

The sound of the fans going wild is forever. It is the moment when we make up for everything we've ever done wrong, overturn all judgments against us, erase any doubt directed toward us, and ascend to our rightful position very close to the right hand of God.

The sound of the fans going wild is an eternal moment, the moment when we would be heroes.

The Fire

On November 3, 1945, five months after Victory in Europe Day and a month after Victory over Japan Day, the Gwinn Milling Company in Columbus, Ohio, caught fire. The fire alarm sounded shortly after eleven p.m., and the fire burned for three days and three nights. The burning mill signaled an end to the age of personal sacrifice, an era that began with the Great Depression and continued with the wartime shortages of butter, nylon, and gasoline. It drew larger crowds than the parades for either of the American military victories. My parents met at the fire.

I loved how they referred to it as The Fire—as if in the course of human events, there has been only one fire, and as if we, their progeny, had sprung from it. "We met at the fire," they'd say. Even as a young child, I saw them drawn inexorably toward the fire like moths, two worlds colliding and exploding to create a heroic destiny. It was so romantic! It was so mythological! It was fate!

The MGM picture *Weekend at the Waldorf* opened at the Ohio Theater on that same November evening, and my mother began dressing for her rendezvous with Van Johnson in the late afternoon. By the age of eighteen, she was an accomplished young woman, a pianist and a premed student. She was also six feet tall and had never had a date. Recently, and with increasing frequency, she would be overcome by a clammy and unspeakable fear whenever she prepared to leave the house, and her heart would start chugging like a train. She was terrified that she was either dying or finally, like her mother, losing her mind.

To safeguard against just that, my mother had been removed from her parents when she was seven years old and raised by her aunt and uncle, Mr. and Mrs. Clarence Gwinn. In addition to raising his sister's daughter, C. E. Gwinn also ran the family mill.

For most of her childhood, the Gwinns had lived in one of the big old houses on Woodlawn Avenue. By the time my mother was in high school, however, her uncle had built a mansion on Sunbury Road, just outside the city—a white clapboard manor with Greek Revival columns, white porches, and rambling stone terraces. My mother loved it. The property was less than a ten-minute drive from St. Mary's of the Springs, the school she attended. The remove of the new home also gave her uncle an excuse to stay in town overnight—to play cards, he said, at the Columbus Club—which made it that much easier for both aunt and niece to entertain their friends at home.

As a result, my mother lived in two distinct—and often conflicting—feminine worlds. At St. Mary's, the Dominican sisters had coached her academically, spiritually, and athletically for eleven years; by the age of eighteen, she'd formed lifelong bonds with her classmates and fallen madly in love with her piano teacher, Sister Maristella. In all other matters, however, "Aunt Clarence," her sister, Dodo, and their friends played Professor Henry Higgins to my mother's Eliza Doolittle. Instead of God, the ladies worshiped money, Eleanor Roosevelt, and Dr. Salk's vaccine.

Aunt Clarence had recently decided that her charge would become a doctor. And so my mother tried to please her guardian, just as she tried to please the nuns. She wore her hair like Katharine Hepburn in *Woman of the Year,* started taking biology and chemistry, and wowed them all on the basketball court. Privately, however, my mother dreamed of a kinder, gentler life. She wanted to convert to Catholicism (the Gwinns were Episcopalian) and join the convent. She was not a religious person, but she loved boarding at St. Mary's in the winter months when her aunt and uncle went to Miami Beach; having spent most of her life in the company of independent and serious-minded women, the convent seemed like a logical continuation. These visions of the nunnery were also a comforting counterpoint to her aunt's unpredictable rages: taking the veil became my mother's version of adolescent rebellion. It was the only way she could imagine disobeying the woman whom she thought had given her everything she needed.

The year before the fire, however, my mother realized that there was a serious flaw to her plan: she had always intended to have a large family. She needed a husband, and she understood this almost as soon as Russ O'Neill moved into the house on Sunbury Road.

A glad-hander with deep dimples, O'Neill was the youngest man ever hired to manage the Gwinn Milling operation. For several months in the spring of 1945, while C.E. was having a home built for his new manager, O'Neill, his wife, and their two toddlers stayed in the suite down the hall from my mother's room on the second floor. Russ appeared to be tall, dark, and handsome until he stood up: in fact, he was not a centimeter over five feet six inches. But when he chased his children around the second floor, growling like a dog, something turned over inside my mother, and all thoughts of the nunnery vanished. The children were equally captivating, and as they ran up and down the hall, wearing down thousands of the silk knots in the Anatolian runner outside her bedroom door, she found it impossible to concentrate on her studies. Russ's affable gaze and teasing smile reminded her of her favorite movie star, Van Johnson. Both were nice. And nice, my mother decided, was more important than money.

Unfortunately, both the men she swooned for seemed equally beyond her grasp. Van Johnson did not live in Columbus. And Russ O'Neill, in addition to being just the sort of farm-raised, self-made man that the Gwinns would look down on, was already married. In fact, my mother loved his wife and two toddlers as much as she did O'Neill himself. Nevertheless, she took great comfort in knowing that nice people and happy families existed in the world.

After the O'Neills had moved into their bungalow near her uncle's mill, however, my mother's anxieties about her datelessness and her uncertain future returned and she became convinced that she was losing her mind. Her aunt was pushing her toward medical school, snappy repartee, and a businesslike marriage. Her teachers hoped that she would become a bride of Christ and serve faith instead of science. My mother longed for a family like the O'Neills. But who—other than the nuns—would want someone as tall as she was? She knew that she couldn't stay at the Gwinns' forever, but increasingly, whenever she prepared to leave the house, she found that she couldn't breathe.

Van Johnson was one of the few reliable antidotes to my mother's panic attacks. Whenever she imagined herself gazing up at the actor, her heart slowed and her breath returned. The afternoon before her uncle's mill burned down, she was dreaming that Van Johnson might reach out of the screen, take her hand, and lead her to the life she imagined. She was fuzzy on the particulars of that life—she trusted Van to figure things out—but it was an existence that would include lots of happy children and rely heavily on the actor's freckles and his easy, boy-next-door charm. Attracting such a future, however, was no mean feat. Everything would depend on the outfit.

Even as my mother examined her wardrobe, a fine, dry dust made of soy leaves and husks had already begun to smolder beneath nearly a hundred tons of drought-parched soybeans seven miles away in silo number three at the Gwinn Milling Company. She couldn't have known that the filaments and tracks that had been stacked like tinder in her genes for generations would need nothing more than a fire to isolate their complement and forge an unlikely bond. All my mother knew for sure was that she needed a new plan for the rest of her life. And, at six p.m. on November 3, 1945, she knew she'd better step on it.

As a young man, my father bore a startling resemblance to Lou Gehrig. He had a lopsided smile that made powerful men want to employ him and pretty women long to starch and iron his shirts. On the night of The Fire, he was twenty-five years old and had played minor league baseball, primarily in the California and Gulf Coast leagues, before enlisting and becoming a paratrooper. During a training maneuver in Panama, he'd landed on his back and was left with an odd tingling in his left arm. Doctors had warned my father that his pitching days were over, but he didn't believe them. He still assumed that he was on his way to the major leagues—hadn't the Brooklyn Dodgers invited him to their camp in the spring? In the meantime, he was in Columbus living with his brother Russ and working at the mill.

From time to time, a pain that was as sharp and breathtaking as an electrical shock traveled down his arm, and only then did my father wonder—fleetingly—what he would do if baseball wasn't an option. The pain and numbness seemed to appear most frequently when he was cold. It was freezing the night of the fire.

By 1945, the Gwinn Milling Company employed several hundred people, and from the end of the baseball season until March, when he hoped once again to be aligning his fingers with the seams of a baseball, my father worked sorting soybeans.

He did not have a great protective affection for soybeans. Had he worked with the wheat, he might have felt differently. He had an affinity for wheat; he took pride in the fact that the same waving fields of grain he'd wandered as a boy could account for the mill's bustle and steam, the crushing and grinding and sieving, the heavy cloth bags of flour. And then there were all those soft loaves of bread that puffed fragrant and honey-colored in rectangular bread pans, all the Parker House rolls, all the cakes and cookies and—especially!—the pies that so pleasurably resulted from all this effort. Perhaps because he'd spent so much of his early life with his mother in the kitchen, my father loved watching women make pastry. The smell of a baking pie or the sight of a flaky crust emerging from a woman's oven full of bubbling fruit or jiggling custard made him homesick.

But my father did not grow up with soybeans, and only became aware of them from the windows of the buses that carried him from one minor league ballpark to another, through the green valleys of Southern California, the fertile high plains of New Mexico, and the scruffy folds of northern Florida. Soybeans need darker, richer soil than Nebraska's: more water and less wind. My father liked the curly green of soybean fields, but in his opinion, the plants lacked the majesty of wheat, and the soy milk and soy flour he'd eaten in the army didn't toot his horn.

These facts alone would not have shielded soybeans from my father's tenderness, which was ambient and usually boundless. But when he picked stones and withered-looking spheres from the long belt that ran from the soy silos to the crusher at the Gwinn Milling Company, my father felt like a bean counter. He hated bean counters.

And so saving the soybeans was the farthest thing from my father's mind when the fire bells announced trouble just after eleven p.m. on November 3, 1945. It was payday—he made sixty-two dollars a week—and my father had just walked home from the lounge at the Deschler Hotel, where he'd spent the evening buying rounds and sipping Southern Comfort. He was wearing only an ill-fitting, salmon-colored zoot suit that he'd borrowed from his shorter and rounder brother; he did not own an overcoat, and my father had moved beyond shivering to frozen by the time he stepped into the house. Russ and his wife were eating pecan pie and playing penny poker at the kitchen table.

They looked so cozy sitting there that my father told them to stay put when he heard the fire bell go off. Both men knew it was the mill—slow burns were not uncommon in the silos, and the alarm had already gone off once that week. But it never occurred to them that an inferno was raging. "I'll scoot out," my father said, "see what's what, and come back and fill you in."

He ran the ten quiet blocks and dark alleys toward the mill. It was cold out—the sort of cold that made his pitching arm spasm and throb—and the air was oily and smelled like breakfast burning. And then suddenly, he turned a corner and it was like broad daylight. He should have turned around immediately and sprinted back to get his brother, but my father instead pushed closer to the soaring orange and yellow flames, trying to get a better sense of the fire's dimensions.

"And that's when I spotted her," he later told us, "on the other side of this hedge of fire, up on a little knoll. Gee, this girl had to be six feet tall and that was it, right there."

My mother felt glamorous at the Ohio Theater. It had been designed by Thomas Lamb, who drafted the plans for the original Madison Square Garden in New York City, and was built as a movie house with an orchestra pit, a curtain that weighed seven hundred pounds, and a Morton Theater organ. With its ornate plasterwork, gold leaf, and stained-glass panels, the theater was a lavish place. Two hours in its plush red velvet seats was enough exoticism for my mother, however. Like most of the generation that would spawn Ohio's baby boom, she and her friends were loyal to the familiar, determined to create a safe and predictable home to which the boys fighting overseas could return. The best part of going to the movies at the Ohio Theater was emerging from its spell.

The familiar was, however, not to be found when my mother and her friends emerged just before midnight on November 3, 1945. It was bright as day and the traffic was as clogged as it was whenever Ohio State played Michigan. The wind was blowing from the northeast, fire trucks were clanging for the cars to pull aside, and the air smelled like scorched Wheatena. Like everyone else—and it seemed like everyone in town was on the street—my mother and her friends bolted east toward the smell, running fast, as if to rescue a smoldering pot.

"It's the mill!" cried the men hanging on the side of the fire engines. "Go back! It's out of control!" But she and her friends didn't stop until they had to, until the crowd and the police barriers stopped them on a small hillock just east of the mill.

The fire was an orange wall of heat and the air felt fat and slippery. Everything—the faces in the crowd, the checkerboard of the orderly streets of their hometown, the tidy horizon—was sliding out of focus. As they crowded around her, my mother saw that her friends were crying—for her uncle's mill! For her! It made her feel like crying, but she was not the sort who cried in public, not the sort for whom men kept large, well-creased handkerchiefs. She was too tall to cry. Even so, the crowds made her chest feel tight and her breath hurt. She was also alarmed by the fine gray mist of soot that was settling like heavy dandruff on the collar of her Chesterfield coat.

"We're not going to be able to get back to the car," she said. In addition to her pragmatism, my mother had her own Cadillac and was often the field commander of her group. "Let's walk over to Russ O'Neill's. We can call my aunt and uncle from there."

My father had been back long enough to get cleaned up by the time my mother and her friends clattered up the front porch steps of his brother's house. The hot shower in the second-floor bathroom had loosened his shoulder and he'd almost forgotten the fire. His thoughts had returned to his sister-in-law's pecan pie. He was halfway down the staircase on his way to the kitchen when my mother pushed through the front door.

Looking up, she saw Russ O'Neill, but taller—his face flushed from the shower, his pink oxford-cloth shirt unbuttoned and loose, his smile, like Van Johnson's, promising good times and happy endings.

Looking down, my father saw tall sons, enough for an infield. He didn't question it, he didn't look back. He knew a sign when he saw it. He took the last six steps as if they were a single hurdle on a hundred-yard course.

"I knew right then and there I was leaping into the rest of my life, honey," he told me once.

My mother, however, took away a different lesson from the evening's events. Several years later—after Aunt Clarence died suddenly, after her uncle married his mistress and suggested that my mother find a home of her own, after my parents eloped to New York City and my mother had me—she offered me a single bit of dating advice. I was three years old at the time, and she had spent several hours dressing me in different ensembles. She had me standing on her vanity, and she was standing behind me.

"Think twice before you marry a man you met at a fire," she said, looking over my shoulder at our reflections in the mirror.

Not surprisingly, I still prefer my father's attitude toward The Fire. There was a day each autumn when everyone in our neighborhood would rake fallen leaves from their yard to the curb for pickup, but my father was not the sort of man to create tidy curbside furrows on a city-wide schedule. Instead, he burned the leaves in a barrel in the backyard, in violation of municipal ordinance. When I was three years old, I remember him holding me in the crook of his right arm as he poked at the barrel with the stick in his other hand. Sparks geysered up when he stirred the embers. Some settled on my snowsuit and burned gray flecks into its pink nylon surface. But most of the sparks rode the hot gusts of air upward, and as we watched the specks of orange glow against the purple-flannel sky my father said, "Now there's how stars are born, Little Doll."

Family Stories

My father had a genius for dodging bad news, bill collectors, confrontations, broken hearts, and the condition that is commonly called "reality." He would not allow the unpleasant or the unresolved into his stories and therefore he had no misgivings and no regrets. Doubt and worry, along with home maintenance, child care, financial planning, and historical accuracy, were my mother's department. She also had strong feelings about what she calls "the truth," a phrase that she uses interchangeably with words such as "fact" and "evidence."

These differences made it difficult for my parents to see eye to eye. They were not contentious people. They just didn't agree with each other about what had happened, what might have happened, and what should have happened—if only the other one had been different. As a result, I grew up in the middle of an argument between two Americas. My mother's America had good silver, a positive cash flow, and higher education. My father's had baseball bats, a Dust Bowl, and a dairy herd. Tirelessly, doggedly, my parents returned to the past—not only to explain the present and predict the future, but also to determine which of them was leading in the long, hard race to shape the story of our lives.

My mother used her forefathers, the Gwinns, to remind my brothers and me of the distinguished line of wealthy, respected, educated people from whom we sprang and to suggest that we strive for more of the same—preferably by becoming doctors and lawyers. Her commitment to unflinching honesty made it necessary for her to reveal that her mother drank, abandoned her children, and occasionally woke up with men other than her husband. My mother was, however, careful to emphasize that my grandmother had discriminating taste. Why, her first husband was a diplomat, and they spent several years in Florence and Rome. She also made clear that her mother's "shenanigans" were not nearly as significant as the family's long history of appropriate dress and upstanding behavior.

Even before they stepped off the *Mayflower,* she said, the Gwinns were cultivated, educated, important people. Once in the United States, they established themselves as tea-sipping Methodists and wealthy landowners, migrating first from Virginia to West Virginia, and then north into central Ohio. At each stop, they established a branch of the family business, the Gwinn Milling Company. Their mills produced a high-quality flour called Gwinn's Jefferson crushed-wheat flour that was, from the end of the Civil War until the great crash of 1929, the local equivalent of King Arthur flour today. A picture of Thomas Jefferson, the spiritual father of the Virginia colonists, was stamped on every muslin sack of flour the family produced; the Gwinns took God, democracy, and themselves very seriously.

Unfortunately, my great-grandfather Othneil Edward was the last of the upstanding Gwinns—the last to have a picture of the framers on his shaving stand, the last to tithe a solid 10 percent, the last to abjure cards, women, and alcohol. As the God-fearing work ethic of his day gave way to jazz and bobbed hair, opium and booze, O.E. saw his children—like so many cakes too rich with butter and too light on eggs or other leavening—stop rising.

Many blamed O.E.'s marriage to Ella ("Lambie") Brown. Her people were farmers and lacked social stature. Others claimed that O.E.'s children proved the consequence of sparing the rod. Whatever the causes of the Gwinn decline, however, the results were undeniably disastrous. When O.E.'s eldest son, seventeen-year-old Brown, was found dead of acute alcohol poisoning outside Smokey Hobb's whorehouse, his mother was able to weather her grief. There were two other sons, after all, and two daughters, so Lambie laid aside her black taffeta and resumed her household routines of canning and preserving and sewing. But Lambie did not recover from the family's second tragedy. Twenty years later, when she went out to the garage to supervise the hanging of the hams, she discovered the blue-faced corpse of her youngest, Walter, who had intentionally asphyxiated himself with the exhaust from the Model T Ford his father had given him. The servants later reported that she simply walked out of the garage, returned to the front porch, settled into her Adirondack rocker, and called for the scrap basket, needle, and thread. With the exception of going to and from her bedroom, she never moved again. For the next twenty-two years, she quilted.

In fair weather, O. E. Gwinn would join his wife on the porch for lunch and dinner. When it rained or snowed, they ate from trays in their bedroom. He talked. She did not reply. The three surviving children married quickly. My grandmother, Lambie's firstborn child, moved to Italy with her husband; her sister, Mary, moved to Florida with hers. Clarence, however, who soon became known as C.E., was expected to join his father at the mill, so he and his wife, Aunt Clarence, ended up only half a block away, on Woodlawn Avenue.

By 1929, when the stock market crashed and O.E.'s own empire buckled, it was clear that the family's surviving son was not interested in making money in order to make a better world. Like many others of his generation, C. E. Gwinn was interested in making money to make money. It signaled the end of a certain Columbus: a place fueled by the passion for social and industrial progress but also tempered by the distaste for discussing or revering wealth. O.E. died of a heart attack several weeks after the great crash, leaving his son with a faltering mill to run, a helpless mother to support, and a sister—my grandmother—who seemed determined to embarrass and confound him for the remainder of both their lives.

My grandmother had by then divorced her first husband and married his friend and law partner, my grandfather William Arthur Moss. He was a tall, blue-eyed Southerner with thick white hair and morning-glory-blue eyes who wore white suits and had a tendency to start businesses that first flourished and then failed. In 1929, he decided that the Next Big Thing was selling hundred-gallon drums of yellow cake mix to army bases and soup kitchens. These facilities abounded in the South, so he moved his wife and three-year-old daughter, my mother, from Columbus to a four-room bungalow in San Antonio. It was here that my grandmother developed a terrible thirst.

Frances Elizabeth Gwinn was a beauty—a tall, brown-eyed blonde with a perfect figure, an unerring sense of style, and rapacious appetites. As a young mother in San Antonio, she had a difficult time balancing the demands of parenthood with her mania for cocktails, reefer, and men. On good days, my grandmother remembered that her dinner parties had been the toast of Florence, Italy, and Columbus, Ohio, and she roused herself to care for her three young children in a style befitting such early social promise. On bad days, she disappeared for long stretches, and my mother and her baby brothers ate cake mix at home alone.

In response to this chaos, my mother placed a high premium on being "all set." The precise conditions for this glorious state have shifted over the years, but the necessity of a well-coordinated ensemble has remained constant: as a result, my mother remembers her life in outfits. This devotion to apparel was noted first by the baby nurse who, due to the great affection my mother had for her white baby shoes, nicknamed her charge "Bootsie." The name stuck, as did my mother's habit of explaining various turning points in her life as the consequence or by-product of some sartorial decision. When she was six, for example, she woke up and realized that she had been left alone in the house with her brothers. She knew that children weren't supposed to be on their own, so she dragged the boys out of bed and started walking from bar to bar, looking for her mother, still wearing the big T-shirt she'd been sleeping in. Eventually, after midnight, they were picked up by the police in downtown San Antonio.

When looking back on this incident, my mother always blames the T-shirt for what happened next. "They probably put us in the orphanage because of the way I looked," she points out. "If I'd just taken the time to get dressed, it wouldn't have happened." When their father returned from his business trip, he sent his wife away to dry out and decided that although his sons were young enough to travel with him, his school-age daughter would be better off living with her aunt and uncle in Columbus. C.E.'s wife had lost a baby, and was willing to take Bootsie in as a surrogate daughter.

My mother doesn't remember how she felt about being given away, but she fondly recalls the dress she was given away *in*: a brown plaid Shirley Temple dress with a smocked yoke. Her father had just bought it for her in St. Louis, during the drive north from San Antonio, and she was wearing it when he delivered her to C.E.'s elegant brick house on Woodlawn Avenue. My mother had been especially enchanted by the plastic picture of the child star that hung from the dress's sash—in her seven-year-old mind, the medallion made the outfit—and she was devastated when her father, who identified the ornament as a tag, snipped it off before she could object.

At that first lunch on Woodlawn Avenue, my mother was enthralled by the Chippendale table that seated twenty-four and was set with linen napkins, a butter-and-cream-colored checked cloth, and a dazzling array of silver. There were big round soup spoons, teaspoons, and demitasse spoons; small and large forks with four tines, and small and large forks with three tines; knives that had blades and knives that looked like flat shovels. C.E.'s watch fob glowed gold in the afternoon light, and Aunt Clarence, who had been ill, appeared for lunch in a silk wrapper. When she called for milk—"a glass of milk for the young lady, please, Roscoe!"—her diamond ring cast prisms across the room.

"My," said my mother, looking around the mahogany-paneled enclosure. Above her uncle at the head of the table was a stained-glass window designed around the letters O.E.G. "Isn't it grand!" she exclaimed, smiling broadly first at her aunt and then at her aunt's sister, Dodo, and her husband, Ned. My mother had a faint Texas drawl and no sense that children should be seen and not heard; after the bedlam of San Antonio, the restrained silence at the Gwinns' table must have confused her. There was, at first, only the sound of the silver ladle against a tureen as Roscoe served the cream of asparagus soup. No one spoke until the entrée had been served, whereupon Uncle held forth on various issues of the day—FDR, the drought, the economics of commodities. This continued until the plates were cleared. Then the room fell silent once more.

In an attempt to stimulate conversation, my mother, who was seated next to her father, crooked her head toward C. E. Gwinn and, in an acceptable imitation of her sassy little heroine, said, "Well, who does he think he is? Shirley Temple?"

When she tells me this story, my mother always adds, "The next time I spoke recklessly was when I said 'I do' to your father."

Aunt Clarence saw considerable room for improvement in my mother, and her table manners were only the beginning. Although my mother had always been called Bootsie, she'd been christened Ella, after her grandmother, Lambie Brown. Aunt Clarence, however, blamed the demise of her husband's siblings on Lambie, and so when my mother moved to Columbus she was born again. Allowed to choose from a list of acceptable names, she selected Virginia—because, she explained, "I liked dotting all the *i*'s." But the name-cleansing wasn't enough: Aunt Clarence believed that only constant vigilance could save my mother from the willful, self-destructive genetic strain that Lambie Brown had introduced into the family. She was also convinced that my mother's hereditary vulnerabilities might be exacerbated by her astrological sign; Aunt Clarence was exquisitely attuned to any evidence of Leo or Brown rising in her young charge.

Soon after her arrival, my mother began receiving daily lessons in self-control. Aunt Clarence would seat her on the edge of a ball-and-claw-footed chair and instruct her to hold her spine straight, her shoulders square, and to tilt her chin imperceptibly—just enough to raise her nose and her gaze higher than most people's. Her chin, she told her charge, should form a ninety-two-degree angle with her long, thin neck. She should stare straight ahead.

Mrs. C. E. Gwinn would then set an egg timer for ten minutes. If my mother moved—if her spindly legs quivered in their white lisle stockings, if her breath caused her blue chambray sailor dress to wrinkle, if she twitched or averted her gaze—Aunt Clarence would bring a yardstick down on the offending body part.

"Leo," she'd shout, like the priest at an exorcism. "Brown!" For years, my mother thought that Leo Brown was a demon with designs on her soul. If my mother erred in any way, the egg timer would stutter as it was forced back up to ten minutes. During my mother's earliest lessons in self-control, it happened again and again. After San Antonio, however, my mother took a certain solace in any predictable outcome. When the yardstick came whooshing down, she supposed it was for her own good. She fought her fidgeting by repeating what her father had told her: life with her aunt and uncle would be better for her; she was going to be a little rich girl, like Shirley Temple in *The Little Princess*. This was something she could work with.

My mother cherished order, and so her highly regimented life with the Gwinns was like a fairy tale at first. She loved the piano lessons and the riding lessons and the carefully served meals. She thrived under her aunt's watchful eye and delighted in pleasing her by earning the highest grades at her convent school. She adored the nuns, her three dogs, and her outfits from Best & Company with their matching shoes and stockings and hats. She arranged her days and her dresser drawers so that each hour and each compartment was tidy and clear, unburdened by clutter, unimpeded by poor planning.

When I was a little girl, these details were all a part of my mother's inspirational narrative, in which she would wax rhapsodic over the joys of a well-made bed or the satisfactions of a well-ironed shirt. Apparently there was no

privilege greater than the privilege of exercising control over one's sur-
roundings—or failing that, of knowing that the emergency-room attendants
would be impressed by the cleanliness of your underwear should you be hit
by a car.

When these tales failed to have their desired effect, she would shriek,
"You don't know how lucky you are that I care!" and "You don't know what
happens to girls who throw their clothes on the floor!" and, worst of all,
"Girls who don't make their beds end up eating cake mix for dinner!" I
thought she was nuts and secretly made a ritual of eating cake mix from the
box with a spoon.

As time went on, however, hints that everything had not been perfectly
under control at the Gwinns, either, began to seep into her narrative. She
would let something slip about her aunt's dangerous and unpredictable
rages, or refer to the fact that her uncle chose to ignore the terrible bruises
left on his young niece by his wife's four-carat diamond. The servants sustained her emotionally, she said.

But my mother also had her own charges to think about when she first
lived on Woodlawn Avenue—a family of bisque-headed dolls whom she
attended to assiduously. The girls were named Ursula, Carol, and Mildred.
Her boy doll was called Charlie. Each had an extraordinary wardrobe,
because Aunt Clarence, and her sister, Aunt Dodo, designed all their clothes
and stitched them by hand. From the time she got home from school until
Roscoe rang the silver bell for dinner, my mother dressed and groomed her
dolls.

She baked them sugar cookies on her play stove and set the small table in
her playroom with porcelain doll dishes for tea. She made her dolls wash
their hands before coming to the table and taught them to use the napkins
that the ladies had embroidered for them. She brushed their hair and pol-
ished their shoes and arranged them in a line on the window seat. There was
no way that *her* dolls were ever going to have to eat cake mix for dinner.

My mother also spent hours reading the books in the third-floor library
that adjoined her playroom. Her favorite, a cast-off from a cousin's medical
training, was called *Operative Obstetrics*. She studied it closely, concentrat-
ing primarily on the illustrations.

"I will have four babies," she told Ursula, Mildred, Carol, and Charlie.
Then, considering the history of losses in her mother's family, she decided
to have a couple of backups.

"Six babies," she said, "and then we'll be all set."

*   *   *

If conformity was the lodestar of my mother's compass, my father was more of a transcendentalist. He believed that doctors and lawyers were a bunch of pussies and shysters and that most institutions existed only to snuff out individualism, originality, and spirit. He told us stories of his Irish forebears' escapades on the Nebraskan frontier to instill in us a sense of yearning and adventure. Our great-grandfather John Hugh O'Neill was, in my father's opinion, the embodiment of the screw-you that is essential to becoming a fully realized individual in America.

Throughout my life, my father would regularly recall details—as well as characters and potentially life-altering events—that he'd previously omitted from his grandfather's story. Some of these details, I've recently discovered, were actually true.

John Hugh O'Neill dared the ocean from Knocknacarry, County Antrim, in 1871. He was twenty-three years old and made his way from New York to Chicago, working first as a laborer, helping to rebuild the city after the historic fire, and then as a police officer. He married Mary Clemens, a cousin of Samuel Clemens, in 1873. Five years later, our great-grandfather rode a horse from Chicago to Nebraska. The trip took twenty-one days.

He applied for a homestead a few miles west of an outpost of Fort Kearny on the south fork of the Loup River. The outpost, which was situated in the middle of a vast, windy flatness devoid of trees (and, usually, even grass), was called Fort Banishment. There John O'Neill built a sod hut, farmed cattle and hogs, read his Bible every morning, and established himself as a formidable baseball player in the local barnstorming leagues. He lived alone until 1884, when the Burlington & Missouri River Railroad came to the area and brought his wife and three young children along with it.

When Mary Clemens O'Neill died of a fever eight days after delivering her ninth child, John O'Neill soldiered on, raising his children alone. He also killed Indians, claimed over a thousand acres of Nebraska land, helped build Our Lady of Lourdes Catholic Church, and continued to play ball. Later, John O'Neill traveled back to Ireland and became the first, and to date the only, foreign correspondent for the newspaper in Ravenna, Nebraska.

These were the facts; beyond them, it is not clear how much of the O'Neill legend was passed down to my father and how much he invented. He told people the stories they wanted to hear. In his view, happiness was the highest truth. For this reason, anyone growing up in our household could be forgiven for believing that our great-grandfather had single-handedly settled

Nebraska, probably helped invent the game of baseball, and—by dint of his example as a European correspondent—basically taught our cousin Mark Twain the writer's craft.

In part this was because the importance of being an O'Neill loomed so large in my father's mind that anything he liked or respected became O'Neill—even if, as was often the case, it wasn't. When, for instance, he told me that his mother, who was called Mollie, mashed her potatoes "just like the old country," he meant Ireland. So I believed that my grandmother Mollie Skochdopole O'Neill was Irish while knowing that she was Czech. And whenever he told me that I had my great-grandfather's brown eyes, he would then sing several bars from "When Irish Eyes Are Smiling." "Irish" was, to my father, another word for "O'Neill," which was not, in his view, a culture or a particular people as much as it was a spiritual condition.

If my father had any knowledge of fiddling, Gaelic, Yeats, or step dancing, he did not choose to share it with his children. To compensate for this lack, we invented our own Irish tradition—a bizarre circle dance that involved squatting and extending first one leg and then the other while crossing our arms over our chests. Our original inspiration was some dancing Cossacks who performed on *The Ed Sullivan Show,* but as it did to our father, "the old country" really meant "any old country" to my brothers and me. We represented our routine as a "family custom," and performed it at weddings, wakes, or any other occasion when ancestor homage seemed appropriate.

At the end of his life, our father acted as if he'd taught us this circle dance. By then, he'd also switched from Dial to Irish Spring soap, developed a taste for Irish sweaters, and had taken to wearing a Tam o' Shanter made of a plaid that, according to the salesperson at a gift store where he stopped while on a bus tour of Ireland, was traditionally associated with the O'Neill name. Even as he mellowed and became more sentimental, however, my father made no effort to revisit his Czech roots.

My father's maternal grandfather, Frantisek Skochdopole, emigrated from Humpolec in Bohemia and arrived in America with two of his older brothers in 1874. He was fifteen years old, and he spoke German, Bohemian, French, and English as well as a smattering of Italian. He was, according to one of my father's sisters, carrying his Bohemian-made Stradivarius, supposedly the twenty-first made outside of Italy. But I didn't know about the violin, or much about the man the O'Neills affectionately called "Ole Skochie," until many years later.

In college, I visited Prague with a friend who was searching for signs of her ancestors in the city's old Jewish Quarter. We found no mention of her family name in the synagogue or on the gravestones in the cemetery; we did, however, find my grandmother's. When my aunt Peg later told me that my grandmother was "probably" Jewish, my father said, "Is that so?" He was not impressed. Like his grandfather's music and the scent of rosewater and poppy seeds that filled his family's kitchen around Christmastime when he was young, a mother whose real name may have been the Hebrew Malka, or the Yiddish version, Mulka, had no place in the story my father told to inspire us—the story about brown-eyed Irish Bravehearts, the one that he believed.

The only O'Neill my father did not mythologize was his own father, Arthur Hugh O'Neill. He did not speak ill of his father. He simply avoided mentioning him. And when he couldn't avoid it, my father's jaw twitched and he pulled his lips together the same way he did when facing a batter who'd somehow gotten ahead of him in the count. His father, who was called Art, had also been a ballplayer and was paid to barnstorm throughout the West in the first decade of the twentieth century. But when he was in his thirties, he was practically blinded in a fight. By this time, he'd already retired from baseball, but when I was young, I assumed that my grandfather simply played by sound and smell. He was, after all, a son of the great John O'Neill.

My father, Charles William, was born on March 18, 1920. The seventh child, he was the first of his parents' offspring to be delivered in the tiny white-frame farmhouse of the O'Neill dairy, on the western fringe of Ravenna, Nebraska. The family had lived in town until shortly before he was born; Art, who was a cold and severe man, had operated the local grain elevator, and worked both as the sheriff and as the commissioner of roads prior to buying his dairy. He may have disliked my father in part because he resembled the irrepressible Ole Skochie, whom Art O'Neill scorned for his Eastern European accent, violin concertos, and fondness for homemade wine. But my grandfather mostly had contempt for my father because of his "spells."

My grandmother always steadfastly maintained that my father was "just a little nervous"—a whopping fiction that the family doctor and the locals, all of whom loved Mollie Skochdopole O'Neill, were happy to subscribe to. As a result, for the first seven years of my father's life, my grandfather tried to teach his son self-control by beating the convulsions out of him.

All the O'Neills were known by one name to outsiders and another name at home. My father was called "Chick," as if he was fluttery and fragile and in need of protection—which he was. His older siblings did their best to watch over him, hiding how afraid it made them whenever their brother's eyeballs rolled back in his head and left him with that white-eyed stare. Their nicknames strengthened their sense of esprit de corps: my aunts and uncles also colluded with their mother to conceal how frequently my father's brain misfired.

Even though they were not completely successful at shielding their brother from his father, perhaps their efforts were the bedrock for the cheerful denial that characterized my father's life. When we were growing up, he described his own youth in snapshots that depicted him as a winner, not as a frail child who had a habit of falling. He hung off the sides of trucks, he helped his mother make cottage cheese, he had a pet pig whom he christened Chester White. On cold, dark winter mornings, when we didn't want to get out of bed, our father would tell my brothers and me about how, as a little boy, he would race to the privy before dawn. The first out of bed wouldn't have to wait in the cold wind, he pointed out, dancing from one foot to another.

"You better believe I woke up first, gaw-darnit. Ran ma legs off to beat the rest of 'em and sat there with Montgomery Ward till they 'bout beat the door down. Grah! Ha! Ha! So who's gonna win the race this morning?" he would bellow, pulling the blankets and pillows from our beds. "Go! Go! Go!"

Leaping from bed, I would imagine that I was running to an outhouse. I transformed the cold linoleum under my feet into the frosty Nebraska ground and raced from the alcove where I slept toward the bathroom, which was next to the room that my brothers shared. There were round white fuzzy rugs along the hallway and I imagined they were sleeping sheep whose backs I had to leap over. Sometimes, when I was very young, I would imagine my father as a little boy, perched over the hole in the plank bench in the little wooden shack with the Montgomery Ward catalog on his lap. His overalls were pulled down to his knees, but he was holding the straps from their bib like reins in his left hand—"You didn't want your overalls slipping down the floor and getting all icy and wet," he said—while using his right hand to turn the catalog's pages. I could hear his brothers and sisters banging the door, begging him to hurry.

By the time I was a teenager, I understood that the catalog was toilet paper as well as reading material, and that its pages were cold and thin and slick. The index and order pages went first, and as the catalog got thinner, my father hoarded the pages that pictured boys' clothes. He tried to imagine the unspeakable luxury of wearing something that his brothers had not worn before him, something brand-spanking-new against his skin. As the heat rose up from the hole in the plank to warm his private parts, my father studied the catalog and envisioned a life beyond his loose hanging world of overalls and blue chambray shirts. He imagined owning a pair of trousers and a belt.

I also came to understand that he was dreaming of being a different somebody altogether—somebody like everybody else. For even if my father won the morning race, his siblings weren't simply yelling about having lost the contest as they gathered outside the privy door. They were also worrying about who would take care of him, scared of what would become of him— perhaps scared of what had become of him that very minute.

"You OK in there?"

"You didn't fall in, didja?"

"Chick!" his brothers and sisters would yell. "You're not takin' a spell, are ya?"

The town of Ravenna, Nebraska, is less than a mile from the former site of Fort Banishment, less than a square mile in size, and was originally settled by Italian, Irish, German, and Czech people. In its heyday, in the 1920s, sixteen hundred people lived there. The railroad that ran to the mineral fields in Wyoming stopped in Ravenna, and the local hotel, which was called the Burlington, was renowned. My grandmother, who was famous locally for her cooking, baked cherry pies and fresh-cheese strudels and tall white layer cakes in her kitchen and delivered them to the hotel herself. But she had also been a schoolteacher before her marriage, and so she educated my father at home until he was nine or ten, due to his nerves and his habit of falling; he was therefore her constant companion.

Together—my diminutive grandmother dressed impeccably in one of the skirts or cotton shirtwaists she made herself, and my dreamy, twitchy father, always in his blue chambray—they would walk up and down the brick sidewalk along Ravenna's main street, which was called the Appian Way. There was a bench outside Smaha's Meat Market, the butcher's where the Chester White hogs raised by Art O'Neill were slaughtered and the pork was stored for the family's use. Every day, his mother would tell my father to stay there while she delivered eggs to Rasmussen Grocery or bartered her cakes and pies for dry goods at Cottrell's Blackbird General Store. Frequently, however, my father would wander off and fall down.

He was never quite sure how he'd gotten cut and scraped and bruised, how his lips had gotten nicked and swollen. When he was very young, he thought that his wounds were related somehow to magic moments, those moments when his vision seemed to sparkle and the world stood still. It happened once when he was leaning against the giant elm tree on Grand Avenue, when the town clock—a two-faced fixture made by Frank Macourek that displayed Ravenna time on one side and showed the time in Bohemia on the other—suddenly sprouted a shimmering halo; the next thing he knew, my father had shaved the left side of his face on the tree's bark and knocked his head against the stone curb. It happened another time when he was watching a man box a kangaroo on the little bandstand at Genoa Street.

When my father told me the story, he said that he remembered an arc of stars shooting like a comet's tail from the kangaroo's oxblood-leather boxing gloves and, not much later, the taste of blood in his own mouth. For the most part, however, he fell at home—while weeding his mother's garden, or gathering eggs, or layering straw and salt between the sheets of ice in the ice-house. Once, he tripped and fell into the threshing blade: "I got beat good for that one."

At the dinner table, the thin line of my grandfather's lips prohibited his wife and children from interfering with my father's downward slide from his chair. My aunt Lucille said that my father ate many meals under the family's heavy oblong table. She and Peg would slip food to him: slabs of his mother's bread, joints of chicken, leftover dumplings fried in butter.

Mollie knew that her husband would have used a definitive medical diagnosis to exile her son from the family forever, possibly by sending him off to a home for the mentally deficient. Sometimes after my father fell he just got up and kept walking; other times, however, he was disoriented and in a fuguelike state for days. When that happened his mother would put him in bed in the little room off the kitchen, out of his father's sight, and instruct Lucille and Peg to take turns sitting by his side, in case he had another seizure.

One evening, when my father was recovering from a bad spell in the little room, his father stormed in and informed him that it was time to be a man—time to slaughter Chester White. Art O'Neill yanked the boy from the bed and pushed him into the kitchen.

"You walk us down to the hog pen, Nellie, we'll see what kinda nerves you got," said his father, who by this time was almost completely blind. He handed his son a baseball bat and pushed him again, this time out the kitchen door and into the cold Nebraska night. His rage buzzed through the air like a plague of grasshoppers as he shoved and kicked his son across the yard.

"I'm right behind you, Nervous Nellie," he yelled. "You get that pig right between the eyes, boy. First shot, by God, you'll kill him or I'll kill you."

This experience—and the ham dinner he was later forced to eat—went a long way toward explaining my father's attitudes about farmers and farms and the taste of pork, not to mention men who swing bats. His brothers and sisters were not surprised that he dreamed of becoming a pitcher. They were, however, surprised that he became one.

Of the six O'Neill brothers of Ravenna—several of whom were gifted and fierce athletes—my father seemed the least likely candidate for the family business of baseball. He was indulged by his older siblings, allowed to hit and throw, but he was small and "nervous," and therefore never taken seriously. Besides, no one could imagine that he possessed the cruelty of a winner.

But his brothers and sisters didn't know how many hours my father spent honing his skills. While they were at school, he was in the fields with only the herd for company, dreaming of making it all the way to the Big Show—oh, how my father loved to imagine the expression on his father's face when his-son-the-baseball-player showered his mother and siblings with riches.

When following the cows, he used branches for bats, hurled stones in the air, and slammed shots at the endless curtain of sky above Nebraska. Again and again and again until the thump of his heart pulsed like applause through every muscle, and, for an instant, the whole world danced and tossed sparks in front of his eyes.

I now know that these are the sorts of glittering moments that usually herald the onset of a seizure. But my father never acknowledged this, and perhaps he never admitted it to himself. Perhaps he was already unconscious when he pitched forward, and never saw the stubble and the dust rushing toward him. He never said.

By the time I was born my father was thirty-three years old and his nervousness was consolidated entirely in his lower lip, which quivered as spasmodically and regularly as a toddler's just before it starts to wail.

Long before I learned words such as "epilepsy," "grand mal," and "seizure," I learned to look the other way.

Give Me Sugar

When I was a toddler, my mother made a pie every day. She usually began at eleven a.m. by locking me in my high chair and preheating the oven to 350 degrees.

"Watch me, honey," she said, as she poured flour into her sifter and held it over the smooth white hills of Crisco in the bottom of her mixing bowl. Watch her? I couldn't take my eyes off her! It was lunchtime and I was famished for the carefully weighed and measured portions that my mother served me daily: one carrot stick and one celery stick, two ounces of canned tuna fish, one half slice of Hollywood diet bread, and one quarter of an apple or pear. But I also relished the slow and careful torture of pastry taking shape under my mother's hands.

I loved how the flour snowed through her sifter, how she knit her brow and pressed its handle as if it were the trigger of a gun. I imagined her taking aim at the people who tracked mud into her house, training her sights on anyone who said "ain't got none" or "them there" or "nigger," and my own hands itched to be part of the pie campaign.

"Bang!" I hollered, slamming my palms into the tray of my high chair and flailing the chubby sausages of my legs for additional emphasis. "Bang. Bang. Bang!"

My mother winced but remained focused on her delicate, flaky crust. She had expected a different sort of daughter—a quieter daughter, a daughter with less fat and more hair, a little girl who was excited by dolls and satin sashes and intricately smocked yokes—a little girl like herself. Pie-making required greater finesse than making babies, but it also guaranteed a more predictable outcome. It reminded my mother of the qualities that she valued, and renewed her faith that those qualities could be learned.

I watched my mother like a stalker. When she talked—and my mother confided in me just as she had in her dolls, discussing her fears and her philosophies and enlisting me as a witness and supporter of her worldview—I closed my eyes and wrinkled my forehead and tried to memorize every word she said.

"My aunt thought I could do better, but frankly, who else was going to marry me?" she asked. "Besides, there is absolutely no doubt that the Gwinn gene pool needed some new blood." Putting aside the sifter, she began assembling the remaining ingredients for her crust: an egg yolk, a dash of salt, a tablespoon of ice water.

"I think it was the forceps, I really do," she went on. "It was a shock at first. I mean! Your head was smashed in. They'd sewn your ear on with black thread and splinted your nose with toothpicks. I thought I'd given birth to the missing link! I hid you under my bed jacket so no one would see, which, I believe, is the polite thing to do. You don't want to inflict your troubles on the rest of the world, that's my philosophy! And remember, Molly, always use ice water for crust, never just water from the tap."

I nodded my head vigorously, dislodging the pink bow that was taped to my head. Although I constantly fell short of our plans for my improvement, I remained a rapt and eager student.

"If you slap the dough around like some bohunk, it's going to be tough and it won't be worth the calories," said my mother, casting a concerned glance my way, "and that's something you'll need to consider." She fluttered her wire pastry harp like the wing of a hummingbird to combine her ingredients. Quickly then, using the heel of her hand, she smooshed them all together to create a ball of dough.

"Bang! Bang!" I screamed.

"Girls don't play war," said my mother, using her index finger to restore the lift in the wave of hair that swept away from her forehead. "What are we going to do with you, honey?" Then she put the dough between two pieces of waxed paper and, using a barrel-style rolling pin, she pushed the ball into a thin, flat circle.

Some days she filled the shell with lemon curd or chocolate silk; other days it was cherries or blueberries or apples. But every day, after weaving a lattice-top crust over the filling and crimping the edges of the pie, my mother swept the scraps of dough together and made another ball. She pushed this second ball of dough flat, dotted it with butter, sugar, and cinnamon, rolled it into a log, and cut it into pinwheels.

"Testers," she said, placing the pinwheels on a cookie tray and pushing them and the pie into the oven. "They'll tell us if we got it right."

My mother couldn't wait until dinnertime to appraise her pastry. She would stand between my high chair and the oven as the cookies baked, holding a pot holder and tapping the toe of her pump. I shared her excitement. Every day she screamed, "Don't!" and slapped my hand when I reached toward the hot cookie tray as she passed by. It wasn't the potential burn that concerned my mother; it was pie protocol and the possibility of excessive calorie intake.

"Don't grab! Don't act like some starving Armenian," she said.

She settled the tray on a rack near the sink and then, carefully, using a small metal spatula, she pried a pinwheel from the tray. She held the pastry between her thumb and index finger. She observed it, blew on it, and bit into it. Her pinkie was raised. The cookie made a hissing sound against her front teeth.

"*This* is how you eat a cookie, Molly," she said, closing her eyes.

By the time I could walk, sugar had taught me that longing is a higher good. Satisfaction was embodied by my mother's pie. It was always at a distance, it was never enough. Achieving it was a perpetual aspiration that burned like cinnamon on the roof of the mouth.

We lived on Schreyer Place in Beechwold, an older, leafy, modest neighborhood north of Ohio State University. Most of the houses were white clapboard and had been built in the Federalist style after the First World War. Ours was older and smaller—only a story and a half—with Tudor windows, a stone patio by the front door, and a steep gabled roof. Instead of being set on a square lot, our house was perched on a little pie-shaped knoll, and while other people had maples or sycamores or elm trees in their yards, we had an enormous blue spruce. For our family, this tree that towered over everything around it would come to symbolize our own superiority and special destiny, but at first we were simply happy to be in the neighborhood.

For my mother, Schreyer Place epitomized warmth and modesty, an antidote to the austere grandeur of Sunbury Road. The tiny house was her domain and she took care of it with a fanatical zeal, scouring its crannies and corners. Pushing her Electrolux, she sensed the approval of neighbors—not to mention the entire baby-booming world—filtering through the huge lilac bushes outside her windows. In the afternoon while I napped, she washed my shoelaces, hung them on the clothesline in the backyard, and felt, for a single moment, that she deserved the cozy goodness of her life.

My father liked Schreyer Place, too. He liked how the neighborhood smelled of laundry on Mondays, of mowed grass on Saturdays, and never, ever of cow dung. When he carried his black lunch box to the car every weekday before dawn, he felt protective of his sleeping neighbors, despite their PhDs, their degrees in electrical engineering, and their CPAs. They just didn't have it in them to do what he did—working the early shift at North American Aviation so he could spend two hours every afternoon with his little girl, helping out with the housework so his family could relax together on the weekends. He earned half what his neighbors made, but by God, didn't he take his wife out to dinner every Saturday night?

Poor bastards, he would think to himself as he backed the car down the driveway, they just don't know how good they have it. But he did, and there was no limit on the overtime he'd work to make sure he never had to slaughter a hog or milk a cow again.

We had linen napkins at lunch and damask ones at dinner. Weeknights we used the silver plate cutlery that my father had given my mother as an engagement present. On Saturday we shopped for food at the North Market in the morning and in the evening we went to my favorite place in the whole world, the Jai Lai Restaurant. On Sunday, we had roast beef for dinner at noon and used the hefty sterling my parents had accumulated, place setting by place setting, as wedding presents.

During the week we would have breakfast together while it was still dark. Then my father would say, "Take care of your mother for me, Little Doll," as he left for work. And then every morning, after washing the dishes, my mother would give me the first of my three daily baths, arrange me in a party dress, and put me in the backyard.

For a while, I was the only child on the street, and I saw its tidy asphalt driveways, concrete walkways, and stone garden paths as part of a watery world of creeks, streams, and rivers; the shade under its trees formed my oceans, lakes, and ponds. Aside from the creek that really did flow in the crease of the ravine across the street from our house, the most significant body of water I'd ever encountered was a blow-up swimming pool. Nevertheless, while my mother used Q-Tips and bleach to purify the seams inside our house, I patrolled its exterior perimeters, navigating a complex system of waterways. Using a curving branch that had fallen from the redbud tree, I searched for goldfish and starfish and my best friend, Karen, who was a mermaid. Other children had blankets, dolls, or stuffed animals; I had sticks and responsibilities. I had to take care of my mother. I had to catch some shrimp for dinner.

Unfortunately, the bounty from my kingdom never brought my mother the relief I intended. "Jesus, get those filthy things out of here, Molly," she would say when, triumphantly, I delivered handfuls of muddy maple wings into her kitchen. "Oh, honey, what are you thinking? Yes, I *do* love shrimp, but those are *not* shrimp. They are maple wings and they are dirty and I just finished the floor! Out! Out!" My mother was baffled by my inability to grasp the obvious, just as I was mystified by her inability to see past it. These shortcomings made both our jobs more difficult.

My father just wanted us to be happy. When my mother confiscated my stick—"Look at this darling doll, honey. If we give it a bottle it wets its diaper!"—he would never say a word, but when I found other sticks, he used a paring knife to whittle the ends for me—"Don't tell your mother!"

"Where are you getting these things?" my mother asked. "Chick, look at this, somebody sharpened the end of it, it's like some harpoon. Now that's dangerous, it could poke her eye out." She broke my sticks in half and buried them in the trash barrel. My father shrugged and winked and set them on fire.

But it was not possible to reign over my kingdom without a stick. So I recovered charred bits from the burn barrel and carried them as others carry splinters from the crucifix. I imagined myself immune from persecution, endowed with magical powers, and I waited for my stick to regenerate. It always did.

"Put it under the pine tree and let it grow," my father would yell from the car. "Hurry up, honey, come on, come on, fast as you can." When I remembered to check on the splinter that I'd hidden, there would be a brand-new stick in its place.

*   *   *

Every afternoon, after lunch, pie, and nap, my mother would bathe me, arrange me in another party dress, and place me in front of the house to wait for my father. At three-thirty he would pick me up and I would stand next to him in the front seat of the Plymouth as he delivered the other members of his car pool to their homes. Then we would go to Greendales and share an ice cream soda. "Don't tell your mother," my father would say.

My father loved ice cream, and he also loved me with ice cream. In addition to their dairy farm, his parents had operated an ice cream parlor in Nebraska, and the privilege to give away extra dips or ice cream sodas never, for my father, lost its thrill. Ice cream was the currency of his affection.

Perhaps ice cream was the only thing for which I would set aside my sticks. Or perhaps, like me, my father felt it best to eat before sitting down to my mother's carefully prepared and measured meals. At Greendales, we would perch on wire chairs at a marble table and my father would use a penknife to clean the black grease from his fingernails as I sucked down the soda. Afterward, he would buy Dentyne gum to erase the smell of sin from our mouths.

"Don't tell," he'd say again. Then my father would let me choose six chocolate turtles from the glass case and, later, usually after I'd gone to bed, he would give them to my mother. "Candy," my father told me as he steered the fat blue Plymouth from Greendales back up the river of Schreyer Place, "is the best defense."

"Ahoy, matey," I shouted as we turned into our driveway.

"Can you put a lid on it, Sinbad?" my father said. "We don't want to upset your mother."

By the time we arrived home every day, my mother would have fluffed out her hair, changed her dress, applied red lipstick, and put dinner on the table.

"Mashed potatoes!" my father would say happily, poking me with his elbow. "Aren't we the luckiest guys in the world?" Then he might flick green peas across the table toward me, or make fangs out of his green beans. Once he took the mayonnaise garnish from the salad in his hand and pretended to cough it up.

"Chick!" my mother would exclaim in mock horror. Sometimes, she did the Charleston across the kitchen, her opaque nylon apron swishing as she kicked.

"Your mother's got the best legs in the U-nited States, Little Doll," my father would say. "That's why I married her. Her legs and her pie."

My father had had infielders and pitchers in mind when he married, but his need to feel like the luckiest guy in the world was greater even than his dream. Following my difficult birth, when my mother was told she couldn't have any more children, my father decided that all he'd ever wanted was one little girl. My mother, on the other hand, *had* wanted a little girl, but she was worried about the one she'd gotten.

"What if she takes after your mother?" she whispered late at night, across the six-inch gulf that separated her twin bed from my father's in their little room at 304 East Schreyer Place. "And what are we going to do if she ends up like *my* mother? Oh, Chick, why didn't I think of that? Oh my God. Chick? Are you awake? What do you think is worse—fat and dowdy? Or elegant but completely insane?"

My mother's concern was not unfounded. Grandma O'Neill was deeply suspicious of any woman who had never chopped the head off a chicken. Upon hearing that my mother, who'd nearly died in childbirth, hadn't risen from her bed and gone out to plow the lower forty, Grandma O'Neill immediately left Nebraska and came to Columbus to care for me. She had no time for my mother's Spock-inspired notions of baby care. She disregarded the charts and graphs and measuring cups, the sterilizers, the timers, and the pepper stain to discourage thumb-sucking. Instead my grandmother picked me up whenever I cried, added sugar and cream and rum to my bottles, and quickly became my favorite person.

"We got another two ounces on her," she would announce proudly to my father when he came home from work.

My mother knew a traitor and a future fatso when she saw one. She pursed her lips, took her liver pills, and bided her time. When Grandma O'Neill went home, my mother's first act of sole custody was to put me on a diet— a situation that, whenever she visited, my grandmother did her best to remedy.

A thick, short woman with soft, dark eyes and a big nose, Grandma O'Neill wore gingham aprons over her flowered shirtwaist dresses, beige shoes with laces and chunky heels, and thick, flesh-colored stockings that resembled Ace bandages. When she stayed with us, she cooked incessantly, and when my mother wasn't looking she would slip me cookies and pastries. Her specialty was Czechoslovakian kolache, a big, yeasty bun with a puddle of rose jam or sweetened farmer's cheese or prune or almond paste in the center. The fact that my mother didn't like kolache did not discourage my grandmother from baking it in commercial quantities: a day's worth of her effort left every surface in my parents' house stacked with honey-colored buns. It was like living inside a bakery, and as a toddler, I would even forget my sticks in order to follow my grandmother around the house.

She also spread yards of waxed paper over the plastic-covered daybed near the kitchen door and lined hundreds of her crumbly, sour-cream roll-up cookies there to cool. She treated the pair of rattan basket chairs in front of our television set in the basement as if they, too, were storage units and filled them with date rolls.

"It's like she's expecting the entire bohunk army to drop by," whispered my mother. "Over my dead body."

The day she left, my mother would fill trash bags full of the pastries that Grandma O'Neill had stored throughout the house. It would then take several applications of Mr. Clean to rub the smell of Grandma O'Neill's chicken soup from the walls.

"I told her I would buy her soup in cans," my mother would say, as she scoured her way across the linoleum floor. "With noodles. But no. She's rolling dough on the kitchen table, cutting noodles. Now I ask you, who does that anymore? Then she's out in the backyard, hanging them on the clothes-line! The noodles! What will the neighbors think? Where am I supposed to hang your shoelaces?"

But if my mother dreaded her mother-in-law's visits, she was more unnerved by her own mother's return to Columbus. Long since divorced, Grandma Moss had come home shortly after I was born. She was living at the Great Southern Hotel downtown. From time to time, she called on the telephone and offered herself as a babysitter. "You have got to be kidding," my mother would say and hang up. But she was haunted by the possibility that her mother might one day simply appear on her doorstep.

"What will I do then, Chick?" she said.

"Don't worry about it, Boots," my father said.

She never articulated her worst fear: that her mother was already in her house, her tendencies toward drunkenness and madness slowly unfurling inside of me. Periodically this thought would lead my mother to moments of near hysteria, during which she would wring her hands and scream.

"The driveway is *not* a river, Molly. Trees are *not* castles. You do *not* have tea parties with mermaids and fairy godmothers," she said. "Do you? Now tell me the truth, young lady."

"Okey dokey," I would say. In fact, Grandma Moss had finally tired of the telephone; she had begun instead to lurk around the neighborhood and had joined my pantheon of playmates.

*   *   *

The first time I met my maternal grandmother I was two years old and I was shrimping on the Mississippi. It was fall. The curb was thick with shrimp and Karen the mermaid was helping me wield my stick, which I was using to sweep up our catch. We heard a tingly, jingly sound, and when I looked up, there was a tall woman whose arms were resplendent in bangles and charm bracelets and whose stiff dark blue voile dress made a whispering noise as she walked.

"You must be Bootsie's," she said.

She was very tall, and her gray hair was pulled back in a bun. I was especially fascinated by her large crocodile purse, which boasted two miniature crocodile heads at the clasp.

"This is my friend, Karen. She is a mermaid," I said gravely, patting the air next to me with my stick. Ever alert to my duties as Queen of Waterworld, I performed an identity check. "Are you the fairy godmother?" I asked.

"Fairy Grandmother," she answered, laughing, and this announcement convinced me that the woman possessed magical powers and was very possibly divine.

I invited her to join the two of us in my castle under the pine tree. Its low-hanging branches concealed a huge interior space that smelled like Christmas, with blue-green walls that rose up and up to a ceiling patched with pieces of blue sky. Once inside the tree, we were completely hidden from the house.

I had used pine needles, dirt, and stones to build various rooms in my castle. I used the same materials—plus clover, grass, leaves, flowers, or the purslane that grew between the line of stones that led to the front door—to make pies for Karen.

"Hmmm," said Fairy Grandmother, when I offered her a taste. "That smells delicious. Why don't we let that finish cooking, darling, and have us a little sweet."

From beneath the crocodile heads, she extracted a glassine bag of pastilles. They were small, slightly rounded discs with a delicate pink candy coating that was, initially, as sweet as a birthday cake on the tongue. But the candies had beads of licorice liqueur in their center, bitter and black and a terrible surprise. I gagged and Fairy Grandmother took me into her lap. "Shhh, just wait," she said, rocking me. "Don't spit it out."

Her dress smelled like lavender. Her breath smelled like malt whisky. Pressed next to her, I drifted, probably as drunk as she was, through the fear and revulsion of the harsh taste in my mouth, the visions of mud and swamps and pirates, the feeling of being lost in the dark, of being paralyzed and incapable of calling for help. But somehow I felt safe enough to wait for the sugar coating to triumph.

Fairy Grandmother had no sense of a child's taste, and she often pushed bizarre and complicated sweets into my mouth: sugared violets, candied grapefruit, chocolate-covered coffee beans. But she also told me marvelous stories to go with them—about the grapefruit she'd eaten in Provence, how the scent had stayed on her fingers "like a little bit of sunshine," about the smell that rose from espresso machines in Florence, and the violets she'd picked once next to a canal in Venice. Her stories, like her candies, were always about risk and redemption and I quickly started to embellish the stories she began.

One afternoon, as my mother was preparing me for my daily outing with my father, I heard the distant jingling of Fairy Grandmother's approach. I was standing on the vanity in the bathroom, just to the left of the sink. My mother was standing behind me, tying the sash of a white nylon dress.

When I leaned toward the tingling sound, she said, "Stand still," and pulled the ends of the cream-colored sash around my waist as if they were reins. She glanced at me sharply in the mirror and, when I was once again immobile, she released the sash and tied it in a bow.

Staring over my shoulder at the two of us in the mirror, she tugged the hem of the dress and said, "If you feel your dress hiking up, pull it down like this. We don't want to see those knees. We want to emphasize the length of dress and deemphasize the girth. See, you look almost cute."

And then the doorbell rang and my mother froze.

"Shhhhh," she said.

The doorbell rang again and my mother pulled the bathroom door shut and locked it. "Shhhh," she said.

"It's Fairy Grandmother," I said.

"Don't be ridiculous," said my mother. "Be quiet." The doorbell rang again and again.

"Shhh," said my mother. There was knocking at the back door.

"Shhh," she hissed, pulling down the blind on the small window that was high in the wall of the bathroom. She didn't unlock the bathroom door until she heard my father drive up, tooting the horn of the car.

When she opened the front door, there was a pint of Lady Borden ice cream on the stone patio in front of the house. It was summer. The ice cream had melted and leaked onto the flat, gray rock. My mother began to cry and, when she defeated my effort to lick the white foam off the front porch, so did I.

Before my grandmother left the Lady Borden on the front porch, I was not allowed to eat ice cream in my mother's presence. When, on the rare and special occasions that she and I went to Greendales candy store or Knight's Ice Cream, she ordered herself a hot fudge sundae and gently explained how, from both a calorie and a cost perspective, a single scoop of orange sherbet was better for me. I didn't object. I didn't even ask for a taste of the glorious black-and-white, hot-and-cold concoctions that my mother ate in front of me. But after my grandmother's visit, we both changed. I no longer accepted my sherbet status and, like a criminal buying the silence of her only witness, my mother allowed me to have them. Concerts, movies, shopping trips—any outing or event that we shared—became a prelude to sundaes.

By the time I was in kindergarten, though, my mother decided to forgive her own mother, and she invited her to Sunday and holiday meals, along with Aunt Dodo, for the remainder of their lives. "Will you pick her up?" she would ask my father as she stood by the open oven and, using two big forks, transferred the standing rib from the roast pan to the china platter.

"Come on, Little Doll," my father would say, and we'd drive down through the Sunday quiet of High Street to my grandmother's hotel. Later, after she'd been evicted for drunk and disorderly conduct, we would pick up my grandmother at the top end of West Broad Street, where the state mental institution was. She was always happy to see me. We had an understanding.

"Give me sugar," she would say, offering me first one cheek and then the other to kiss. "Now, darling, you simply must tell me about our little friend Karen."

My father's response to my underwater kingdom was even more gratifying. In addition to recognizing Karen the mermaid, he also gave me fishing lessons. He had a collection of fishing rods in the garage and one night after dinner when I was very small, he taught me how to cast. We stood at the crest of the little knoll of our front yard, hurling lines down to the street.

"That's your river, honey," he said. "Go get your fish! Lookie here!" Standing next to me, close enough for me to feel his weight shift from his left foot to his right as he squared his hips to the street, he raised his elbow and then, with a mighty force that seemed to rise from his hips and gain velocity before exploding from his left shoulder, he hurled the line, snapping his wrist.

The fading evening sun sparkled off his green metallic casting rod as it cut the air like a furious magician's wand. There was a mosquito sound, a whirring trapped close to my ear. I heard, but didn't see, the line unraveling toward the narrow sign high on a pole far across the street that said "Schreyer Place." A dull ping reached us through the evening air.

"Yes," said my father. When I looked up, his arm was still extended, his gaze fixed on the street sign. "Got 'em," he said.

He squatted behind me, close enough to guide my arms and, I feared, close enough to wrinkle my taffeta dress, as well. The dress had a Peter Pan collar and a yoke that was smocked in satin and embroidered with tiny pink and yellow rosebuds.

"Don't worry about your dress," my father purred. "Lean on me, I'm not going to let you fall."

I was squeezing the black handle of the pole he'd given me and squeezing my eyes shut, too. He loosened my hand, separating my fingers like a pitcher's splayed against the red seams of a baseball.

"Eyes on the river," said my father. "Don't close 'em, keep your eyes on the river, Molly. Look at your target. Here we go."

His right hand covered mine and, after squaring my hips and pointing my belly button to the street sign, he used his left hand to lift my elbow as his right knee pressed into my right shoulder blade.

"Blow," he said, exhaling hot into my ear. "Eyes on the river!" Even before our wrists snapped against the rod, I felt as if I were being pulled and began to stumble. The line fell like a pebble near the curb and tears gathered against my eyelids.

"You moved your feet," said my father. "Where are your eyes? Your eyes are on the curb, honey, not on the river. Your line's gonna go where your eyes are. Let's do her again, come on, no cryin', cryin's not gonna get you a fish."

We did it over and over; my father—with his ingenious blend of taunt, encouragement, and relentless focus—was a natural coach. He moved away from me, inch by inch, cast by cast, until his arm across my belly, his hand over my hand, and his knees against my back were more a warmth than a presence. I was half as tall as the casting rod, scowling toward the street, searching for the white of the street sign in the gathering dusk. I was wrapped in a silence like snow, conscious only of my grunts, the whir of the reel, the thud of the lead weight landing, farther each time, unaware that my mother had finished the dishes and had come out to the porch. Then I heard her voice and it was worried.

"She'll ruin that dress, Chick," she said. But her voice was far away, like a fire truck downtown, as I lifted my elbow and launched the rod—as well as myself—into the air.

There were scraped elbows and knees, a slow trickle of blood from my nose, grass stains, and a wail from behind us—"Now that's just infuriating, Chick. Uncle gave her that dress!"

"I told the darned kid to keep her feet on the ground," my father replied guiltily.

Within moments, it seemed, there were turtles. My father was opening the box from Greendales, and the smell of chocolate stains against frilly paper entered the air. My mother was saying, "Umm, oh my God, these are just delicious," and adding, through a mouthful of chocolate, caramel, and pecans, "Oh, she shouldn't, Chick, let's get her a zwieback."

But he gave me a turtle anyway and they giggled like thieves—my mother zany with dietary abandon, my father flush as a con man holding loaded dice.

Years later, after the reality of raising six children on a blue-collar entrepreneur's earnings could no longer be softened by chocolate turtles, they forgot how we were when I was very young. My mother would say that she married my father because he was the only person who ever asked her out on a date. He would say that he married her because he felt sorry for her. Or he would claim that he married her for her money, and she would reply, "Well, the joke's on him, the Gwinns couldn't disinherit me fast enough after I tied that knot." But I know that none of this is true. I remember my parents happy.

It was Saturday night, and I was standing next to my father on the front seat of the Plymouth, breathless with anticipation, waiting for my mother to finish dressing. It was Saturday night, and the three of us were going to the one place where we could all be exactly who we wanted to be: the Jai Lai. I was wearing a rose-colored taffeta party dress and a pink cardigan. My father was wearing his new suit and a brown felt hat. The New York Giants were about to play the Brooklyn Dodgers at Ebbets Field, and he was listening to the pregame show on the car radio. He'd pitched for one of the Dodgers' minor league teams.

"They're gonna go all the way this year, Little Doll," he said, and his lip quivered as it did when he was nervous. But then the kitchen door squeaked open and my mother's high heel and slim ankle, followed by her long, shapely calf, appeared.

"Would ya take a look at that leg!" said my father. "Who's the luckiest guy in the U-nited States?" My mother moved slowly down the three steps from the kitchen to the driveway. She was hugely pregnant, immaculately dressed, and wearing sparkly clip-on earrings.

"Shake a leg," yelled my father, and he honked the horn.

"Chick!" said my mother, looking around to see if any neighbor had been disturbed. "Shhhhh."

Honking was considered crude. Traffic stopped frequently along High Street, the main thoroughfare in our neighborhood, so that drivers could exchange pleasantries. Rather than an inconvenience, these pauses were seen as an opportunity to savor. People shifted into neutral and looked around. They read the hand-painted signs for specials in the window of Albers grocery. They tried to see what was new in the window at the S & H Green Stamp Store. They noted the date on the poster that announced the spaghetti dinner at Bishop Watterson High School. They did not, under any circumstances that were not life-threatening, honk.

"What are you thinking of?" asked my mother, in the same tone she might have deployed with me if I had done something ill-advised but sort of funny. Her tongue was pressed into her left cheek, and she was trying not to laugh; even so, after she'd wedged herself into the car, she nervously scanned the block again. Although she was still buoyed by my father's inability to see anything but the best, she also believed that the world beyond her little family was one big court of judgment that might, at any moment, issue a ruling that could shatter our lives. Then she pulled my dress down to cover my knees, pulled up the anklets that had already slipped into my black patent leather Mary Janes, and reached across me to pull a loose thread from the lapel of my father's suit.

By then, however, my father had arranged a piece of Black Jack gum over one of his front teeth. He raised his hand over the car horn and grinned maniacally.

"Chick!" my mother said, letting out the breathy, unself-conscious laugh that my father and I loved. I jumped in the seat and clapped. "Hey, take her easy, there, Little Doll," said my father. Their hands met on the back of the seat behind my head and, still grinning like a jack-o'-lantern, my father backed the Plymouth down the driveway into Schreyer Place.

The Jai Lai was the best restaurant in Columbus, a huge, dark place with thick carpets, arched Moorish doorways, and heavy wooden chairs. It was also my invisible kingdom made manifest. Dozens of aquaria were set into its dark walls, so that the entire dining room was lit by their light blue-green glow. And as my parents sipped highballs and my father fired up a Lucky Strike, I was allowed to explore this plush, underwater cavern by myself— "Just stay where we can see you"—to be summoned back to the table by the waiter only when the food arrived.

The tanks were gigantic, and each contained an intricately wrought diorama that blended aquatic life with marine fantasy. In one, a squid would sail by like streaming spaghetti against a backdrop of sea fans and a half-sunken pirate's ship, while on another wall, a mermaid would wave from atop a chunk of coral. Electric-blue fish and bright pink ones glided by my nose when I pressed it against the wall of the tank, shrimp danced on their tails, and crabs scooted sideways when I tapped my finger on the glass. I believed that the Jai Lai was the source of the tributaries that I patrolled. I also thought that the restaurant was the center of the world's shrimp supply. After all, we always had shrimp at the Jai Lai. Shrimp cocktail. Shrimp in avocado. Baked stuffed shrimp. Shrimp scampi. Butterflied, breaded, and deep-fried shrimp. After chocolate turtles, shrimp was my mother's favorite thing in the world.

"Another plate!" said my father, again and again.

"Oh, Chick, I can't!" said my mother.

I stood between them on the curving banquette, the leather cool against the backs of my legs. My mother always waved at the friends of the Gwinns who crowded the restaurant and smiled shyly up at those who stopped by the table. My father licked his thumb and peeled bills off the fold of cash he drew from his pocket. He bought drinks for people he didn't know, and tipped the waiter each time he emerged from the kitchen with more shrimp.

He said, "Hey ya, Whatsy!" to anyone who passed the table. "Grah grah grah!" This sound—a sort of purring, growling, and snorting noise that ran across the roof of his mouth—may have been my father's way of laughing at others, or perhaps he was offering himself up as the butt of their jokes. The *grah grah grah* generally covered his inability to recall a name and was often followed by a teasing, sotto voce commentary, tinged with derision.

"Hey ya, Whatsy! Grah grah grah!" he'd say heartily, as if greeting a long-lost friend. And then he'd turn his face and whisper, "Ole priss looks like he's got a load in his trousers, huh?"

"Chick!" my mother exclaimed happily.

"Ahhh haa haa!" I sang.

Ensconced in our thronelike banquette at the center of the world, my mother's eyes sparkled like her earrings, my father grinned and winked, and the pile of empty shrimp shells between them grew ever higher.

"So sweet," my mother said, closing her bright red lips around a cold pink shrimp.

"Like sugar," said my father, peeling the legs and the shell from a tiny rock shrimp and then flying it, as if it were an airplane, into the open hangar of my mouth.

No one made me eat my green beans. I didn't even want dessert. Like my parents, I just wanted that salt-tinged sweetness in my mouth to last forever.

My Baby Sister

My mother said that she was disinherited because she married a nobody—"No money, no education, no prospects, no nothing but good looks"—but I always thought that it had more to do with her lack of self-control. She couldn't stop having baby boys. For seven years—from the time I was three until I was ten years old—she promised me sisters and delivered brothers. It was an embarrassment and an outrage and I would have disinherited her, too, if I'd known how.

The boys arrived like a litter of Jack Russell terriers shattering the quiet order of our days and prompting the young neighborhood matrons to comb the *Ladies' Home Journal* for advice on prenatal gender selection. If only we could have pooled our efforts! A significant portion of my early childhood was dedicated to persuading my mother's uterus to grow a girl. And yet every eighteen months my mother carried another boy home from the hospital and swore that it wouldn't happen again.

"Statistically, the next one has to be a girl," she said. "If I didn't believe that, I'd stop right now."

Had I not taken her at her word, I might have responded less helpfully to the shrieking, red-faced, hairless primates she kept introducing into our lives. As it was, I cheerfully shared my parents' subjugation. The tyranny of sleeping babies taught me to live in whispers. Almost as soon as my brothers began to appear, I set aside my sticks, resigned from my position patrolling the imaginary waterways, and became a full-time mother's helper. I learned to fold tiny terry-cloth unitards with snaps down the front and along the inseam of each leg. I learned to fill glass bottles with formula and warm them in hot water over low heat on the stove. I learned to whisk the lumps from baby pabulum, to mash bananas, to cut meat in tiny bites, to make custards and puddings.

I never, however, learned to cope with the aromatics of my brothers' invasion. The stench of their dirty diapers, which soaked in a white enamel pail next to the toilet in our tiny bathroom, permeated our lives. The faint scent of the family's Dial soap and the residual Cheer detergent that clung to the bath towels stood no chance against the ammoniated vapors that seeped from the terrible pail.

"Just put the diaper in and shut the goddamned lid," my mother would growl after passing me a soiled wad and returning her attention to cleaning, oiling, and powdering the fleshy curves and creases of whichever one of the kicking and flailing baby boys she'd laid on the counter next to the bathroom sink. Although my journey from her side to the diaper pail was fewer than three steps, I approached the matter like a spastic mime doing a scarf dance, my diaper-bearing arm extended toward the open pail while the rest of me reared back toward the fresh air on the other side of the open bathroom door.

"Stop waving the thing!" said my mother. "What in the name of God is the matter with you?"

If she had to ask, there was, I realized, nothing to be gained from discussing the situation. And what can one say, really, to someone like my mother? Someone who broke her promises. Someone who never, directly, apologized. Someone who kept sniffing her infants' downy heads and saying, "Nothing is sweeter, Molly, come smell." Birth by birth, my mother had grown paler and thinner. She had blue-brown circles under her eyes and looked, increasingly, like the reedy and pitiful mothers of children pictured in the Unicef appeals that arrived in the mail. She also frequently had blame on her breath.

"You're stinking the whole house up," she yelled at me when I was slow to reach the diaper pail.

Later, after dinner, she yelled at my father, "Can you get them out of here? I need a moment's peace. I have *got* to get this place cleaned up. My God, Chick, it looks like Tobacco Road."

I added marital counseling to the services I provided my parents. "Turtles," I would whisper to my father as I stood on a stool next to him drying dishes after dinner. "Let's drive down to Greendales and buy her chocolate turtles."

I fine-tuned my early detection system so that nary a zygote could escape my notice. At the first signal—which generally corresponded with seeing a little appointment card from Dr. Donley, ob-gyn, taped to the refrigerator door and my immediate feeling of nausea—I began talking about my sister.

"I love the name Karen," I would say while we sat on the edge of the bathtub, staring at a small boy sitting on his potty chair. "Don't you, Mommy?"

As soon as her pregnancy was confirmed, my mother would begin her campaign to make room in the diaper pail for new offerings by purchasing a bag of Nestlé chocolate chips and initiating potty-training procedures with her youngest toddler.

"Just sit there," she instructed, rising to return to the kitchen. "If he does anything, give him a chocolate chip."

"How about Kathy?" I said, hoovering down a handful of chocolate chips so that I could concentrate on the task at hand. "Or Suzie? Suzie O'Neill, that's cute, Mommy, what do you think?"

"Pink," I counseled when, on Saturday morning, my parents sifted through the bargain bins at JCPenney. "Not blue, remember?" And when she packed her small, plaid, hard-sided suitcase for the hospital I slipped several of the outfits I'd worn as a baby between my mother's nightgown and her quilted satin bed jacket. "How about Linda?" I said. "Or Cindy?"

"Get her turtles and roses," I reminded my father as he helped my mother down the front walk to the car, adding, for emphasis, "*pink* roses."

"Brenda!" I shouted as the Plymouth pulled out of the driveway. "Lisa! Laurie! Sandy!"

"WELCOME HOME BABY SISTER," I wrote in big letters on white shelf paper. When my mother returned with another baby boy, I finished off the bag of chocolate chips and went down to the basement, where baking supplies were stored, for a chaser of brown sugar. Spoonful after spoonful, I wondered what I'd done wrong. As time went on, however, it became clear that my mother was the problem, and I took matters into my own hands.

My brother Mike was more than a broken promise. He was a shattered covenant, a vein-bulging, breath-stopping tantrum who was born in an eczema-crusted skin and acted as if he were trying to scream his way out of it. He exploded like a dirty bomb in a baby carriage, his rages tearing through Schreyer Place, forever shredding the local belief that a child's smile requires little more than Mom in the kitchen and fluoride in the drinking water.

Mike's fury was implacable and imperious. He was immune to kindness. At the stage when most infants begin to offer gummy smiles, Mike learned to curl the right side of his upper lip in disgust. He spewed vomit on anyone who attempted to ease his discomfort. Mike's discomfort was as central to his sense of self as was the blue flannel blanket that, when he was barely verbal, my mother accidentally ripped while attempting to launder.

Another child, someone a little greedier, more eager to please, and not quite as smart—a child like me, for instance—might have been placated when my mother demonstrated how the single blanket had become two, hence doubling the blanket asset. Not Mike. "You killed my blanket," he howled. Just as she'd ravaged the sanctity of his cozy existence in her womb by giving birth to him, my mother had destroyed the integrity of his transitional object. And for both of these crimes—as well as for the infuriating fact that he was expected to share his mother with others—she would pay. "He's *just* impossible," my mother would say, and then burst into tears.

Mike had fabulous brown eyes fringed by lashes that were thick and black enough for a Maybelline commercial. He also had several deep, Russ O'Neill dimples, and all of this thrilled my mother and fooled her at first. But quickly she saw it: the implacable frustration under his Gerber Baby good looks, the unbearable itchiness of a spirit trapped in an ill-fitting body, the errant gene that drove her mother to drink and her uncles to suicide. Mike was a Gwinn.

I heard her climbing up from the basement one morning. She took one heavy, deliberate step and then, much, much later, she took another. When I opened the door at the top of the stairs to check on her, she was still standing on the second step from the bottom and holding the big wicker laundry basket in her hands. The basket was full of clean diapers and little blue baby clothes.

"It's . . . beyond . . . me," my mother said. I was four years old. Later, she would say that she suffered from postpartum depression. Back then she said,

"Can you just watch your brother for me, Molly?" and "Molly, I need you to lend a hand." Perhaps Mike heard the dread in my mother's step or perhaps it was simply the slowness of her gait that increased his endless roaring, his gum-gnashing plea for her attention and devotion. When I tried to comfort him—"Here, honey, why don't you just chew on this pencil for a little while, that's a good boy"—he spat. When my father picked him up, his toothless firstborn son bit him with such force that his gums left bruises.

"Jaayyz," said my father, admiringly, "this kid's got some power." He was mesmerized by Mike's grip and size. He spent less time playing with me and more and more time studying his infant son for any indication of superior eye-hand coordination.

"He's *just* impossible," I said, shaking my head and looking up at my father, bitterly. "It's beyond me," I added.

As Mike railed and howled throughout her next pregnancy, my mother tried to console us both with extravagant assurances about my forthcoming sister. The gratitude I felt at my mother's growing belly was matched only by my excitement. The phrase "after your sister comes" was a promise greater than Christmas. In kindergarten, Miss Richards helped me use the fat, flat-bottom red crayon from my Crayola eight-pack to draw *X*'s through the days leading up to the Ides of March, the date that Dr. Donley had set for my sister's arrival.

From what my mother told me about the events to come, I also got the impression that babies were like swollen tonsils: eventually they had to be removed. "I may have to go to the hospital while you are asleep," my mother said; I was prepared. Mike, on the other hand, was not. And on the morning of March 15, 1957, when he awoke to find her gone, Mike was so shocked that he actually shut up. He searched the house until he found one of our mother's maternity tops in the wicker laundry hamper. Then he began to sob without making a sound.

The blouse was a delft blue number with a large white sailor collar that was trimmed in red rickrack and had shiny red Bakelite buttons. So deep was his despair, so profound was his hatred of Mrs. Kell, the Amish lady who'd come to take care of us, that Mike condescended to sit on my lap. He didn't spit or bite or try to scratch the itch of his oozing eczema by rubbing his skin against me. He simply clutched the maternity top and rocked and mewed like a runt abandoned by the side of the road.

We sat on the daybed that was wedged between the table and our father's little Formica-topped desk in the kitchen and watched *Captain Kangaroo*.

"Mommy will be right back," I said, stroking the blouse. "She's just gone to get our baby sister." Inhaling the smell of his dark curls, I held him tight and rocked the silently sobbing weight of him. I loved him in the way that one loves those who no longer matter: poignantly.

"Just you wait," I said, and perhaps I already sounded like the sister of a baby sister. For despite the wet-leafed gray morning that was visible through the kitchen windows, regardless of the blue-tinged light from the television set as *Captain Kangaroo* gave way to *Tom Terrific,* I felt the golden glow of a well-earned reward. I felt magnanimous.

"I'll take care of the baby," I told my brother. "You can have Mommy all to yourself."

We were still sitting in the same chair when my father called from the hospital. *Mighty Mouse* was on the television and Mrs. Kell picked up the heavy black telephone from its spot on the desk and stood next to us, holding it while Mike and I gripped the receiver between us.

"Mommy's fine, honey," said our father. "And just you wait till you see this little fella. His name is Patrick Joseph, he tipped that scale at nine pounds four ounces, a real bruiser, honey, but easy, happy, nothing like Mike, I can tell you that right now. And coal black hair. He's one handsome guy, takes after his father, ha, ha, ha."

I would like to say that I ripped my mother's maternity blouse from my brother's arms and tore it to shreds. Instead I simply returned it to the laundry basket and set my sights on the next pregnancy, resolving to be more attentive, more vigilant in the future.

"Lori," I said when, in the fall of 1958, my mother mentioned that she was going to see Dr. Donley.

"Debby," I wheedled when she placed Pat on the potty and handed me a bag of Nestlé chocolate chips.

They had traded in the Plymouth and were driving a rusty green Dodge station wagon by then, and I ran alongside it as my father and mother headed to the hospital on April 3, 1959.

"Caddie!" I said. "Like Caddie Woodlawn!"

"Kevin," my father said when he called later that night. "John Kevin but we'll call him Kevin. Just you wait till you see him, honey, a little fella, seven pounds three ounces, more blond hair than a lifeguard, a real looker, honey, and happy as a lark, just like his dad."

The next year, I was romancing *National Velvet* and lobbied for Elizabeth while crouching in front of Kevin and holding a single chocolate chip between my index finger and thumb. My campaign for an Elizabeth Taylor namesake paralleled my mother's fifth pregnancy through its final months in the hot summer of 1960 and continued right up to September 15, when my father, once again, called from the hospital. I didn't even say hello. I said, "We can call her Lizzie or Beth, Dad, or even Eliza!"

"Robert," said my father, "Robert Gwinn. You just wait till you see this one, honey. Another nine-pounder! Biggest eyes I ever saw, and calm! The only one not carrying on in the nursery up there. Real good disposition, just like his dad."

My next campaign was canceled due to miscarriage, and I had three years to revise my baby sister strategy. Encouraged by my mother, whose hopes for a second daughter remained undaunted, I unpacked all of the infant finery that the Gwinns had showered on me when I was born. There were cashmere blankets and silk baby quilts, little quilted jackets, gowns with pink satin sashes, tiny taffeta and chiffon dresses embroidered with rosebuds and daisies. I washed each piece and hung it on the clothesline.

By this time, my brothers had commandeered the quiet room under the pine tree and turned it into a fort. I'd retreated to a cave formed by the tumble-down branches of a rosebush behind the house. While I waited for my sister, the rosebush offered complete privacy as well as unparalleled views of the clothesline. I curled under the branches watching my pretties bleach and dry in the sun, reading *The Secret Garden,* and imagining the private world we would share, my little sister and I.

Her crib was already arranged in the alcove in which I slept, a pink angora throw artfully tucked over one corner of the bars. It was a maple, mission-style crib that was decorated with a decal of a teddy bear in light blue pajamas on the headboard. I recruited my best friend, Anne, who had, by that time, moved into the house next door to ours, to serve as lookout as I applied pink nail polish to the teddy bear's pajamas.

"Hurry up," hissed Anne from her position by the windows above the driveway that separated our houses. Our mothers were at her house, practicing their piano duet, and while I painted, Anne listened to the progression of the music and urged me on. "They're on the second-to-last page," she warned. "She'll be back any minute."

Anne had an older brother and two younger sisters and I relied on her memory of the months in which her sisters were formed in her mother's stomach. Prior to her involvement, my sister-making strategy had, I realized, been fairly superficial. Anne was helping me take it to a new level. She confirmed the importance of pink blankets and clothing but emphasized the importance of ingesting pink, as well.

"My mom drinks milk of magnesia to make girls," she whispered as we huddled near my sister's crib, spying on our mothers, who were seated in folding chaise lounge chairs by the side of the house, talking and folding laundry.

"Do you want some more coffee, Mrs. O'Neill?" Anne yelled out the window. And then, turning toward me, she hissed, "She does! Mix the milk of magnesia with some Cremora! Hurry!"

"Coming right up!" she yelled out the window.

Soon I was serving my mother coffee at every conceivable opportunity: in 1962, during the second trimester of her pregnancy, my mother was the most highly caffeinated person on Schreyer Place. "Here, Mom," I would say, proffering an aqua-colored Boontonware cup filled with chalk-colored brew while she scrubbed the linoleum floor in the kitchen, stripped the beds, or, bucket and brush in hand, patrolled the walls for fingerprints.

"There's something wrong with the percolator," she'd say at the first sip, and she'd wrinkle her nose. "Why don't you paste the Green Stamps in the books so we can go down to the redemption center?"

Anne was eight years old and I was nine, but she knew many things that I had not yet learned—things, I realized, that might have hampered my earlier efforts at sister-making. I had not previously known, for instance, the importance of Kotex removal.

"Your mom probably hides it in a big box, usually blue," Anne counseled. "When she goes to the grocery we'll find it and bury it in the ravine. If we don't, she might catch menstruation, which is a disease mothers get when they are old, and then they can't have girl babies."

My gratitude was boundless. "What do you think of the name Anne?" I asked my mother one afternoon as we sat at the kitchen table folding diapers together.

"I think Anne or Olivia," she said. Our accord was as complete and delicious as the excitement we shared. The gender imbalance in our house—there were five males by then and just the two of us—disturbed us both. The female contingent lost before it even voted on choices of entertainment, television channels, or household chores. In addition, while my father's attitude and my brothers' tender ages cast maleness as playful and forever young, a sense of drudgery and old-fogy-ness shrouded the female experience in our family. But a baby girl would change everything. It had been worth the wait.

"Anne or Olivia," I repeated, while carefully creasing a cotton diaper and folding it three times to achieve the perfectly aligned configuration so prized by my mother.

"Olivia or Anne," replied my mother dreamily as she refolded the diaper.

"Paul," said my father on the telephone several months later. The heavy black telephone that lived in the arched nook in the hallway had been replaced by a lighter-weight model that was beige, like the new linoleum on the kitchen floor and the new Formica on its counters. The television had been moved to the new rec room in the basement, and the new telephone resided on my father's desk. His chair was a molded white plastic thing on a swivel base and, as the single syllable he'd pronounced hovered between the telephone receiver and my ear, I could feel the chair pressing a cold red line into my thighs beneath my rumpled, pleated skirt. Mike was wrestling me for the receiver, Pat was pulling the curly cord. Kevin, who was almost four years old, was unrolling one of my knee socks, and Robert, who was three, was probably chewing on one of my saddle shoes. I was ten years old.

"Well, it better be Paul That's All," I screamed and slammed down the telephone.

Anybody could see that my parents were in way over their heads; even before their sixth child was born they could barely pay their mortgage.

My father had lost his job at North American Aviation and had started an excavating business. He bought a backhoe, a bright yellow model that we named Henry, and, since he could not afford a truck or a trailer, Henry was, for a time, our father's primary mode of transport. There were no other backhoes in evidence on Schreyer Place. To me, the heavy equipment desecrating our driveway seemed like yet another manifestation of the testosterone that was ruining our lives.

The neighborhood had changed since we'd first moved in. Most of the older people had retired and moved away, and their houses had been bought by assistant professors and dental residents at Ohio State University, or junior engineers at Battelle Memorial Institute. The new neighbors were all like my friend Anne's family—they tended to have three or four children, mostly girls, as well as tidy habits and predictable schedules. Fathers drove to work on weekday mornings. On Saturday, mothers drove to the grocery and while they were gone, the fathers cut the grass, usually using a hand-powered push mower that made a noise like a winding clock. Upon the mothers' return, the fathers carried the brown bags from Albers into the house. Then they put Spic-and-Span in a galvanized bucket, added hot water, washed the family car—usually a Rambler or a Ford woody—and buffed it with TurtleWax.

The presence of Henry in front of our house, caked with mud and grease and reeking of diesel fuel, indicated our family's lack of appreciation for TurtleWax as well as our probable lack of health insurance, college savings, and retirement benefits. The neighbors couldn't imagine what sort of people would continue to sentence innocent children to such chaos and insecurity. This bedlam was compounded by the fact that whenever the bank threatened to repo Henry or the house, my mother would have to return to the laboratory at Mount Carmel Hospital where she analyzed blood samples. She would work nights and weekends until the crisis passed, which generally meant until the spring thaw, when the earth once again became tender enough for the chunky iron teeth on Henry's bucket to dig waterlines and gas lines. Sometimes my father worked at the gas station. For a while he sold Royal vacuum cleaners, door-to-door. Regardless of their enterprising natures, my parents couldn't afford another child, male or female, which left me with only one alternative: I decided that Paul would have to be my baby sister.

It helped that he was born with deep blue eyes, a quiet disposition, and a head full of blond ringlets. I called him Polly, which others took to be Paulie, but that was their problem. I dressed him in the gowns and pinafores and petticoats that I'd worn as an infant, the ones I had so assiduously prepared for his arrival. I protected his curls from even the hint of a barber and tied pink bows in the cascading blond Afro that resulted. Others might have considered my denial worrisome, even pathological. I prefer to think of it as my first overt act as an O'Neill. After all, my father always told us not to listen to other people. He said to trust our instincts and act accordingly. He said that reality is what you recognize. I recognized my baby sister.

My parents did not challenge my conviction; they were otherwise occupied. Within weeks of the baby's birth in late February, we were ankle-deep in mud season. My mother was working in the evening and spent her days cleaning dirty footprints, washing windows, and screaming, "Don't-you-dare-set-foot-in-this-house-stay-in-the-yard-give-me-that-bat-you-just-wait-till-your-father-gets-home-I'm-gonna-kill-you-so-help-me-God-Molly-can-you-lend-a-hand-they-are-beyond-me-my-God-they're-gonna-end-up-in-boys'-industrial-school."

My father and Henry were digging water and gas lines from five a.m. until sunset six days a week. He showered and ate dinner when he got home and then he went to visit each of the neighbors who had complained about his sons. After threatening some frail professor or engineer with bodily harm, my father would return home and pitch batting practice in the backyard. Later still, he returned phone calls to his customers, wrote invoices, and drove to Greendales to buy my mother chocolate turtles.

Perhaps my parents didn't have the time to notice the sartorial presence of their youngest child. Maybe they felt guilty for having broken their promises to me, or maybe neither one of them had the heart to dash my dreams of sisterdom. As for my brothers, although they were still very young, they already acted en masse. They were wild, they were a tribe, they were the Apaches of Schreyer Place, and the last thing anyone felt they needed was another brave.

By the summer of 1963, Paul was old enough for a stroller and, after dressing him carefully, I would settle him in our light blue Taylor Tot and push him far beyond our neighborhood, up past Dominion Junior High and around the bend where the street changed from worn asphalt to a lighter, smoother surface and the houses became newer and lower and more often made from stucco, stained wood, and stone. There, in a development near Indianola Avenue, we were not known. We were not children of a ditchdigger, we were not outcasts in a faculty ghetto, we were not a delusional ten-year-old and an ill-used baby brother. On those new and expensive and anonymous blocks, we were sisters.

Achieving this pinnacle of contentment among strangers caused me to become a bit cavalier about Polly at home. Had Anne and I not been so busy lip-syncing the Top 40 countdown on WCOL before dinner that fateful night in July of 1965, my charade might have continued for decades. But no, I was so preoccupied with making a microphone by attaching an empty orange juice can to a broomstick that I neglected to exchange my brother's seersucker dress for a more androgynous sun suit before dinner. The frenzy to be fully propped prior to the airing of our favorite songs—"Sounds of Silence" by Simon and Garfunkel and "We Can Work It Out" by the Beatles—blurred my judgment and cost me dearly.

We were at the table, eating mashed potatoes, peas, and "city chicken"—skewered cube veal broiled with lemon—when ten-year-old Mike, whose many obsessions by then included a constant desire to run his hands through his younger sibling's hair, attacked Paul's curls. Paul screamed and clapped his hands to his head—a motion that launched his dinner plate into Pat's lap. I leaped to my youngest brother's defense, upending my chair in the process. Pat seized the opportunity to dump the contents of his plate into his lap, as well, saving himself his usual dinnertime showdown with my father. My mother snapped—"Damnit, Molly, how many times do I have to tell you that Mike cannot sit next to the baby?"—and, rousing himself from his perpetual and generally imperturbable calm, my father finally noted that his youngest child was looking alarmingly fetching. Turning slowly toward me, my father wagged his finger.

"You're gonna turn that kid into a darned, um, unhappy person," he said. A couple days later he took his five sons to get buzz cuts.

This was not the first time that I'd paid a high price for a moment's inattention. Five years earlier, when my mother had been four months pregnant, Mike was hit by a car in front of Our Lady of Peace Elementary School. He was in first grade, I was in fourth. Eager to provide us with the comforts of organized religion, our parents had formally converted to Catholicism and had taken us out of Indian Springs Elementary, the public school, and enrolled us in the parochial school a block away. Our Lady of Peace was located on a busy street but, for reasons known only to the pastor, Father Foley, it had no patrol boys protecting the school's crosswalks with flags on long wooden sticks.

"I put my trust in God," he told my parents. "Trust me." And perhaps because they needed to trust something, they did. Just to be on the safe side, however, they also told me to wait at the foot of the school's wide concrete steps after my teacher, Sister Maria Goretti, had dismissed us.

"Wait until Mike comes out," my mother would remind me. "Don't cross Dominion Boulevard until you have him by the hand."

Most days I did wait. But on the way to school on the morning of November 9, 1961, I had discovered a clubhouse made of leaves behind one of the houses on the other side of the street, and as soon as our class was marched down the steps that afternoon, I pulled my friends across the street for a quick tour of the facility. Mike's class was just coming down the stairs when I returned. Standing across the street on a piece of lawn that rose up behind a row of parked cars, I spotted his brown stocking cap and corduroy jacket. He was confused, looking around for me.

"Mike!" I yelled. Hearing me, he dashed between two of the parked cars and into the street. Then I screamed, *"Nooooooooooooooo!"* so that Mike had skidded to a stop and was standing still when the Mercury, driven by a woman who was doing nearly 40 miles per hour, hit him full on.

As if launched by a bionic trampoline, my five-year-old brother flew into the air. His composition book, his Baltimore Catechism, the pages of paper with wide lines that were filled with his penmanship exercises, all fluttered down like beige-colored leaves as Mike rose higher and higher. The sound of screeching brakes and my screams collided over Dominion Boulevard as he floated down, down, down. As he fell, his jacket billowed around him, but he was still wearing his stocking cap when his head slammed into the chrome statue of Mercury on the hood of the car. Blood spurted like hot grease against the woman's windshield.

"The nuns made me cross the street," I told my mother.

"It's not my fault," I said.

"They wouldn't let me stand there."

"I told him to wait for me."

"It's not my fault."

But I knew that it was. Eighteen hours later, as surgeons at Riverside Hospital continued to tease minute bone shards from my brother's brain—hundreds of splinters would be removed from the depressed fracture of his skull—I crouched in the narrow stairwell between the first and second stories of our house, listening to my parents cry.

This was Mike's place. When he had tantrums, my parents would confine him to the carpeted stairway, and his imprint was everywhere: crescents from his hammering fists and black scuff marks from the heels of his shoes scored the walls. There were even teeth marks on the banister. I crouched silently on the second step, straining to hear my parents' conversation.

They said it didn't matter if, as the surgeons had predicted, Mike never walked or talked again. "It doesn't matter if he's a vegetable," my father declared. "All I care about is that he's alive." "How can you say 'vegetable,' how can you?" my mother asked, and then they cried some more.

I was still crouched there when, an hour later, my mother screamed, "Jesus!" and my father said, "Jesus Christ, Boots, you're miscarrying. We've got to get you to the hospital." And that, I was later told, was how I lost my baby sister.

Although he recovered, Mike seemed determined to reverse the miracle of his survival. On his first day back to school, in May, he managed to climb to the top of the jungle gym during recess, lose his grasp, and smash his head open once more. A month later, while I was baby-sitting and Mike was terrorizing Kevin and Robert, he ran through the kitchen and continued right on through the glass storm door, falling down the concrete steps outside in a Niagara of blood and glass.

"Where were you?" my mother asked when I called her at the Jai Lai, where she and my father were having dinner. She reopened the investigation into his original accident for years. We might, for instance, be in the kitchen together, on a winter afternoon, sharing the details of our days. She would be telling me about which neighbor had complained about which brother as she mashed the potatoes. I would be outlining the plot for the play I was writing while dribbling Thousand Island dressing over wedges of iceberg. Steam would be fogging the windows of the warm and intimate world we shared in these moments and suddenly my mother would say: "Tell me what really happened."

Months would pass and then, after an evening shopping together when we were tucked into a booth at Jerry's drive-in, sitting close enough to feel the warmth of each other's thighs, conspiring over hot fudge sundaes, she would say: "Tell me."

Or in the middle of the night, as she comforted a sick or fretful baby in a rocking chair next to the alcove where I slept, she might suddenly blurt out: "I just want to know the truth, Molly."

But I couldn't tell her.

Of course, I had a distinguished history of lying to my mother. I lied to ease her worries, I lied to make her laugh, I lied to entertain us both. Under normal circumstances, I lied without compunction, without a second thought, and with significant élan. Like my father, I believed that life could be reordered by simply being rephrased. And if that was the case, then admitting exactly what happened would mean that I almost killed my brother and that I *had* killed my sister, the baby that my mother lost. How could I admit to such a crime?

Frequent surreptitious doses of brown sugar and swigs from the maple syrup container provided some relief, but nothing can wash the blood from a murderer's conscience, and a secret becomes a space between people, a chasm that eventually forgets its original purpose and takes on a life of its own. Decades passed before I even attempted to bridge the gap that grew between my mother and me.

"Think how different it would have been if you'd had that baby," I said a few years ago as we drove through the old neighborhood together. "Remember how much we wanted another girl?"

"That baby wasn't a girl," said my mother as I turned her white Cadillac onto Schreyer Place. "Where'd you ever get that idea?" she asked.

A Social History of Crab Melts

"**D**id your mother show you how to do that?" asked Mrs. Yokel. My Girl Scout troop had set its sights on earning the cooking badge, and the troop leader was amazed by my flawless crack-and-cradle technique. I was ten years old and could have been juggling uranium inside an infinity symbol for the awe in her voice as she watched me relay the yolk between each half of a cracked eggshell. I pretended not to hear her.

"It's a cinch," I said, smiling in a way that I hoped resembled that of the carefree mothers I saw on TV, serving their families Tang for breakfast. "But you should never crack an egg directly into the large mixing bowl," I continued. "The tiniest bit of yolk can keep a whole bowl of egg whites from becoming meringue. That's why you should always crack your egg over a small bowl and let the white out by rolling the yolk from one half of the shell to another. Like this."

"Do you cook with your mother, honey?" asked Mrs. Yokel again.

I evinced my best Mona Lisa, a poignant and tight-lipped grimace meant to convey fortitude in the face of unimaginable suffering. Yes, I cooked with my mother. I was her deputy, for heaven's sake, an impeccably trained domestic and a living example of the failure of child-labor laws in our country. But what really stoked my Cinderella complex was less the servitude itself than the healthy, high-end cooking that I'd been pressed into service to create. Griddled pork chops, skewered veal, French-style green beans, and potatoes lyonnaise, indeed!

Other families ate tuna noodle casserole. They had macaroni and cheese, or meat loaf, or chicken pot pies for dinner. But my parents did not believe in mixing food together and baking it under crusts of crumbled Ritz crackers, cornflakes, or Velveeta cheese. They practiced a separation of food groups. We had meat. We had potato. We had vegetable. We had salad. We had dessert. Each was distinct and none was overcooked. It was humiliating.

My father believed that junk food was a communist plot. My mother explained to us that only trashy people ate food that was mass-produced and wrapped in plastic. Well, if she only deigned to eat potato chips delivered in a can by the Charles Chip man, that was fine for her. We wanted Ruffles with ridges in stylish individual bags.

Our parents' attitude toward dinner was not only embarrassing to us, personally; it was an affront to the central Ohio of the 1960s. At that time, Columbus was the test-market capital of the United States for food products. Automobile designers and sitcom producers may have been wondering whether it would play in Peoria, but food manufacturers and restaurateurs were asking a different question: "Will they eat it in Columbus?"

For over fifty years—from 1922, when White Castle hamburgers were launched, to the introduction of the Wendy's and Subway chains in the 1970s—rare was the food product that was not test-marketed in my hometown. Albers, the grocery store a few blocks from our house, was the Eden of our forbidden. Although inflexible on the menu at home, my parents exerted nothing beyond financial control over what we put in our mouths outside the house. At Albers, on Saturday morning, new product samples were free.

Here, sugary cereals and salty snacks were dished up with impunity. Here, alluring slices from the frontiers of processed cheese and lunch meat were rolled up and offered to us on toothpicks. What's more, here our opinion *mattered*. My brothers and I stampeded the service counters. We wanted to be part of history, and we recognized our chance: we were usually sampling new food concepts at least a year before they were available nationwide.

Marketers have different theories as to why the taste of Columbus was the epitome of average when I was growing up there. The population of the city has always been young, and in its test-market heyday, the city was also ethnically indistinct. Marketers claim that the local economy has long been balanced between the production of goods and the rendering of services, and that a well-balanced demography follows a balanced economy. But these facts alone do not explain the city's uncanny ability to anoint the next Frito or its habit of voting for winning presidents. With the exceptions only of 1944, 1960, and 2004, the candidate who won Columbus won the election. No city has a better record. Being average is considered a civic virtue in Columbus. "We tend to do everything in this city at about a B-grade level," Mayor Tom Moody once told the *Chicago Tribune* proudly.

Taste-testing was also a grave responsibility. I never sported my carefree smile when tasting new products at the grocery store or standing in line for free samples at prototypes for Kentucky Fried Chicken, Krispy Kreme doughnuts, or Arthur Treacher's Fish & Chips. No, on those occasions, I would close my eyes and try to align my heart and mind with the rest of the country's. I knew that millions of dollars, the taste of dinner, and the future of the American landscape rested in my tongue.

Sometimes, late at night, I still wonder if the obesity epidemic might have been avoided if I'd given a thumbs-down to my first McDonald's french fry. I torture myself with the possibility that roadside America might still be sprinkled lightly with a few family-owned eateries, places where meals are a matter of heart and always made from scratch and by hand. Back then, however, I was only worried about responding as others did. A good taste tester is not, after all, a person with a finely calibrated palate. *Au contraire!* The tongue that food marketers dream about is not distinct in any way. It is average.

And that is exactly what my brothers and I wanted to be. We wanted to set an example for the country by eating like everybody else. The men who noted our responses to new products on Saturday mornings, the ones with pocket protectors and clipboards, listened to us. The smiling women who performed cooking demonstrations also thought that our opinions were important. We called these women Betty Crocker. We wished we had a Betty for a mother. We began to rebel at the family table.

Day after day, my mother's connection to the privilege of her past—to say nothing of her footing in Schreyer Place society—was becoming increasingly tenuous. Nevertheless, she greeted each morning with renewed conviction that a well-balanced, well-served breakfast could change everything. There

was no instant oatmeal. Oh no, we were a steel-cut-oat family. A sweet butter and heavy cream family. A perfectly timed three-minute egg family. Let
the rest of the world begin its day the easy way, eating Wyler's grape jelly on
toasted Wonder Bread. We would scale the craters of Thomas's English
Muffins. Homemade preserves would be laid before us in a Waterford crys-
tal compote dish with a silver spoon. There would be fresh-squeezed orange
juice.

To my mother's delight, every morning, several hours after her husband
had departed to dig Columbus, five of her children would sit down to breakfast. They would chew as quietly as possible, mouthing phrases such as
"Morning, Mom," and "Please pass the sugar," and "More orange juice,
thanks." We were trying not to wake up Mike. The oldest boy in the family
arose each morning, slammed into the kitchen, sneered at each of us, glared
at our mother, and screamed, "I HATE THE BREAKFAST."

He began low with the word "I." His voice rose to an excoriating screech
when he pronounced "hate," and then softened when he pronounced "the
breakfast." It was as if the object of his hatred were beside the point. Pat and
I pretended not to hear. The little kids watched his hands and covered their
heads with their own for protection.

"I HATE THE BREAKFAST."

"No, you don't," said my mother firmly. She still felt guilty that she had
not said just these words to his third-grade teacher, when she'd called to discuss the possibility of tying Mike to his chair. And yet how could she pretend not to know what they were up against?

"Sit down!" she ordered. But day after day, my brother's morning mood
beat my mother into Bettyhood. She would offer Mike different grades of
"toasted" or alternative toppings for his muffins, various degrees of doneness
for his eggs. She would threaten. She would beg. And when he was sure that
she was his and only his—when the rest of us had left the table and she'd sat
down close enough to him so that he could see the battered-dog plea in her
eyes—Mike ate the breakfast.

My mother prayed for inclement weather. When it was too wet or too
cold to dig ditches, my father stayed home. He made pancakes and Mike
always ate them without comment, without coaxing, and without recrimination.

"I don't know what you're talking about, Boots," my father would say,
"Mike's a darned good eater. Pat's the problem. That kid's got you bamboo-
zled. That kid doesn't know who's boss."

Pat did not like home cooking; he had a visceral distrust of anything that was produced in the family kitchen. He viewed junk food as an inalienable right and as the only safe and sane source of human nutrition. He saw Mom as a culinary cripple.

Luckily, Pat had a generous and forgiving nature. Just as he defended Jan-the-clubfoot and Billy-the-harelip on the playground, he upheld my mother's right to cook. "It's OK, Mom," he'd say, after gagging on his dinner. "It's not your fault." But protecting his mother's feelings and eating her cooking was not the same thing.

By the time he could talk, Pat refused anything but bologna and canned peaches. Innately, it seemed, he understood that these were the only two items in our family's larder that had been sanctified by the food-processing industry. While my mother battled the Gwinn-ness in her imperious eldest son, my father went toe to toe with Pat, who was born looking like a miniature O'Neill. Barrel-chested and built low to the ground, Pat had tiny hands and feet, and pale skin. With his black hair, he bore a startling resemblance to Beaver Cleaver. "I want what I want and all what I want," he'd announce, banging his silver spoon into the bone-china baby dish on the tray of his high chair.

"You're not coming down till you clean your plate," my father would say, leaning low to press his face into the younger version of itself every night at dinner. "Ya hear me?"

But years would have passed and the high chair would have splintered around my brother's full-grown, full-back girth before he would have allowed healthy, handmade sustenance to enter his person. His attitude did not change when he graduated to a chair at the table. We ate at five-thirty, and by eight some nights, Pat was still sitting in his seat and my father was rooting through the kitchen drawers.

"Boots," he would say, "where's the darned funnel? You think you're cute, Buster? Well, we'll see who is going to eat his lima beans tonight. Boots! Where's the blender? By God, this kid's gonna eat if I have to pour it down his throat."

Pat was not impressed. His mouth was closed. His teeth were clenched and opening them would have required a vise. My father was not good with hand tools. My mother didn't like cleaning up vomit. Like a patient batter, Pat played the odds. He sometimes arrived bruised, but he always got on base.

By the time he was in kindergarten, Pat had distinguished himself as a libertarian; he believed that he could do whatever he pleased and he extended this philosophy to everyone in his radius. Among the other children in the neighborhood, he was a leader and a trendsetter. Local mothers often left their purses on the front seat of their cars during neighborhood Girl Scout troop meetings; when Pat targeted them as an excellent source of candy money, an army of small bandits gladly donned their Zorro capes and Lone Ranger masks to serve as accessories to his crime. By the time he was in second grade, Pat was enlisting the same children in his fireworks business.

"Just run this sack of M-80s and this box of cherry bombs over to the junior high for me. There's a kid wearing a jersey that says Frankie Robinson; give it to him. He's going to give you a five-dollar bill." Fireworks were illegal in Ohio. Pat purchased his supply from high school kids and stored his inventory under pillows of insulation in the eaves of our sun-baked attic.

"You could have blown the house up," said my father, folding his wide belt and grabbing Pat by the wrist.

"You're going to end up in boys' industrial school," said my mother. Upstairs, listening through the heat grate, our bottoms itched and we felt like dancing as Pat took his beating. "Stop it!" my mother screamed. "You're going to hurt him, Chick."

Pat never cried and he never lied. He took full responsibility for his actions and he was undeterred by punishment. He was an entrepreneur. When my parents demanded explanations, his was simple: "I have to eat," he said.

My response to my parents' food philosophy was far more covert. I ate what I was served and then, when no one was looking, I ate whatever else I could get my hands on. My primary poaching ground was the cupboards in the basement, which served as a pantry. There my mother kept baking supplies: the sugar sprinkles that, when shaken from their container directly onto my tongue, could boost a mood; the brown sugar that—spoonful by pilfered spoonful—delivered me from the densely packed pandemonium of family life into a quiet room of my own.

I shared my brothers' dietary frustrations, and yet I also shared my parents' concern about my wild and crazy brothers. I had to save us, and when I was in fifth grade, the Ohio Power and Electric Company showed me how. They invited my Brownie troop to a cooking demonstration in the atrium of their company headquarters downtown. A four-burner electric range was placed like an altar in the center of the soaring room, and as soon as we had settled into our folding chairs, the overhead lights were dimmed and a spotlight beamed on the range. Then, waving like Miss America, a home economist in an apron *tap-tap-tap*ped her way over to the stove, where she began peeling and chopping carrots. She was wearing pumps. Her smile never wavered. She got nothing on her apron. She was the ultimate Betty and her life was a breeze.

"This is as easy as pie, girls," she confided as she placed the carrots, along with water, butter, and sugar, in a saucepan, covered it, and put in on a burner. An orange glow began to surge through the coils of the burner and she explained how the water would boil and how that, in turn, would cause the butter and sugar to dissolve.

"Girls, when I take the lid off, those carrots are going to be tender and sweet and shiny," she said, and her tone reminded me of the women my mother scorned, the ones who couldn't balance a checkbook and called their husbands "Daddy."

"I still can't believe how easy this is," she trilled. "It's nothing! It's a cinch!"

The other girls may have been impressed by the ease, safety, and hygiene of the electric stove; I was mesmerized by the cook and her carrots. The idea of sugaring a vegetable was thrillingly subversive, and the teacher—with her vacuous smile and easy delight—was the mother I wished I had. Glazed carrots touched a chord down deep in the cavern of hunger and desire inside me. My heart raced, my palms tingled. The possibility of cooking the way other people did filled me with the sort of determined, freight-train will that makes winners of mere mortals. I saw my future and it was in the food service industry.

I began spending my evenings locked in the bathroom, practicing my smile and saying, "It's a cinch!"

"What can I do?" I asked my mother, prancing into the kitchen.

My mother was clearly dubious. However, in addition to my established tasks—setting the table, making the salad, pouring the milk, and carrying plates to the table—she taught me to peel and mince and chop.

"I can't believe how easy it is!" I said, beaming up at my mother as a cheerleader might smile up at a taller and less fortunate girl.

"Remind me to call the orthodontist," she said. With the furrowed brow of a scientist at work, she taught me to dip chicken in buttermilk, to dust it with seasoned flour, to fry it in Crisco. Holding her tongue between her lips in the manner of one afraid to breathe, she demonstrated her technique for forming hamburger patties gently, lest the meat be mushed. By watching her, I learned how to sauté cutlets to a neat and uniform gold, how to broil chops until they were juicy. The results were impressive, but I found her earnest precision wearying. Cooking, I decided, was only as fun as the cook was.

"It's nothing!" I trilled, offering my mother a taste of the béchamel sauce that I'd learned from a package of Carl Budding's chipped beef.

"Obviously not," said my mother, arching her eyebrows.

I chose to overlook her sarcasm. I learned to whip cream to soft peaks, to meringue egg whites, to beat oil slowly into egg yolks. And, of course, I learned how to separate eggs. But even as I started to cook for my mother, I was also learning how to cook against her.

My brothers and I quietly stockpiled ingredients to use on the rare evenings when our parents went out. I memorized the recipes that appeared on the sorts of food my mother would never buy—processed cheese, for instance, canned chili, or Spam—and used these guidelines to make gooey casseroles and cream cheese dips. I also made cakes and brownies from the mixes that I bought with my baby-sitting money and hid in my closet. While other children smoked cigarettes and made prank phone calls, my brothers and I sat down to the sorts of dinners that other people ate.

Stealth and efficiency were paramount, and I always eradicated all evidence of back-of-the-box gourmet activity from the house. I swept the kitchen. I scrubbed the counter and the stove. I opened the windows and waved sections of the *Columbus Evening Dispatch*. I used Lysol. And then I cooked the meal that my mother had instructed me to prepare so that its aroma might linger. Our escapades were never detected.

My younger brothers worshipped me. In exchange for my promise to prepare a dish they'd seen on television or at the home of one of their friends, they offered unimaginable deals. "I'll tickle your back all during *Lassie* if you make SpaghettiOs with cheesy Manwich sauce," offered Pat. Mike said, "If you make sour cream onion soup dip, I'll be nice."

Crab melts as I know them were born on a cold, wet Saturday in March of 1964, not long after the Beatles appeared on *The Ed Sullivan Show* and exactly one week after we participated in a taste test of Arby's roast beef sandwich. I was eleven years old. That morning, my father stood at the top of the basement stairs and yelled, "Come on! We're going to Albers!" My brothers were watching *Mighty Mouse,* and the older ones immediately understood that their commitment to the cartoon had to be balanced against the needs of our private dining society. Our parents were going out that evening. We needed supplies.

"Coming!" cried Mike, who was eight years old, and Pat, who was seven, hopped up with an alacrity that should have made my father suspicious.

"It's almost over!" cried the five-year-old Kevin.

"Five minutes," echoed Robert, who was four years old.

"Da-aaa-had," whined Paul. Paul was only two years old, but the threat of sobs in his high, wavering voice made him sound like a little old lady. It was a terrible sound, an entire history of oppression in one nasal soprano.

"Five minutes," my father agreed quickly, adding, as he closed the basement door, "Jesus. What's with that kid's voice, Boots? Adenoids?"

I was upstairs cleaning, and I could hear my parents talking through the heating vents. "I need a rag over here," my mother said. "My God, will you look at what I'm getting out of this crack?" She was working the perimeter of the kitchen floor with a paring knife. Before summoning my brothers, my father had been following her with a scrub brush. "You better get a can of Ajax when you go to the store." I was using a dust mop to thrash my brothers' dirty clothes out from under their beds. "Spic-and-Span, too," my mother added, her voice rising happily through the heat vent. Just as happily, I folded the dirty clothes and put them back into my brother's drawers.

On school mornings, I usually kicked their clothes under the bed from the middle of the floor, where my brothers had left them. Saturdays were different. My father tended to lapse into nostalgia for his days in the army when he helped clean the house. It was not uncommon for him to imitate the superior officers who had once tormented him by performing a thorough inspection of my janitorial services. I didn't mind reswabbing a deck here or there, but the possibility that he might withdraw my off-base privileges concerned me. I could not afford to miss a cooking demonstration at the grocery store.

The Betty at the Ohio Power and Electric Company had lifted the scales from my eyes, but it was the Saturday-morning Bettys—the women who did cooking demonstrations at Albers grocery store—who showed me the creative potential that could be unleashed from a can of cream of mushroom soup, a box of Jell-O, or a loaf of Velveeta cheese. They were there every Saturday, at the juncture between the meat and the dairy counters, and they were the professors of my continuing education, a virtual wellspring of inspiration. Using only an electric skillet or a toaster oven, the Saturday-morning Bettys transformed groceries that could be found even in my mother's kitchen into the sort of toothsome trash that made my mouth water.

One week, they combined freeze-dried onion soup, ketchup, and hamburger meat to make a sloppy joe mixture. They mixed Rice Krispies with margarine and tiny marshmallows to make treats, and stirred flour, brown sugar, butter, walnuts, marshmallows, chocolate chips, and coconut together to make no-bake Rocky Road bars. It was captivating. It was exhilarating. All

I had to do was watch and learn. I wouldn't have considered missing a single lesson. On rainy Saturdays, therefore, I cleaned with a thoroughness and speed that could have rocketed me to the top of the housekeeping industry.

"Do under the toilet seat and all around it with bleach," said my mother through the heating vent. Our seamless partnership—the mother, the father, and me, the deputy mom—meant that she did not need to differentiate between the orders she gave me and the shopping reminders she gave my father.

"You better get another bottle of Lysol. I don't know which one of them isn't lifting the seat, but it is absolutely disgusting up there," she continued.

"Get ground chuck, not hamburger. Maybe a rump roast for Sunday, or rib or tenderloin, whatever looks best. Bananas, but green, not black; try to control yourself, Chick. Apples, canned peaches, frozen peas. Potatoes, ten pounds, two heads of iceberg, get the French-style green beans if they have them, peanut butter, and a jar of honey. Get preserves, not jelly. Colby cheese, not cheddar, and definitely not the individually wrapped stuff. Canned tuna in water, not oil, it tastes like cat food," she said, and then:

"On second thought, maybe you should use bleach, Molly, one of them's got an aim problem. The wall behind the toilet is a nightmare. Chick, you've got to show them how to do it right and if they can't, they're just going to have to sit down on the toilet. You better get another bottle of Clorox. I think we are okay on Cheer. Try to give me enough time to get the refrigerator cleaned out and get the floor waxed," she said. "And, Molly, what do you want to make the boys for dinner?"

I had no plans. I preferred to be inspired by the market. And that day, like so many others, the inspiration came in various forms. Upon our arrival at Albers, my appetite was immediately piqued by the scent of the tater tots that were being taste-tested that day.

"Yuck!" I said to sample number 1.

"Yum!" I said to sample number 2. My brothers followed suit. The salty taste of potato covered with a film of fry grease confirmed our mission: junk food for dinner.

"Thank you, thank you very much," said the man with the clipboard. He sounded like Ed Sullivan acknowledging our fine performance, and I could almost hear the fans going wild. Perhaps more important, I could not hear our father working the aisles—not to mention the angles—of the grocery store.

It was bad enough that he did the food shopping on rainy days—no other father in the neighborhood cooked and cleaned and went to the grocery store. But this embarrassment was compounded by the fact that my father had not fully grasped the difference between the quiet, smell-free Albers shopping experience and that of the old North Market, where, when I was very young, he'd spent Saturday mornings talking to farmers, sniffing meat, and poking his finger into beefsteak tomatoes.

"Heya, Whatsy! Grah! Ha! Ha!" he shouted, pushing his cart through the grocery store, "Workin' hard or hardly working? Graaaah ha ha!"

His loud, cheerful voice seemed to jump from aisle to aisle and to swing from the big aluminum lights that kept every corner of Albers bright. It gave shape and urgency to our mission.

"We have to get to Betty before he gets to produce," hissed Mike, who, for all his tantrums in private, was exquisitely attuned to public opinion.

My father's habit of bargaining for bananas humiliated Mike. In fact, my father's behavior was so unusual that the produce clerks wondered if they'd been selected as patsies for a stunt on *Candid Camera* the first time my father approached them for "a case price on ripe, grahh ha ha, come on now, good buddy." Eventually, when they saw him coming, they trotted out the back door, rescued boxes of produce from the Dumpster, and conducted the sort of auction that my father relished. My brothers and I understood this. In our shame, we turned to Betty.

On the day that crab melts were invented, Betty was making pizza. The smell of American cheese melting into ketchup sauce on a hamburger bun emanated from her toaster oven as my father cried, "Hey ya, Whatsy, whatcha got for bananas in the back?" With dreams of dinner dancing in our heads, Mike and Pat and I didn't even hear him as we stampeded from taste-testing to the cooking demo, pulling the younger children behind us. Paul was already whining. He had his sights set on crab. "I want crab!" he squeaked. "Molly, I want crab." But our noses and mouths were too exercised to pay him any mind.

Betty was working on a new batch of pizzas when we arrived. She was using a bottle cap from a Diet Rite soda to stamp pepperoni circles from a slice of bologna: *Thunk! Thunk! Thunk!* sounded the cap against her Formica-topped worktable.

"It's a cinch!" she said, flourishing her pepperoni.

Gurgle! Gurgle! Gurgle! In the electric skillet, ketchup boiled. "Now, I just added some onion soup mix and garlic salt and oregano to that ketchup, folks," she said to the crowd and then, handing me a wooden spoon, she added, "Do you want to stir that for me, honey?"

By then, of course, all the Bettys of Albers knew how I liked to stir. Standing beside her, I beamed my own assurances of a carefree, husband-pleasing recipe to the crowd of young matrons and five little O'Neills. Betty smiled indulgently at me. Paul, however, standing in the front row, was not appeased.

"I want crab," he whined in his rasping soprano.

"Just you wait until you taste these, honey," Betty said, but her breeziness momentarily faltered at the sight of the locks of golden Afro that had escaped the hood of Paul's parka.

"My baby brother," I whispered.

Betty said, "Ahh, isn't he precious. You know, last week I thought he was a girl." Then she showed us how to spread the sauce on the hamburger buns, how to unwrap the cheese slices and lay them over the sauce, how to dot the top with pepperoni rounds. "Or mushrooms, or peppers, whatever you want, honey," she added, as she slid a tray of pizza facsimiles into the toaster oven.

Within moments, a pizzalike smell began to work its way into our noses. In the front row of the audience, Paul rasped, "I want crab." In the distance, our father upped his ante. "Yes! You have some bananas," he sang to the appropriate tune at the top of his lungs. "You've got some with—black spots in—the back!"

But we were no longer related to him. We belonged to the Betty Crocker of burger bun pizza, the goddess of ketchup sauce and individually stamped lunch meat pepperoni. Our senses were saturated. Our hearts were bursting. And our minds were an electric hum of shopping strategies and backup plans: What were the essentials for tonight's dinner?

"OK, little buddy," said Pat, throwing his arm around Paul's shoulder. "We're gonna put you in the seat of Dad's grocery cart and all you have to do is say, 'Dad, I want individually wrapped slices of Kraft American cheese,' OK? Just say it over and over again."

"I want crab," said Paul. He sounded like a disappointed diner in line at the nursing home.

"No, you don't," said Pat, calmly. "You want cheese. Say 'I want cheese.'"

"But I want craaaaab," said Paul, his voice rising and cracking around the tears that seemed imminent.

Crab was not a staple of the O'Neill table. In fact, we'd never even sampled crab, and none of us had any idea what had inspired our youngest brother's appetite. When I knelt in front of him to discuss the crab issue, he could not tell me why he wanted it so badly. Perhaps, like the rest of us, he was simply born too good for tuna fish.

My father pushed his overladen shopping cart up to us and Paul began pulling the leg of his corduroy pant, lamenting for crab.

"I want craaaaab," squeaked the little boy. He was sobbing by then. "I want craaa-aaa-aaab." My father glanced around for someone to blame. The triumph he'd experienced in the produce department—he'd scored a case of aging bananas at half price! What a deal!—seemed to collapse. His lower lip trembled. He ran his left hand through his hair and shook his head. It was as if we were already home, as if my mother were already asking him what the heck she was supposed to do with fifty pounds of black bananas. He looked stricken and disoriented.

I took charge.

"Dad. Listen. I'll make it for him for dinner, no problem. We're just going to need, let's see, two cans of crab, some hamburger buns, some ketchup, and some individually wrapped slices of Kraft American cheese," I said, picking up the baby and hugging him to my hip. "You want cheese melted on your crab, don't you, honey?"

Except for Paul, none of us expected to like crab. Crab was simply part of the bargain I had made. The decision to mound the mixture of canned crabmeat, mayonnaise, and cream sauce on a bun was self-protective—"He's gonna want a bun when he sees our pizzas," said Pat—and I added the cheese because Paul reminded me to. "You promised," he shrieked. "You told Dad you needed cheese!"

We only had enough ketchup and bologna circles for twelve pizzas, leaving twelve half buns. So I topped the remaining buns with crab and cheese and put both trays under the broiler. Soon the house smelled like low tide in Naples and the little O'Neills had worked up quite an appetite.

Go, Dog. Go!

M any families have an inspirational text, a book that both mirrors their
hopes and ambitions and acts as a spiritual how-to guide—the Bible,
for instance, or *The Road Less Traveled*. Ours was *Go, Dog. Go!*, a children's
book by P. D. Eastman. It was published in 1961 and is a story about dogs—
big dogs and little dogs, black dogs and white dogs, dogs on foot, on skates,
on bikes and on scooters, dogs in the water, in trees, and in cars. *Go, Dog. Go!*
is mostly about boy dogs, all of whom resemble hounds. It is a book about
dogs going places.

There is one girl in *Go, Dog. Go!* She is a French poodle and a redhead,
and she spends all of her time trying to get one big goofy-looking hound to
notice that she's alive. She first appears looking quite fetching in a simple
blue boater, embellished with a single yellow daisy.

"Hello!" she says to the big boy dog.

"Hello!" says he.

"Do you like my hat?" she asks, standing on her tippy-toes and wagging the pom-pom tip of her tail.

"I do not," replies the boy dog, drawing himself to his fullest height. "Good-bye!"

"Good-bye," sniffs our heroine. But her disappointment spurs her to ever-increasing heights. While the boy dogs wander through a garden maze, zoom around in their cars, ride a roller-coaster, visit a construction site, and go to the beach, she works on her hat. It has become much larger and has a big pink feather when we meet her next. She is riding a scooter and so is the object of her affection, who is now wearing a black derby and carrying a cane.

"Do you like my hat?" she asks.

"I do not like it," says the hound. "Good-bye again."

And so it goes. The boy dogs go-go-go. The girl dog adds more things to her hat. Finally, her bonnet is a skyscraper festooned with ribbon and ticker tape as well as a potted plant and a big dog bone. Lollipops spring from its lower levels and, dangling from small rods, candy canes, spiders, fish, mice, and birds jiggle.

"And now do you like my hat?" asks the girl dog.

"I do. What a hat! I like it! I like that party hat!" says the boy dog.

I, in fact, looked more like a St. Bernard than a poodle, and I had little interest in building hats. But my appetite for recognition was greater than any dog's, and in the spring of my eleventh year, I courted it with a red pogo stick. I bounced for hours and days and weeks. I bounced without thought to its effect on my knees, without consideration of the potential loosening of my brain, without regard to the miles of round pockmarks that trailed behind me up and down our street. The steady *boing-boing-boing* of my effort drowned out my mother's yelling, my brothers' pandemonium, and the voice in my head that would not stop saying, "No, I do not like your hat." When I worked out on my pogo stick, all I could hear was the springing sound, the beating of my heart, and Walter Cronkite announcing on the six o'clock news my inclusion in *The Guinness Book of World Records*. Distance, time, number of jumps—I owned every category as I bounced around Schreyer Place, appearing and then disappearing in window frames throughout the neighborhood. Other mothers raised their hands and waved. My own merely raised her eyebrows.

I moved on to tetherball, a game for which I possessed an innate talent, both in terms of height and the delight I took in smashing the ball. Recognizing my abilities, my father installed a removable pole in the center of the driveway. "But if the boys want to play basketball," he warned, "you have to take it down." I moved on to track and then springboard diving. I distinguished myself in each arena, but never in the way I hoped.

"I don't need to drive to some swimming pool to see you bounce around in a tank suit," said my mother. "What happened to your pogo stick?"

I began swimming competitively when I was ten and for several summers I practiced in Uncle Gwinn's pool, thrashing out laps and imagining that each one brought my family closer to inheriting his estate on Sunbury Road. My efforts, however, did not change the fact that, with one car, my parents could not juggle swimming meets and Little League games. I switched to summer art programs: I could walk to those classes.

As an artist, I specialized in clay statues of little boys with serious simian aspects as well as oil portraits of gorillas. "Adopt a Boy for Free," read the sign under the group portrait that I propped against the concession stand that Anne and I operated at the curb: "Lemonade 5 Cents."

"I wish you'd do something I could use in the living room," said my mother, crinkling her nose at a statue of a man holding a chicken on his head and another on his knee. "What *is* this anyway?" She was happier about my foray into the dramatic arts. The Elizabethan festival I organized in the backyard occupied my brothers for weeks one summer, and the same was true of the plays I wrote and directed in the garage. But, along with my skills in the kitchen, my dramatic renditions of the family's inspirational tale were my most reliable source of accolades. When the three youngest children clamored for attention, when they shrieked or sobbed, I had only to don a simple boater.

"Let me handle this," I would say to my mother. "Do you like my hat?"

"NO!" my younger brothers would scream.

I might add a sash to the hat and ask again, "Now do you like my hat?"

"NO!" the little boys would scream again. I considered them my children and took great pride in my ability to shut them up. It was always just a matter of time. I would stack bows and fake flowers and small stuffed animals on my hat and mince around, barking, and my younger brothers would scream in unison, "No, we do not like your hat!"

With the addition of Barbie doll parts and toothbrushes and Tinkertoys, my hat would grow to perilous heights. Still, Kevin and Robert and Paul did not like my hat. Even the addition of Lego and Tonka toys and the toilet brush did not win their approval. Not until I added the mop head to my hat did they scream, "NOW WE LIKE YOUR HAT!"

My pride could not have been greater if I had taken the Olympic gold in pogo sticking.

The neighbors did not like our hat. They did not like the backhoe in the driveway. They did not like the pogo-stick holes that punctuated their yards. They did not like the sound of my mother's screaming, which began before dawn when my father left for work and continued until he returned at dusk. To the buttoned-down Protestants of Schreyer Place, my mother's attempts to motivate and control her sons sounded a little too born-again. "Jesus!" she would cry out, and "So help me God!"

The neighbors especially did not like the plague of small turds that beset their gardens in the summer of 1961.

"Jesus!" exclaimed my mother, who was planting hot-pink petunias in the flowerbed next to the driveway.

"Possums?" wondered Mr. Stutz, glancing accusingly at the concrete frog that he'd positioned as a decoy at the corner of his vegetable garden.

"Boys," said Mr. White, who lived three doors down. Mr. White, who was terribly tall and thin, wore horn-rimmed glasses. He had three daughters, Karen, Lauri, and Suzy, and a wife who had approximately fifty pounds and ten years on him. He cultivated roses for the annual competition at the Park of Roses and he was no dummy: "O'Neill boys," he said.

In fact, my brother Pat had discovered the pleasure of defecating *en plein air* and, more than likely, many children on the block were following his lead. Pat's charisma was bemoaned up and down Schreyer Place. At six years old, he had a way of bringing out the exhibitionist tendencies in those around him. In addition, he always seemed to be nearby whenever a gunpowder-scented explosion rocked the block. His schemes were bad for property values.

One sweaty August day, while attempting to build a swimming hole for the White girls in their backyard, Pat was unexpectedly summoned home. He neglected to shut off the hose, and by the time the girls' father returned from his job at General Electric, his roses were afloat.

"What is the matter with you?" shrieked Mr. White, jabbing his finger into my mother's perpetually pregnant belly. His concave chest heaved, and his voice was squeaking even more than usual. "You can't take care of the ones you already have!"

A stillness like the yellow-tinged ones that proceed summer tornados in central Ohio immediately settled over the neighborhood. Children were called home earlier than usual. There was no hide-and-seek after dinner. After showering, cleaning his nails, and eating dinner, my father moseyed over to the Whites'. The rose gardener was six inches taller than he was, but with his legendary speed, my father grabbed the man by the collar of his shirt, pulled him down to eye level, and said, "If you ever talk to my wife that way again, I'll give you something to talk about."

"My God, Chick," cried my mother when my father walked back into the kitchen, "what will people think?"

They may have thought that a preemptive strike was their best defense: soon the O'Neill boys were banned from most of the backyards in the neighborhood. I could travel freely, but my brothers had no place to go. Instead, the neighborhood came to them. My brothers were cute and funny and idolized by their peers, so my father didn't need to build a playground in our yard, but he did anyway. He installed a swing set that rivaled the one at the elementary school, a whirligig, a sandbox, and a slide. He created arenas for dodgeball, kick ball, and four-square. Children packed our backyard as if it were a day-care facility. Anne's mother refused to ban the O'Neills, so the games spilled over into the Stutzes' yard, as well.

"Now, I ask you," my mother would say in the afternoon as she and Mrs. Stutz sat on their chaise lounges, folding laundry together in the shade between our houses. "Is this not past the point of human endurance? I mean, really."

"Now, I ask you," she would say in the living room as we sat together after my brothers went to bed. In the evenings, while my father wrote invoices at his desk in the basement or talked to customers on the telephone, my mother would read or knit and seek my opinion on the outrages of the day. Such as the time when Mrs. Armbruster from across the street invited everyone but my brothers to her son's birthday party and later attempted to deliver the leftover cake to our back door. "Would you have accepted it?" my mother asked me, looking up from the pages of Teilhard de Chardin's *The Heart of the Matter*. "It was made from a cake mix," she added.

We debated such dilemmas night after night, parsing the affronts and analyzing the pettiness. "Now, I ask you," my mother said, "what did I do?"

"It's not your fault," I said at regular intervals. Night after night I reminded my mother that she was blameless—indeed, admirable above all homemakers of Schreyer Place. Why, she washed and ironed the sheets every day! Her sons might *act* like candidates for the boys' industrial school, but they looked like a happy back-to-school ad from JCPenney. "Everybody but other parents and teachers and, well, I guess, all adults just adore them, Mom," I said.

Night after night when my reassurances failed to cheer her, I said that I had to polish-my-shoes-iron-my-blouse-pack-the-boys'-lunches-for-tomorrow and ran to the kitchen to eat brown sugar from the box.

"Now, I ask you!" my mother called after me. "What did I do to deserve this?" Consumed by self-doubt, she surrendered space in her kitchen cupboards to Oreos, Lucky Charms, and Cap'n Crunch, and more and more space on its counters for my improvisations.

Then, in 1963, my mother understood her mistake: the neighbors had fallen for her impersonation of a blue-collar wife. The realization dawned when I won the good citizenship essay contest and one neighbor sniffed, "I guess the truck drivers have the geniuses."

"I mean, really," said my mother, "they think we're *descended* from ditchdiggers." She was flabbergasted.

In order to correct this misconception, she immediately painted the living room antique white and had the corduroy and canvas upholstery on the furniture replaced with brocades. She threw out the folksy rugs and ruffled café curtains and ordered thick white wall-to-wall carpeting and elaborate window treatments. She needlepointed pillows, knitted complicated afghans, and hung reproductions of mother-and-child paintings by Mary Cassatt in museum-quality frames on the walls.

We spent hours every weekend digging through antiques stores in search of the furniture and cloisonné boxes and porcelain statuary she'd previously rejected from her aunt's estate. Our shopping trips inevitably ended in the furniture department on the top floor of Lazarus department store, where we would study the various model rooms and count the days until their components went on sale, my mother mentally tabulating how much activity her Lazarus charge card could bear. Just as she never deviated from a recipe when she cooked, my mother faithfully reproduced the tableaux from the furniture department at Lazarus or from the pictures she admired in *House Beautiful* magazine when she decorated.

"Why don't we sit in the living room," my mother would suggest the next time someone dropped by bearing leftover cake.

"Don't go in there!" she'd scream whenever one of her children edged toward the living room's closed door. Next she set her sights on the dining room, and soon 25 percent of our tiny house was rendered inaccessible, a museum created for public opinion and the occasional Sunday or holiday. In the evenings, however, we continued to sit in this preserve, my mother and I, after my brothers had been put to bed.

"Take your shoes off before you come in," my mother called from the pink velvet chair in which she sat. "Now, I ask you."

My father felt sorry for the neighbors who did not like our hat. They were jealous, he said.

"I see," said my mother when the telephone rang during dinner and my father began shaking his head and mouthing "I'm not here!" as if he were auditioning for a silent movie. "They are jealous because the bill collectors never call *them*."

"Aw, come on, Boots," said my father, "they're bored! Poor things have nothing but—what?—two weeks at Lake Erie to look forward to?"

"It's sad," agreed my mother. "They don't even realize how exciting it is to wake up in the morning wondering if today is the day the bank is going to foreclose on the house! How thrilling it is to be called into the principal's office to discuss your sons' predelinquent behavior! They don't know how wonderful it is to live dangerously—their cars have windshield wipers and brakes that work!"

"Aw, come on, Boots. I told you just to pump the brakes, they'll work. Just pump them!" my father said. It was an undying refrain. "You have to take the long view," he continued. "Where do you think these drips are going to be ten years from now? How many Nobel prizes you think they give out for filing taxes by April fifteenth? What's the last movie you saw starring a balanced checkbook?" When he was passionate about something, my father narrowed his eyes, jabbed the air with his middle finger, and ended by saying, "That's my philosophy." He pronounced the word as if it had more to do with dental charges than Socratic reasoning. "It's not over till you win," he said. "That's my flossy-fee."

We took a great, if unspoken, comfort in seeing life as a perpetual beginning, experiencing the errors and triumphs of any given moment as no less reversible than a hit or an out in a first at-bat. Victory, in my father's view, was a direct result of ambition. Ambition was a central tenet of his flossy-fee— "I don't care how smart they are," he said of our neighbors. "If they don't have any gumption, they don't have any brains."

The regulation-scale backboard and basketball hoop that he installed above the garage door became the manifestation of our gumption: proof that we had it, evidence that others lacked it. It was so obvious! "Ole Marconi didn't even measure, just slapped the hoop up!" said our father one summer evening as we coasted down Schreyer Place in our brakeless Ford station wagon. "What's gonna happen to that poor kid of his when he goes to shoot at school? He'll be coming up two inches short, that's what!"

"Lookie there!" he said, pump-pump-pumping the brake pedal to slow the car so that we might have a better view of what Ole Chandler settled for (a cheap hoop with a bell) and what Ole Litzinger was letting happen to his facility (rusting hoop), and worst of all, what Ole Whatsy had done when creating a half-court for his sons. "No backboard!" said my father. "That's the kind of guy he is!"

My brothers took up the cry.

"What kind of person lets his net rot?" said Mike, shaking his head sadly at the Eckles' basketball hoop across the street.

"Mr. Caldrone didn't even set his post in concrete," said Pat. "So here you have a guy who is basically telling his kid not to stuff it because if he does, the whole pole is going to come down."

"Because he didn't have the gumption to dig a hole and lay the gravel and set up the cement!" said Mike, sounding the way adults do when they discuss parents who neglect their children. "I don't know what's wrong with these people."

Given the space required to build a regulation half-court outside our house, my mother's plans to redecorate and restrict additional inside square footage, and the alarming rate of my brothers' growth, our future on Schreyer Place appeared to be limited. At least it was in my father's imagination. "This street's fine for pinheads and bean counters but not for anyone who needs elbow room," he said one Sunday. "Everybody in the car!"

Thus began our Sunday afternoon habit of motoring about the countryside, which was, by the early 1960s, largely composed of subdivisions whose water and electric lines were dug by none other than the narrator of our weekly tour of a better life. For nearly a decade, we drove around looking at houses we could not afford. My father would pump-pump-pump the brakes at any sign that read "Open House." My brothers would pour out of the car and appraise the basketball-court potential of the driveway and analyze what it would take to construct a major-league ball diamond in the backyard. Inside the Tudor-Colonial-Federalist-contemporary-traditional-split-level, I would choose a bedroom for myself and, enamored of the possibility of having a door that closed, would work it until its hinges squeaked. My mother would pace off rooms and imagine furniture placement and window treatments.

My father would say to us, "What's everybody think?" Then, turning to the realtor, he would say, "OK, you got yourself a deal, good buddy, you got a business card?" and they would shake hands.

Back in the station wagon, the closeness of our quarters seemed cozy and dear. How fondly we would think back on these days once we had closed doors and hundreds of square feet of wall-to-wall carpeting separating us from one another! Once ensconced in our mansion, we could laughingly recall the water that, on rainy days, had sprayed through the rusted floor of our family car. Strolling our estate, we would reminisce about the neighbors who'd tormented us on Schreyer Place, those pea brains who'd had so much bile and so little ambition!

"Do you really think we can do it, Chick?" asked my mother as my father turned from High Street onto Schreyer Place at dusk. She leaned across the two toddlers who stood between them on the front seat of the car, and, from the backseat and over the head of the baby that I was holding in my lap, I could see that my mother was flushed. She was not frowning. She was not yelling. The fading light of the day sparkled in her eyes. For a minute, it was just the three of us again, and we were headed to the Jai Lai.

"Sure we can!" said my father, swaying as he began the three blocks of brake-pumping necessary to safely make the turn into our driveway. "That drip with the real estate license said we could."

The stack of business cards that he collected from real estate agents grew steadily in the front left-hand corner of my father's top dresser drawer. I assumed that, like me, my mother viewed the collection as reminders of things to do. At the top of that list was the matter of paying for our new home, which was the sort of niggling detail that would not concern my father. Uncle Gwinn, on the other hand, was detail-oriented and had experience with mansions—he lived in one—and so I assumed that he'd help us get one, too. The complicated pastries that my mother baked for her uncle were, I thought, her way of sealing the deal. I assumed that she was baking for better housing, and I supported her efforts 100 percent.

A day after Aunt Clarence's death, Uncle Gwinn had moved another woman into his home. The former proprietor of a slimming salon, the new Mrs. Gwinn was of Italian extraction. She served lasagna for dinner on Sunbury Road and wore a platinum-blond wig. Le Tout Columbus was appalled, and so was my mother. Nevertheless, my mother had spent most of her life trying to earn her uncle's affection, and even "The Wig," as my mother referred to her, was not enough to change this long-ingrained habit. When her uncle called and asked her to make him a dessert, my mother hopped to. And, as ever, I hopped to, too. Just as I'd assisted in baking the pies, cobblers, layer cakes, and cookies she made for our family, I became the sous chef for the Sunbury Road Collection.

For her uncle, my mother reproduced grand, classic recipes—complicated charlottes, difficult tortes, and delicate constructions of puff pastry and mousse—with her characteristically timid yet unswerving exactitude. And like any ambitious apprentice, I dreamed of assuming sovereignty over the ingredients that she instructed me to prepare—the level measures of flour and sugar, the egg whites for meringue, the egg yolks for custard, the grated nutmeg and scraped vanilla beans, the tempered chocolate. Yet for a few years, I resisted my urge to improvise. It was serious business to me. I didn't beam my practiced smile or claim that it was a cinch when baking for Uncle. I followed my mother's orders assiduously and I didn't appreciate it when, after speaking with him on the telephone, she began making jokes about our campaign.

"Oh, I'd *love* to make dessert for twenty and deliver it this afternoon, Uncle," she would say, while holding a washrag in one hand, a dirty diaper in the other, and grasping a diaper pin between her teeth. "What would you like? A Spanish wind torte? Parisian dacquoise with butter cream?"

"How about a little something from puff pastry?" she would say, balancing a basket of laundry on one hip and a toddler on the other. "That should only take me twelve or fourteen hours."

"No problem!" she said, slamming down the telephone after her uncle called the O'Neill Patisserie several days after Mike's car accident. "My son is dying. I lost a baby. We don't have health insurance. So let's make charlotte russe." Quickly then, pursing her lips, my mother said to me, "Get Kevin and Robert going with some Tinkertoys or something and then separate two dozen eggs for the lady fingers."

There were other indications that she and I were not, in fact, dreaming the same four-bedroom-two-bath split-level dream. At night, in my bed in the alcove above the kitchen, I listened to my parents argue about money. "What about the downpayment?" my mother would rail, and I would wonder, briefly, if she was relying on my father rather than our cakes. Once she even suggested that she was resigned to remaining on Schreyer Place. "Could we build another bedroom in the basement?" she asked my father one night. "Could we afford that, at least?" I couldn't imagine that she was serious.

I should have been suspicious when my mother yielded creative control over my brothers' birthday cakes. But I was impervious to her fatigue, her surrender, her screw-it-all lapses. Instead, I saw my mother's relaxing standards as her way of recognizing my skills. With the zeal of an artist freed from paint-by-number pictures, I turned away from my mother's recipes and dreamed of cakes that were more whimsical, more contemporary, more personal, more fun.

Awash with grander visions—visions, by the way, that closely resembled the cakes topped with pipe-cleaner figures and tissue-paper carnations that were pictured in women's magazines—I sniffed at the sedate cakes pictured in the Time-Life cookbook my mother favored. I did not like those frilly and predictable cakes. I did not like them at all. I dreamed of cakes with more insight and courage, cakes with bold lines and colors, cakes that reversed the conventional cake-to-icing ratio.

I realized this final ambition. Informed more by fantasy than by kitchen science, I would add pudding mix or butter to cake batters for additional moisture, which caused the cakes to sink rather than rise. I filled the resulting craters with icing. "Why are you making a fourth batch of butter cream?" my mother would ask. Not one to reveal my secrets, I would simply smile my white-picket-fence smile. Inspired by the Play-Doh creations that covered many surfaces in our house, I made my frostings thick enough to sculpt. Then I cast columns, birds, trees, and little people, and mounted them on my cakes.

"Jesus!" said my mother, the tendons in her thin forearm rippling under the effort of moving one of my creations from the kitchen counter to the table. "I'm not sure I can pick this thing up."

"Wow!" exclaimed my father and brothers, who had a greater appreciation for cakes topped with Lionel trains, Lincoln Logs, and Lego. I beamed in gratitude and tried to ignore the large hunks that remained on everyone's dessert plates, the sugar glaze that entered my brothers' eyes, the looks that were exchanged between my parents.

"You *could* follow a recipe," my mother said. But she was wrong, I could not. At thirteen years old, I could come up with ingenious solutions to structural challenges—devising, for instance, a method for burying Tinkertoy supports inside my cakes, or adding barrels of Crisco and boxes of powdered sugar to my frostings to enhance their cementing properties. But I could not follow a recipe. My mother did not understand me at all.

Oh, but one day she would appreciate my vision, my fortitude, and my talent. One day my creations would do what hers had failed to do: they would reverse our family's fortune and quadruple our square footage. The birthday cakes I made my brothers were merely études. One day Uncle would like my cake.

My opportunity appeared as a stick in my brother Kevin's eye. My mother had just gotten off the telephone with her uncle and we were about to begin baking when a howling Kevin ran into the kitchen preceded by a makeshift arrow. In a game of cowboys and Indians, Mike had heaved the sharpened stick into a clear patch of backyard. Midflight, Kevin appeared in the arrow's path.

"Jesus!" screamed my mother. "Oh my God. And you had the most beautiful eyes! Who did this? Don't touch it! Where's my purse? Jesus, we've got to get you to the emergency room. Molly, get the rest of them in the house and just make some sort of cake for Uncle, whatever you want."

There was not much blood and Kevin wasn't even crying as my mother carried him to the backseat of the car—"I want you to hold the stick, do you hear me? Don't let it wiggle around, honey"—but my other brothers were very quiet as they filed into the house and down to the basement. They tuned the television to *Flippo the Clown,* but they kept the volume low. My mood, on the other hand, was far from funereal. Before my mother had even backed the station wagon out of the driveway, I saw svelte chocolate tiers stacked in my mind's eye and began to imagine the cake I would bake for Uncle.

Using a length of thread, I would slice each layer. I would smooth some surprise filling between the halves—a bittersweet frosting here, caramel there, an amalgam of coconut and minced pecans there—and sandwich them back together.

Uncle would be startled from his complacency by such an unexpected juxtaposition of flavors. "I like it!" he would say. Imagining his response, I baked and carved, filling the sunken center of some layers with milk chocolate butter cream and filling others with butterscotch instant pudding. The stickiness of peanut butter resolved certain technical difficulties. "What a cake!" I could hear Uncle saying. "I like that party cake!"

Finally, my cake had gone as high as it could go. I iced it, adding festoons of butter-cream piping with my pastry bag, and fortified its ramparts with a mosaic of toasted almonds and semi-sweet chocolate chips. Then I dusted it with coconut flakes and powdered sugar. When I stepped back to admire it, even I could see that it was more Leaning Tower of Pisa than Taj Mahal. But I trusted Uncle to understand its intent and applaud the effort it represented.

"Jesus," said my mother. Clouds of confectioner's sugar rose from my cake as she pushed open the door and carried Kevin into the kitchen. Like a tower built on shifting tectonic plates, my cake swayed slightly as she walked across the floor. "Oh my God," said my mother. Her lips seemed to twitch and her eyes seemed to fill with tears.

"Isn't it amazing?" I said softly.

"Oh, yes," said my mother. The pressure of the day had, I could see, taken its toll on her. Her entire body seemed to convulse and tears began to roll down her face. "Yes, it is most certainly amazing," she said.

Later that night, as she and my father sat in the kitchen talking, I lay in bed upstairs, straining, as usual, to hear every word they said.

"I mean," my mother said, gasping with laughter. "You would not have believed it. Really. I could barely carry the thing! It must have weighed twenty pounds by the time she got through decorating it. And the look on Uncle's face when he saw it. I mean, Chick! She'd built this thing that looked like, like—like a pile of horseshit. I'm not kidding you, a big pile of horseshit, spackled with hay! And there we are, trying to carry this monstrosity into the house and the dinner guests are already pulling up in their Cadillacs."

So! My mother was finally having fun in the kitchen, but at my expense! We had not been baking for better housing—we'd been baking for revenge! In that terrible moment, the closeness of the walls seemed to press in even more tightly than usual and I understood that Schreyer Place could go on forever.

"Oh boy, oh boy, oh boys!" sang my father after dinner one night, long after Kevin's eye had healed, as my mother carried a cherry pie from the kitchen.

Pies had, by then, become a special occasion. Unable to find the time or the Zenlike focus necessary to make a respectable pastry, my mother had stopped baking pies every day for her family. That afternoon, however, she'd woven strips of pastry like a lattice over her hastily assembled cherry filling. I'd watched her in the way that I'd been watching her since she left me alone with my grand visions, alone with the burden of attracting a mortgage broker, alone to bake for Uncle. Silently, sullenly, alert to any indication of her imperfection, I'd watched my mother use a pastry brush to paint the crust with milk—"so it will glow. Egg white makes it shine, milk or cream makes it glow, remember?" she'd said—and watched as she'd placed the pie in the oven.

"Who's the luckiest guy in the whole world?" asked my father as my mother set her pie on the dinner table. "Cherry season," said my father, grinning up at his wife while she blushed and smiled down at him. "Fresh cherry pie!"

I let them bask that way for a moment, warm as they were in the sense of a mystery that began with bees buzzing between cherry blossoms and seemed destined to end in kisses that tasted like cherry pie. And then, with a spite as yet unmatched in my life, I informed them that perhaps the world was not what it seemed.

"Those are canned cherries," I said. My mother started to cry.

Bongo, Colo, and Me

Like someone who lingers in an emergency room to gather images for her own nightmares, I tuned in to Chet Long on the evening news in the winter of 1966. I was thirteen and I was obsessed with the deteriorating relationship between Bongo and Colo, two lowland gorillas belonging to the Columbus Zoo. After seven years of uneventful cohabitation, things had turned ugly between the pair, and night after night I sat in my father's La-Z-Boy and watched as Bongo's latest outrage against the little girl Colo was aired on the local news.

After the gorilla keepers delivered their dinner, Bongo stared Colo to the other side of the cage so that he could dine first.

"Yummmmm," rumbled Bongo on the videotape as he tucked into the calf's liver that his keepers had purchased at Kroger and sautéed with onions in the kitchen of the ape house.

"Gross!" I screamed, banging my white go-go boots against the foot extension of my father's chair.

I watched as Bongo filled his fat, sausage-size fingers with beet greens and cherry tomatoes, green grapes, bananas, and pineapples while Colo cowered—hungrily, I was sure—on the opposite side of the cage. Sometimes, over his shoulder, Bongo would hurl his empty banana peels in her direction.

Bongo was a typical bully. He kicked Colo. He hit her. He pushed her around. Sometimes, just for fun, he kicked apart the beds she made herself from straw.

"Typical male," said my mother, passing through the basement with a basket of laundry. She was critical of the much-lauded gorilla keepers of the Columbus Zoo, and in the decades to come, the experts would, in fact, reevaluate their position on cage design and begin to view aggressive behavior differently. But when I was thirteen, the gorilla program at the Columbus Zoo, although famous worldwide, was still in its infancy. Mistakes were made.

"I don't know why they can't separate them," said my mother, curling her lip as Bongo threw a banana peel toward Colo. "I don't care if that is what happens in nature, no one should have to look at that at the zoo."

"Poor Colo!" I whimpered, as the second round of videotape from the Columbus Zoo showed her nervously gleaning Bongo's leftovers for something to eat. Bongo was disgusting. Bongo made me sick.

"Why don't they *do something?*" I wailed, hot tears at the injustice welling in my eyes. "Why doesn't someone help Colo?"

After all, Colo was not just any old gorilla. On December 22, 1956, Colo had been the first lowland gorilla ever born in captivity, and it was the biggest thing that had happened in Columbus since the fire at the Gwinn mill. *The New York Times* ran frequent updates on Colo's progress, *Time* and *Life* magazines devoted pages to her story, and Mayor M. E. Sensenbrenner sprinted around the city handing out cigars that said "IT'S A GIRL!" to holiday shoppers. One employee of the little zoo erected a star of Nazareth over the ape house. Some, but not many, thought that was going a little too far.

I was taken to meet Colo soon after she was born. That day, still in her incubator, Colo was wearing a pink dress, ruffled rubber pants, and a frilly pink bonnet. She had a wide, gummy smile, and when she directed it my way a cosmic connection was established; at the age of four, I understood all too well that Colo did not belong in a party dress.

Like me, Colo was three when her caregivers brought a boy into her nursery. At first, it seemed that Colo was the luckier one. Her keepers, after all, didn't just go to the hospital and accept some writhing, high-strung little ape. Instead, they searched the African lowlands for the perfect companion. Bongo, who was also a toddler, was found in Cameroon and he was everything the gorilla keepers had wanted for Colo. Bongo was laid-back, Bongo was a looker, and—most important—Bongo was a boy. My father was holding me the first time I saw Bongo, and as we gazed at the imperturbable little gorilla through the window of the ape house, I half expected my father to say, "Real easy-going. A little hairy, but he's got a great disposition, honey, takes after his dad." I worried about Colo.

Colo, however, didn't seem to mind sharing the limelight. When the people who had once lined up to see her began pointing their Brownie cameras at Bongo, she simply went about her business. Yes, they sometimes heaved building blocks at each other and, as they grew, they splintered pieces of nursery furniture over each other's head. But for quite some time, Bongo, not Colo, wore the scars.

The change began when Bongo and Colo were moved out of the nursery and into the general gorilla population area. My friends and I thought that their new home looked like a jail cell and the books and scholarly articles that have since been written on the pair say that this was no coincidence; at one point, the zoo had consulted with the Ohio penitentiary on security matters. These grim new quarters consisted of a 250-square-foot cell lined with white ceramic tile and covered with wire mesh on three sides. There was only one piece of furniture: a cement bench at the rear of the cage. Bongo claimed it and ignored all Colo's suggestions that he time-share or simply behave like a gentleman and give her the seat. By this time, Bongo had grown to Godzilla proportions—he was five feet eight inches tall and weighed about 425 pounds, while Colo remained five feet two inches tall and weighed less than 200 pounds—and he'd decided there'd be no more Mr. Nice Guy.

I was nine the first time I saw Bongo and Colo in their new house. My brothers were shitting all over the neighborhood, and Bongo had taken to throwing feces at the mesh walls of his cage. A glass barrier had been hastily erected to protect zoo guests.

"GROSS!" I howled when a gorilla patty splatted on the glass close to my face.

"GROSS!" screamed the other little girls, three years later, on my sixth-grade class trip. The little boys, on the other hand, made farting noises and stumbled around, bent at the waist, their arms swinging low to the ground when they weren't heaving handfuls of dirt—a routine they continued on the playground back at school. The battle lines were drawn. I became exquisitely attuned to Bongo tendencies in my younger brothers.

With a growing sense of horror, I watched Colo cower around the perimeter of her world, desperately seeking asylum or escape. Neither was possible. Colo had no place to go. Neither did I.

*   *   *

By the summer of 1966, I was surrounded by balls. There were hard balls and soft balls, soccer balls, dodgeballs, kick balls, volleyballs, tetherballs, and Nerf balls. There were golf balls and tennis balls, rubber balls, plastic balls, leather balls, Ping-Pong balls, and croquet balls.

My former sanctuary under the rosebush had been turned into third base for the nightly ballgames that my father convened. My hideaway under the pine tree had become the lobby for the baseball broadcasting station that was housed in the tree's highest branches. In the basement of our house, the table I'd used for my art projects became a casualty of the rainy-day stadium. The basement facility was also used for after-hours practice and pregame warm-ups. Resolutely, I corralled the passion I'd once poured into cakes and unleashed it on the study of Latin and fantasies of a toga-clad life in the Forum. While I memorized Latin declensions upstairs, Pat's voice rose up through the heat grate as he announced the spectacular plays of those he imagined each of our brothers to be.

"We got Bob Gibson on the mound—Robert, that's you—Ladies and gentlemen, I'm telling you this is Cy Young material! Would ya look at this kid hurl!" he bellowed. "But he's no match for Yaz! Kevin, you're Carl Yastrzemski. Look at that cut. Jaaayz, that's outa here! No! We got Reggie Smith all over that ball—Mike! You're Reggie!—and we got Tony Perez moving in. Here I come to back the play!" The announcer always sang the final sentence of his commentary to the tune of Mighty Mouse singing, "Here I come to save the day!" The names of the best baseball players from the late 1960s are, in my mind, still tangled with passages from Caesar and Cicero, Petronius and Pliny the Elder.

At nine and ten years old, Mike and Pat still admired my hat—even if, in my own mind, it was now nothing more elaborate than a simple laurel wreath. As balls assumed a greater importance in their lives, they pretended to be gladiators at the Coliseum in Rome to please me. "I came, I saw, I conquered," Mike shouted to me from the pitcher's mound that my father had created in the center of the backyard. Then he slammed a ball into the backstop of the garage, and the sound of splintering wood, my father's admiring "Jayyyezzz! Take 'er easy," and the frightened squeal of the glider on a neighbor's back porch conquered my brother's ode to Caesar, and to me.

"And Nero lets it rip!" declared Pat, throwing a lit match on the stream of gasoline from the can that he and Mike had accidentally spilled while mowing the ballpark. *Et tu, Brute?* I muttered when my father, after hearing of the inferno that had rolled down our front walk and along the curb of Schreyer Place, took off his belt and motioned Pat to the basement.

"Cogito, ergo sum," I said, sticking my fingers in my ears and repeating the phrase and its translation like a mantra. "I think, therefore I am."

The space between my makeshift earplugs was one of the few refuges afforded me by life among the O'Neills of Schreyer Place. "No, come right home," my mother said, when I campaigned to participate in afterschool activities. I countered with a request for a list of tasks that I could perform in order to earn freedom in the hours before dinner, but to no avail. "I can't think that far ahead," said my mother, "I just need you on deck." I received special dispensation, however, for visits to Aunt Dodo and Grandma Moss, both of whom had had strokes and both of whom were living at the Beech-wold Nursing Home. The facility was conveniently located between our house and Coles Pharmacy, which had a superior selection of candy bars; for a few years, no one other than its paid employees entered the nursing home with greater regularity than I.

"I said!" exclaimed Aunt Dodo, when I walked into the second-floor room of the old, center-hall brick Colonial that my relatives shared with two other aging women.

"I said!" she would repeat, smiling and nodding toward the chair next to hers. I would sit down.

"What did you say?" I asked.

"I said," she said, leaning closer to ensure confidentiality, "I said to Tillie." Tillie, who had been my aunt's best friend, was long since dead. I imagined a great secret, a deathbed confidence. Day after day, I leaned closer and whispered, "What did you tell her, Dodo? What did you tell Tillie?"

"I said," she said. "I said."

Her stroke had left Aunt Dodo with a limited vocabulary but she was never at a loss for words. "I said!" she declared, sounding like a critic about to quote her own rave review when I carried my paintings and sculpture to show her after school. "I said," she purred when I brought the lavender-colored hard candies she liked. "I said," she growled when one of the women in her room stole the candies. "I said," she sputtered when I showed up wearing one of the Chanel suits that had once belonged to her and that my mother had had altered to fit me. "I said," she hissed, grabbing for the sleeve of the worsted pink wool suit. "I said to Tillie," she spat.

I prodded Dodo to tell me exactly what she had said. "You said . . . ?" I would ask leadingly, while unwrapping a Nestlé Crunch bar, breaking it into individual squares, and stacking them into the towers of three that I pre-ferred. "You said?" I would prompt, as I pulled a Reese's Peanut Butter Cup and a Heath Bar from my purse.

My grandmother's vocabulary was more extensive but her confusion was more pronounced. "Do you know who this is, Mother?" she was asked when her son came to visit. "I think it's one of mine," said my grandmother. She mistook me for my mother, for her childhood playmates, and, often, for her caregiver. "Oh, nurse!" she would sing gaily at my approach. "Is it time for my medicine? I believe it must be!"

Communicating with Uncle Gwinn was not substantially different. In the summer of 1966, he was diagnosed with leukemia; my mother would drive us to his house on Sunbury Road in the afternoons so that we could swim in his pool and she could spend time with him. I did my laps and my brothers did cannonballs. If he emerged from the house at all, Uncle Gwinn greeted me in Latin. *"Quid agis,"* he would call out. *"Bene,"* I would answer. Then he would ask me to read passages from Cicero aloud to him.

"You will go to Harvard," he pronounced.

"To Harvard?" I asked. The university, at that time, accepted only men.

"To Harvard," he said. "I've set up a trust for your education."

"A trust," I said.

"For Harvard," he confirmed, turning up the collar of his smoking jacket against the rare breeze of an August afternoon in central Ohio. "Har-vard" may have been C.E.'s "Tillie," but his confidence bolstered my Latin mania and led me to carve a quiet, scholarly spot from the chaos of Schreyer Place. Setting a door on two sawhorses, I made a desk in my closet.

Aside from the bathroom, my closet was the only place I could enjoy a closed door. When I was not at the rest home or on deck for domestic serv-ice, I divided my time between these spots. In my closet, I prepared for my life as the future Emily Dickinson by memorizing Latin wisdom. In the bathroom, I floated in the tub while imagining being burned at the stake by Bongo-like barbarians.

"Aut disce aut discede!" I gasped valiantly from my pyre. "Either learn or leave!" I said to my tormentors as the flames licked the folds of my toga.

"I GOTTA GO!" a brother would scream, banging on the flimsy hollow-core door and jumping up and down. *"Hurry up!"*

"Para leves capiunt animas," I whispered sadly, floating in a prunelike afterlife in the tub. "Small things occupy light minds."

My father was befuddled by my habit of lapsing into Latin. "What the heck is she talking about?" he asked my mother.

"What do you care?" replied my mother, who had Bongo concerns of her own. "You don't care about girls! You don't care about education! You don't care about anything but balls! Balls, balls, balls. My Gawd!" she said, thrusting her lower jaw forward in simian fashion and imitating our imitation of our father's quivering lip. "Out in the backyard with the balls every single night after dinner! That's your idea of fatherhood? Balls? Well, it's not *the neighbors'* idea, I'll tell you that! And it's not mine, either! Children can read! Children can learn to play the piano!"

My father was rattled by this outburst. Soon after, he ordered a book from Time-Life about the human mind and began to school himself on the particulars of the brain. Night after night, he sat at the kitchen table poring over the book.

"Lookie here, honey, what's this ink spot remind you of?" he asked as I searched the kitchen trash for the economy-size orange juice cans that, along with Dippity-do, I used to straighten the wave in my hair.

"Rodin's 'Thinker,'" I said, with a practiced flip of my wet, shoulder-length hair that sent additional splatters across the page. "Well, now it looks more like Colo," I added. "Colo in profile."

My father used a pencil that he'd sharpened with a paring knife to note my response on an index card. His tests continued—"Tell me what you see in this picture," he said, "a vase or two faces?"—but the data he collected did not bring us closer.

"We *have* a pencil sharpener, Dad," I said. Undaunted, my father tried to engage me with information.

"Your gorilla has more than an opposable thumb," said the Time-Life scholar one night, looking up from his book as I stood over a pot of boiling water at the stove, my head covered with a towel as I steamed my face. "He can learn sign language and make deals. Heck, he sounds smarter than some of the people I work for."

"Very interesting," I said as I rushed from the stove, past my father, and into the bathroom to attend to clogged pores. Anyone who ran his finger under lines of text and formed words with his mouth as he read to himself was, in my view, too Bongo to be taken seriously. This realization gave me new insight into my father's preoccupation with bananas.

My best friend, Anne, had elected to study Spanish instead of Latin and she was also having difficulty understanding me. I was sorry that my friend had taken the easier way into Romance languages. This pain sharpened when Anne made the junior cheerleading squad and, despite my athletic superiority, I did not. But we still crowded into the bathroom to raid the medicine cabinet after school.

"It's only because of my hair," said Anne, brushing her honey-colored bangs and smoothing the waves from her Little Dutch Boy do. But I knew that my failure to make the squad had something to do with my physique, as well. "If you help me iron my hair, I'll help you bleach yours," Anne said. I demurred, but I still held the doorknob while Anne lifted her ribbed knit shirt and taped Band-Aids over her nipples. When she said, "Can you tell?" I assured her that the evidence was well concealed.

I did, however, begin to refuse her offers to tape me down. *"Beneficium accipere libertatem est vendere,"* I told my friend. Tears for the years we'd shared welled in my eyes; tears for the future we would, clearly, not share rolled hot down my cheeks. "To accept a favor is to sell one's freedom." I also pitied her for succumbing to the easy temptations of Spanish—piñata, indeed! At school, I gathered my toga around me and began marching toward the eternal, the superior, the classics. Anne rolled the waistbands of her skirts so that they defied the dress code and surreptitiously applied frosted-pink lipstick at her locker in the morning. In other areas, however, we remained united.

"GO AWAY!" we screamed together when my brothers banged on the bathroom door.

"GO AWAY!" we yelled in unison when they kicked at my closet. We dreamed of bold and independent lives. We imagined the apartments we would share in New York City, the rock bands we would play in, the books we would write, the weddings we would have when Anne married Paul McCartney and I married John Lennon. And all of this seemed immanent in the afternoons when we left my closet and, standing in my alcove as if it were a stage, lip-synced our favorite numbers from the Top 40 countdown on WCOL. We held a broom handle between us and sang into its tip. Our eyes were closed, our lips near enough to eat the lyrics from each other's mouth.

"Hey there, Georgy girl," I sang, grabbing the mic and pointing at Anne. Grabbing the mic back, she would respond, while wagging a finger at me: *"Don't be so scared of changing and rearranging yourself!"* And so it would go, curiously apt, as the broomstick moved back and forth between us.

"Wake up, Georgy girl!" I shrieked.

"Come on, Georgy girl!" howled Anne. We were euphoric. We were powerful. We were Colo before Bongo took the bench. We were Georgy Girls!

And then my brothers stormed the stage. Perhaps it was the opening strands of "Red Rubber Ball" that proved irresistible to them, or perhaps it was the habit of following me that pulled them from the backyard into the tiny space where my two twin beds, a dresser, and a dressing table were crammed. It was clear that they could not help themselves as they crowded us from the microphone. There were so many of them—Mike and Pat were nearly as tall as Anne and I, respectively, and although the three younger ones were still small, like tiny roadies, their gyrating took up space and radiated heat. As they teamed up to sing "Wild Thing," the wide arc of my brothers' air-guitaring drove my friend and me back, back against the windows of my alcove, far away from center stage.

During the winter of 1966, my brothers still responded when Anne and I coughed as Colo had when Bongo was still small. A certain sort of gorilla cough is an objection and a warning, and when Anne and I coughed and pulled our eyebrows low and stared at them fiercely, my brothers would immediately cede the stage. But I knew our return was only temporary. I could feel the Bongos among us. And as the *thwack-thwack-thwack* of balls in the backyard grew stronger and steadier, I felt the Bongos getting closer.

My father said it was not Bongo's fault. We'd just attended my Girl Scout troop's father-daughter outing to the zoo and were driving out of the parking lot when he expressed his sympathy for the wife-beating gorilla.

"Well, it's not *Colo's* fault," I said witheringly. I raised my eyebrows, clicked my tongue, and exhaled as my mother did when she was disgusted. By 1966 my mother was disgusted most of the time and I was disgusted on a regular basis. My father's attention was, by then, focused exclusively on grooming ballplayers. By the time I was thirteen, we were strangers and I was repulsed by the smell of grease and diesel and Camel cigarettes in my father's pickup. I was infuriated that he had driven this rusting vehicle on our date, ashamed of his work clothes, disgusted by how stupid he was.

"Even *you* can see that it's not Colo's fault," I said, and I turned to stare out the window. The car was headed in the opposite direction from home, south along the Scioto River toward Route 161. We were, my father had told me, driving out to Plain City, the Amish community that was twenty additional miles to the west where he had to look at a big job.

"Not everything is somebody's fault, honey," said my father.

"You're just on Bongo's side," I said. *"Ad absurdum."*

"I don't think you can blame a caged animal, honey. I mean, here you have a fella used to swinging around the trees, keeping his own hours, and now he's locked up in some cell and has a bunch of PhDs telling him what to eat and when to sleep and sticking a thermometer up his behind. Heck, I'd be throwing my poop around, too, if I had to live like that."

"*Gross!*" I said.

"Lookie there," my father said, pump-pump-pumping his Ranchero to point at a modern ranch that was situated on a bluff overlooking the river. "Five bedrooms, ten acres. Belongs to some Italian fellow, and he built a lot of it himself. See all that stone? He does stonework. Those dagos like stone, I'll tell you that. Forty-two grand. If I get the gas and water lines on this subdivision out by Plain City, we're gonna be able to do it, honey."

I no longer played Our Better Life with my father, and that day, as usual, I stared out the window so that I didn't have to see his lower lip quiver. As we drove through the flat, orderly farmland of central Ohio that soft spring evening, he exhorted me to smell the fields, damp and freshly plowed, that fanned out from either side of the road. "Smell that, honey," he said, rolling down his window, tossing the glowing end of his Camel out onto the road, and inhaling deeply. "That's the smell of hope, right there."

"Smells like manure," I said, turning to watch in disapproval as the embers from his cigarettes danced away from the truck. "Every litter bit hurts, you know, Dad."

The sun was gold along the road and then the evening turned suddenly mauve as we reached the outskirts of the little Amish town. Most people traveled by horse-drawn buggies in Plain City; few homes had electricity. The darkness was, for a moment, profound. And then, a few yards ahead and high above us, a great chain of lights popped like the flashes of dozens of giant cameras and remained burning against the purple sunset sky. A raspy voice announced someone's name over a loudspeaker. There was applause and the sound of young boys cheering.

And then we were right up on it. We both saw it at the same time: a perfect patch of green, framed by red-brown baselines, bounded on two sides by a tall green fence and on the other two sides by stadium seating, with white dugouts and bases, a perfectly elevated pitcher's mound, a concession stand, and a press box, each built precisely two-thirds the size of its professional counterpart, all of it glowing under the lights. The Plain City Little League facility looked like a miniature major league park.

My father whistled softly, pump-pump-pumped the brakes to stop his Ranchero, and said, "Would you take a look at that, honey? Would you take a look at that?"

Plain City was soon to become the shape of my family's dream, a place that would show each of us something essential about ourselves, define us in relationship to one another, and catapult us toward our future. But I didn't know any of that as my father shifted into neutral and lit up a Camel. I was simply wondering what I had done to deserve such an embarrassing father.

"Non semper erit aestas," I muttered derisively. "It will not always be summer."

How Little League Saved the O'Neills

An elderly man named Mr. Walter lived next door to us on Schreyer Place. He was a gardener who specialized in delphinium, but he also had beds of foxglove, Shirui lilies, Pitcher's thistle, poppies, and Japanese irises. Mr. Walter liked flowers that were tall and fragile—flowers that were especially vulnerable to the balls that began sailing over his fence as soon as my brothers were old enough to launch them. But Mr. Walter was also a religious man, and he did his best to forgive. At first he would smile sadly, gently toss the balls back over the fence, snip his broken blooms, and place them on the altar to the Blessed Virgin near his garage.

"I gotta hand it to the ole fish eater," my father said. "He's no hypocrite."

But as my brothers gained the skills to actually swing for his fence, Mr. Walter lost his capacity for forgiveness. He stopped throwing the balls back. Instead, he trotted out, rescued the offending sphere, and removed it to his house. It was as if he thought himself to be up against a finite supply of balls. But of course he was not. Shortly after my father came upon the stadium in Plain City, he ceased supplying frivolous balls and threw all his resources behind Spalding baseballs, which he began purchasing by the case.

"The poor old thing," said my mother, staring through the kitchen window as Mr. Walter scurried after a ball that had toppled several budding allium. She was feeling particularly sensitive to futile efforts at the time. The previous Christmas, she'd saved to buy her mother two dresses and a coat so that she might get out of her bed at the Beechwold Nursing Home and, once again, come to our house for Sunday dinner. Delighted, my grandmother donned first the long-sleeved dress and then the short-sleeved dress and finally, after using embroidery scissors to remove its sleeves, her new winter coat. My grandmother had been mystified by my mother's response to her alteration. "Why, darling," she said, "I didn't want to hide the sleeves of the beautiful dress you gave me."

My mother's efforts on Aunt Dodo's behalf were similarly unrewarded. After my aunt's stroke, when it was no longer possible for her to live alone, it was my mother who had found a tenant for Dodo's house and my mother who, by scrimping and saving from our family's meager resources, covered the rest of Dodo's tab at the nursing home. But did Dodo thank her? No. She narrowed her eyes and growled, "I said, I said," whenever my mother visited.

And we all found it depressing to consider the attentions my mother had lavished for decades upon her uncle. The day before he died, the previous winter, his will had been changed, and the new document bequeathed his entire estate to his companion of the platinum blond wig, making no mention of my mother or the promised trust funds for her children's education.

The Gwinn family lawyer produced the earlier version of the will and encouraged my parents to contest, but they refused. "That money never brought anybody any happiness," said my father—and my mother, for once, agreed with him. She didn't see herself slugging it out in court with The Wig. This did not mean, however, that she took comfort in my father's habitual assurances that all would be well. It simply meant that she had stopped dreaming of windfalls and petitioning Jesus Christ on behalf of her family and had begun to focus on saving herself.

Chopin was her chosen method for deliverance. Every afternoon as my brothers careened ever closer to Bongo-hood, she and Mrs. Stutz sat on the piano bench in our living room and practiced selections from *Chopin for Four Hands*. Undeterred by their daughters' rendition of Top 40 hits from upstairs, the two women practiced. Unfazed by the sound of ball against bat, unmoved by tantrums, crying babies, or the Fuller Brush man ringing the doorbell, they worked on their fingering and timing for half an hour every afternoon. Lost in their halting renditions, my mother and the mother of my best friend were oblivious to the mafia spirit that was growing among my brothers.

In addition to marketing fireworks, Mike, Pat, Kevin, and Robert were by then stealing and reselling girlie magazines, wreaking senseless havoc on local gardens, shoplifting baseball cards, regularly deploying intimidation tactics against other children, and swinging like Tarzan from a vine across a drop of nearly forty feet in the ravine across the street.

Others might have been more worried about the library of purloined *Playboy* magazines that my brothers kept hidden in a disused sewer several blocks from our house, or how they organized a perfume drive by encouraging children to steal their mother's perfumes and then mixed all the scents together and poured them on backyard gardens throughout the neighborhood. My brothers did not like vegetables. But their vine-swinging, with its blatant Bongo connection, concerned me most.

Pat was the brains. Mike was the muscle. Kevin and Robert were the foot soldiers. As a gang, they enforced baseball card trades that, eventually, left Pat with a museum-quality collection of ten thousand cards and left most kids in Beechwold lousy with doubles of players who never made it past their rookie year.

"We're here to discuss that old Honus Wagner that your dad gave you," Pat would say pleasantly. Most of their marks were too naive to know that fewer than fifty of the 1909 Wagner cards were distributed on cigarette packs before the Pittsburgh shortstop, who deplored tobacco, was able to stop their production; others were too eager to be part of the fun Team O'Neill to refuse. For those who hesitated, Mike stood behind Pat, curling his lip. Robert, who at six years old had wide blue eyes, buckteeth, and an elephantine memory, was a natural mediator. He stood to the right of Pat and spelled out the terms:

"We'll give you real stars for that old thing. Pete Rose! Johnny Bench! Hank Aaron!" Then he'd glance quickly at Mike and add, as if concerned for the mark's safety, "You should take the deal." Kevin, who was seven and already the coolest kid in school, would then flash his Robert Redford smile and say mildly, "We don't want to have to tell your mother about the *Playboys*."

Resistance was futile. Protests, pleas, sobbing, and any effort to escape the circle of brothers would be drowned by the sounds of *Chopin for Four Hands* and shrieking renditions of Top 40 hits.

*   *   *

In May of 1967, Pat woke up at three a.m. His four brothers were asleep in their bunk beds; his was the only twin bed in the room. He was ten years old, he was restless, and he couldn't think of anything else to do, so Pat crept out of the house, walked three blocks down Schreyer Place to High Street, the major north-south artery of Columbus, and lay down in the middle of the street. He stayed there, in his cowboy pajamas, until he felt the vibration of an approaching vehicle and then he rolled to the curb.

My father didn't hear his second-born son leave the house that night, but he suspected that Pat was up to no good. This suspicion was, in my father's mind, confirmed one Saturday morning on the way to the grocery store.

Paul, who was four, was standing on the front seat between my father and Pat and nagging my father in his terrible high voice about things he wanted from the store. He wanted Lucky Charms. He wanted crab. He wanted a blow job.

"Will you get me one, Dad?" squeaked the little boy. Paul still spent most of his time with me, making art projects and lip-synching Top 40 tunes. Occasionally, however, he tagged along with his older brothers, and he'd taken to imitating them. "I want a blow job," he said.

Without taking his eyes off the road, my father reached past his youngest son and slapped Pat in the face.

As usual, my father mistakenly identified his second-born son as the per-petrator—rather than just another victim—of the family's woes. Clearly the inmates were running the asylum while the warden played Chopin, and Pat was their leader.

That spring, my father abandoned his easy, boys-will-be-boys flossy-fee and adopted a fierce and vigilant Puritanism the likes of which had not been seen in Ohio since Howard Hyde Russell founded the Anti-Saloon League in Oberlin in 1893. What I felt as the hot breath of Bongo on the back of my neck and my mother interpreted as the ascent of Barbarians for Balls, my father defined as hormones—particularly Mike's and Pat's hormones—on the rise. This surge, he told my mother, needed to be harnessed.

"You have *got* to be kidding, Chick," said my mother. "They're just little boys."

"You better start wising up," replied my father, wielding his Time-Life book as Carrie Nation once wielded her hatchet through Ohio. "If we don't nip this in the bud, you're going to see the little kids acting stupid, too."

"Puberty is not communicable, Chick," said my mother.

My father, however, would not be swayed. He saw my brothers huddle and then scatter inexplicably at his approach. Spotting a small square packet in Pat's back pocket, he performed a body search. My father was undeterred when his effort failed to produce the condoms he suspected and yielded, instead, several dozen sticks of the Topps bubble gum that came packaged with baseball cards. "They are up to something, by God," he said. That the bond between my brothers lay in pornography, cigarettes, and extortion would have been unimaginable to my father. He assumed a confederacy of hormones.

"I've seen enough bulls around enough cows to know what's what," he told my mother. "The next thing you know, it's the girls and then it's all over. That's it. The whole ball game."

"You have *got* to be kidding," said my mother. "You were twenty-five years old by the time I met you."

"I know what I know," said my father. He knew, for one thing, the cost of losing control. Just the thought of it caused the world to sparkle for a second, as it had when he was a little boy and about to fall down. The difference in the spring of 1967 was that the shimmering fantasia that passed before his eyes when he worried about his sons quickly settled into a sparkling image of the pint-size ballpark at Plain City. Baseball, thought my father, was the answer.

And just as Howard Hyde Russell had known that he needed something more than mortal might to battle hell's own demons, my father knew that he needed more than backyard ball games to save his sons. As the days lengthened, he moved the nightly games to the diamond at Dominion Junior High, recruited players beyond his own family, and began to issue challenges to teams from the local recreation center and the churches.

My father may have been determined to save the rest of his sons from Pat, but Pat quickly proved to be the most eager convert to my father's cause. He loved the game in the same wordless, absolute, and selfless way that my father did and shared a similar resolve: if he wasn't destined to be one of its stars, Pat would support those who might be. As my father recruited players, Pat quietly offered incentives in the form of bubble gum, candy, and even his own baseball cards to my father's hottest prospects. Pat gave similar bonuses—also unbeknownst to my father—to the players who responded well to coaching.

As a coach, my father mixed praise, ridicule, terror, and an unflagging commitment to each boy, and the combination created players who loved him too much to lose.

"Keep your shoulder in there!" he hollered, hurling pitch after pitch to each boy.

"It's not going to hurt you," he yelled.

"If I see you start to bail, by God I *will* hit you with this ball," he said. Within weeks, my father's ragtag team started trouncing players who were older than they were. Parents came to watch their children perform gravity-defying relays and pickoffs that sent their bigger, stronger opponents kicking dirt back to the bench. When other little boys were swinging wildly for the fences, my father taught his players to parlay their lesser strength into well-placed little hits. And when the players were successful, Pat slipped them bonuses—a string of firecrackers or a box of sparklers—on the sly.

"My boys are crazy about him," said one father, who taught physics at Ohio State and sounded puzzled by his son's feelings for the ditchdigging coach.

"He really knows how to bring out the best in boys," said another neighbor.

"I can't tell you how grateful I am," Mrs. Hammond told my mother. Her youngest son wore Coke-bottle glasses. "If it hadn't been for Chick, Terry would never have had a chance," she said.

For years my mother had courted a shift in Schreyer Place opinion. She had never, however, imagined that balls would be the source of the change, and she was not entirely happy.

"Balls! Balls! Balls!" she screamed at my father after my brothers brought home lackluster report cards and then headed out to the backyard to complete the batting and fielding drills that my father had ordered. "I hope you're satisfied," she added.

In fact, my father was not satisfied. A sandlot and casual pickup games could not, in his opinion, stoke the fire of competitiveness hot enough to fry hormones.

"You crowd the male of the species and you get hormone problems," he told me one night after baseball practice as I surveyed the sandlot for stray pieces of equipment and errant children. My father had a habit of leaving children behind. Once, he forgot Robert at the grocery store and another time, he left Paul digging in the sand behind home plate in the sandlot. My mother worried less if she knew that I was checking the ballyard before we came home. "Hormone problems are no joke," he continued. "Look what happened to Bongo."

After the first spring season of sandlot ball, my father motioned Mike and Pat into the cab of his Ranchero. "There's a summer Little League team out of Whetstone Recreation Center," he said. "You two are going to try out, you are going to make the team, and then we're going to the tournament in Plain City."

*   *   *

By August of 1967, Plain City had become our summer home. We knew what part of the grandstand had the worst splinters, where the mosquitoes were thickest, and which concession-stand workers were most likely to throw a couple pieces of penny candy in with the purchase of a nickel candy bar. We were the most popular family in the Little League community.

"Now, batting for the Frisbee Bears, the right fielder, MIKE O'NEILL!"

The man who announced the games at Plain City had the sort of voice you hear describing afternoon ball games on AM radio, the sort of voice my brothers aspired to when they announced their own moves. With each announcement, the man grounded the listener in the moment and raised the possibility of eternity. The way he said "Now" imbued the word with the momentousness of a potentially historic event. His inflection with "batting cleanup for the Frisbee Bears" was low and all business. But then, as he pronounced the player's name, his voice rose in force and excitement. From the silver-tongued sportscaster who worked in a small green booth that was built in a tree above the home team dugout, "MIKE O' NEILL" sounded no different than "BA-A-ABE RUTH" would have. The small players of Plain City acted accordingly. Some waved to the fans and tipped their caps as they moved from the on-deck circle to the batter's box. Others rubbed dirt into their palms.

For these eleven- or twelve-year-old boys, playing Plain City was like playing Yankee Stadium or Fenway Park. Throughout the spring and the early summer, they played their games in the round sandlots typical of schools and recreation departments around Columbus in the late 1960s. Only if they were lucky—only if their teams prevailed—did they get to enter the Plain City tournament, to play on the perfectly groomed diamond with a grass infield, to see their name on the scoreboard, to hear it enunciated by the announcer.

Mike—the first O'Neill to play the perfect park, and the original repository of my father's ambitions—did not usually acknowledge the crowd when his name was announced. Instead he would glance toward my father, who always sat in the front row along the third-base line watching the game as intently and dispassionately as he would have watched a game an hour's drive south at Crosley Field in Cincinnati. From the beginning, my brothers understood that there was no daddy-ball to be played with my father. "Don't look at me, just get up there and hit," he would say, if my brothers asked him to intercede with their coaches. "The better you play, the more you'll play." After glancing toward him, Mike would continue to take small cuts with his bat as he walked to home plate.

The game did not get his full attention until the possibility of personal failure seemed imminent to Mike. Once, playing the outfield in the bottom of the ninth when his team was leading 3–0, for instance, a beautifully hit line drive had landed at his feet while Mike watched an Amish man cart-train his horse on the track that surrounded the ballpark. In the batter's box, he tended to be more interested in the scenery than he was in keeping his eye on the ball until he was down two strikes. But once he had gone to a full count, Mike was all business.

Even from the stands, the change was visible and dramatic: the little boy at the plate became Ted Williams, elegant, fierce, and indomitable, and often he parked the next pitch. Trained on the simple physics of bat against ball, his fury and irritability easily parlayed pitches into line drives over the right-field fence, two hundred feet from home plate. Mike loved to corkscrew around pitches because it made him feel like his hero, Willie Mays. He loved to loft the ball past the announcer's booth and to hear the man's exclamation—"and it's outa here!"—as he took off to first. And as he rounded the corner toward home, Mike would again glance toward my father. In response, my father would nod and clap twice, like a base coach acknowledging a fellow pro. The rest of the family would cheer. I would scream my throat raw.

The howling was existential. Furious at the all-ball, all-the-time turn of events in our family life, I sat in the stands savaging Tootsie Roll after Tootsie Roll from the concession stand. The candy, like the cheering, had therapeutic value. For Robert and Kevin, however, cheering was Bongo training. Sitting next to me in the stands while their oldest brother made his name in Plain City, the younger boys developed a habit of inhaling deeply and beating their small chests.

"Smell that air!" said my father approvingly. "It's good for you." And he stood—first to fill his lungs with the dew-on-corn aroma of another Plain City night and then to accept congratulations on behalf of his firstborn son, the slugger, the legend, the star.

"*This* is our country vacation, Chick?" said my mother. "You've got to be kidding me."

Yes, that is exactly what it was. While others looked forward to summers at Lake Erie, in Door County, or on Cape Cod, the O'Neills were living for Plain City—at least the male ones were. The Little League park had, for several decades, been run out of love by a retired coach and it was the best little ballpark in the Midwest. It was also a society. Within days of our arrival that first season, we were courted with invitations to the most coveted events of the Plain City social season, the pregame picnics and concession-stand rendezvous, the postgame meetings at the ice cream store. The community spotted my father's ball savvy immediately. They wore overalls; he wore green polyester slacks and a pink golf shirt. They came from small rural towns and drove pickup trucks; he came from Columbus and arrived in his Ranchero—which, after all, was half a car. They began seeking his advice in matters of hit-and-run strategies, bunt situations, and the importance of the sacrifice fly.

"Grahhh ha ha. Hey ya, Whatsy!" sang my father happily as he made his way from the third-base line to the concession stand, shaking hands with the men, winking at their wives, kissing their babies, and slapping their little boys on the seat of their pants, saying, "Go get 'em, slugger." It was as if he were running for mayor. The only potential constituents my father didn't court were the little girls who hung over the fence calling the players by name. For his daughter, spending thousands of hours at the ball field was an acceptable fate, but my father saw other girls as a dangerous distraction. "Go walk your dog," my father said to the girls, in a voice that suggested he was kidding. "Tend to your knitting. Grah-hah-hah! Go bake a cake!"

"So refined," said my mother. She arched her brow and shook her head and attempted to make common cause with other wives and mothers, but her intended audience found my mother's behavior confusing. Most of the women of the Plain City Little League subscribed to *Reader's Digest* and packed picnics for their families; they didn't know what to make of a mother who read her books in the unabridged versions and allowed her children to eat at the concession stand.

After a doubleheader's worth of nagging, my mother frequently turned the brass clasp on her wicker purse and threw dollar bills at Kevin, Robert, and Paul. "I give up!" she said. "Eat all the junk you want." The significance of this shift was not lost on me, either. Sitting on the wooden bleachers at Plain City, I'd already been moved to the sidelines of the family destiny; now my mother was unwittingly stripping me of my role as sole provider of junk food and therefore robbing me of the most significant leverage I had over my brothers. Certain that I was careening toward Colo's fate with not one but potentially five Bongos in the making, I sat in the stands reading *The Catcher in the Rye*. I pretended not to hear the women whispering about what a lovely sister I was. "What other fourteen-year-old would care enough about her brother's interest to read a book about a catcher?" they marveled. I did my best to avoid eye contact with my mother, as well.

Plain City formalized the pairing of my parents' six children. First, Mike and Pat were teammates on the Frisbee Bears; several years later, Kevin and

Robert would be teammates on another team, and they were already viewed as part of the Plain City minor league system. But Paul and I, at either end of the birth order, were not part of the O'Neill machine in Plain City in the late 1960s. He was too young and I was a girl. Night after night, we walked around the park together, feeding horses and waving at the strange Amish people. We sat on the picnic tables and drew pictures and colored. One evening that first summer, during a particularly fierce game against the London All Stars, Bill Buchanan, the older brother of another Frisbee Bear team member, joined us. He was already sixteen and the editor of the high school newspaper. He played tennis, not baseball, and was cute and shy. Along with every other girl at the high school, I liked Bill.

"OK, let me see you catch this one!" he said to Paul, tossing a white tennis ball away from the table and high into the air. Paul raced to get the ball, stumbling in the dark and almost tripping over his pigeon toes.

"Again!" Paul demanded, running the ball back to Bill. "Again!"

Again and again, Bill tossed the ball, and the farther it went, the closer his free hand crept toward mine across the picnic table. By now it was past midnight. The Frisbee Bears were playing for the championship. Throughout the summer, with Mike slugging and Pat working occasionally as their closing pitcher, the team had been indomitable. But on the night of the championship game, as Bill Buchanan's hand edged toward mine, the Frisbee Bears were having trouble tromping the London All Stars. The game was already in the twelfth inning when the announcer said the only thing that could have moved me from the picnic table: crackling above the crickets and the mosquitoes, he said my family name.

"Pitching now for the Frisbee Bears and batting fifth, PAT O'NEILL!"

"Come on," I said, and we ran, Bill and I, dragging Paul between us, arriving flushed and breathless to stand behind the backstop as Pat took the mound.

Pat didn't have the height, the power, or the natural ability of his older brother. He was built too low to the ground to have a future in the game—except perhaps as a catcher, and he didn't have the hands to play behind the plate. But Pat had a curveball. And that night, a curveball was all it took to keep the London All Stars hitless into the top of the thirteenth inning. He threw nine pitches. He retired three of the London All Stars. Bill Buchanan and I cheered.

I leaned into the backstop like an animal pressing against the mesh of its cage as the first two batters for the Frisbee Bears grounded out. Perhaps everyone thought that the boys were playing not so much to win, but to prolong that last moment of summer, that magical instant before a fate is decided. I know I did. Mike, the third batter to come to the plate for the Frisbee Bears in the top of the thirteenth inning, launched a ball that bounced off the right-field pole and disappeared past the warning track, deep into a cornfield.

The game was over. Our roar could have awakened Ty Cobb from his grave. But then the umpire unexpectedly ruled the hit a ground rule triple, and the game was suddenly not over.

Mike was on third base. Kevin Kernin, a player who was known to be slower than the seven-year itch, was at bat. He swung at the first pitch and the ball, mishit, twirled about ten feet in the air and about a foot and a half in front of home plate. The world was completely silent as the catcher leaped up. From the corner of my eye, I saw my father's arm windmilling far down the third-base line as the catcher positioned himself beneath the dropping ball, the ball that could end the inning, falling slowly, quiet and certain as destiny, as Mike dove between the catcher's legs and slid into home. He grabbed the plate as the catcher dropped the ball.

"THAT'S IT!" screamed the announcer as Bill Buchanan threw his arm around my shoulder and the Frisbee Bears tumbled out of the dugout and onto the field.

"That's the ball game!" said the announcer. *"O'Neill wins it for the Frisbee Bears!"*

The victory in Plain City that night was huge news on Schreyer Place, where my father had not only helped a handful of other little boys earn a spot on the Frisbee Bears roster but had also counseled and chauffeured them. The neighborhood was still talking about the team's triumph—it was written about in the *Booster,* the local paper, and because it was, at the time, the longest game in Plain City history, it was also mentioned on the nightly news—a year later, when we moved away.

After a decade of searching, we finally found a new house. We moved to East Cooke Road in September 1968. As we were packing the last boxes of our belongings into my father's Ranchero, Mr. Walter began delivering cartons of the balls he'd collected. There were dozens of them, years and years of balls, packed neatly in large boxes, labeled by date of seizure. Like everyone, Mr. Walter was sad to see us go. Little League had redeemed us.

The O'Neill boys were obsessed with Plain City for a decade. They lost their interest in a life on the streets and played to hear their names announced, to hear the ball explode off their bats, to hear the fans going wild.

Sadly, the brilliance of my father's flossy-fee regarding the importance of spaciousness, pecking order, and structured play in the development of male primates gained no more recognition in the scientific community than it did among the female members of his own family. It's a shame. Colo could have been saved years of discomfort.

Once, when we were sitting at Riverfront Stadium together and my father and I were, again, close and comfortable for several hours, he told me the personal basis of his theory. A week before his high school graduation, my father and several of his teammates along with their girlfriends skipped school for a day. They went to a hotel where, hours later, they were discovered by the school principal. They were promptly expelled from school. My father did not graduate, did not get to accept the trophies he'd earned—all-state awards in baseball, football, basketball, and track. In addition, contact with the baseball scout who had already approached him was lost when, in an effort to protect him from the local scandal, and perhaps a local shotgun, my grandmother put my father on a train to California. His former high school coach was coaching at Pasadena Junior College and my father enrolled in the school, but it was several years of playing before he was again tapped to play professional ball.

"It wasn't the war, honey," he told me near the end of his life, "it was those two years and I don't even remember her name. I just know it damn ruined all our lives. Hormones."

Eventually, gorilla experts reached conclusions similar to my father's, and, backed by a huge endowment, the Columbus Zoo constructed Gorilla Villa, a sprawling new home for their great apes. In the area, individual quarters that provide privacy for the residents bank a huge, round outdoor arena where steel beams, ropes, and varied terrain offer climbing areas and room to roam. The mesh that surrounds Gorilla Villa frames the view like the mesh of a backstop. The grass inside Gorilla Villa is very green. It reminds me of Plain City. This association offended my brothers deeply at first.

"You are comparing a monkey cage to the *cathedral* of Little League," said Robert, shortly after the gorilla habitat was opened. "Not a chapel, not a church, the cathedral, OK?" Eventually, however, they saw my point.

Within days of being moved into the new habitat, Bongo became a new man. In a world that offered him privacy and space, he was restored to the mellowness of his youth. Colo left him, anyway. After twenty-five years of sharing cramped quarters and producing three offspring with the huge silverback gorilla, she took up with another silverback the first time she was given a choice and she never looked back. Bongo bellowed for several weeks after her desertion but he, too, eventually found a soul mate, a younger female named Bridgette, against whom he never raised a paw. Together they produced a baby boy named Fosse. Bridgette died soon after the birth, and in a series of events that has not yet been duplicated, Bongo raised his tiny son, holding him in the palm of his hand as an infant, pulling him along as a toddler, grooming him, feeding him, making his bed. Other females were introduced, but Bongo would not surrender his son, nor would his son leave Bongo's side.

These events were not widely discussed until Father's Day of 1989, when the *Columbus Dispatch* named Bongo "Father of the Year" and ran his picture on the front page. I was working at a newspaper in New York City at the time. I saw the story on a wire service and sent a copy to my father and several of my brothers with a note that read:

"You have *got* to be kidding me!

love anyway,

Colo."

Size Matters

L
ike so many reversals of fortune in our household, the move to East Cooke Road was unexpected. My father had turned as soon as he saw the sign—"For Sale by Owner"—in front of the sprawling yellow stucco ranch house in the summer of 1968. "We'll have horses!" he exclaimed, skidding across the gravel apron and into the driveway.

Even coming from my father, the promise of horses was perplexing. The house that we were approaching at a perilous rate as my father began to pump-pump-pump his brakes was, in fact, a "ranch," but only in the subdivision sense of the word. It was no Ponderosa. East Cooke Road—which was curiously situated in the sea of lower-income housing that lay between Interstate 71 and the Northland Mall—was a mile-long island of bucolic ambition, a strip of several dozen large houses sited on four-acre lawns that rose into woody hillocks here and dipped into creek beds or ponds there. Thanks to the grease-creased maps and surveys that he kept under the seat of his Ranchero, however, my father was able to see beyond the obvious. "This lot is zoned 'rural,'" he told us.

"I'm going to give you all I have on me as a deposit," he said to the owner, digging deep into his pockets and pulling out change and wadded bills. His offering, which added up to less than one hundred dollars, represented the full extent of his liquid assets. "That should hold you till I can go out and collect," said my father. "Grah ha ha!" The owner, presumably as worried about the black families who had begun moving onto an adjoining road as he was bewitched by my father's charm, agreed.

My father hated "collecting." He believed that if people appreciated his work they would simply pay him without his having to ask. And, because they liked him so well, often people did. Even so, the ditchdigging fees for hundreds of gas and water lines remained in pockets other than his. Having made his downpayment, however, my father applied himself to attracting his receivables, and within a month we were members of the landed gentry.

On moving day, as my brothers and I carried boxes of balls into the second garage, behind the house, my fathered roared up the driveway towing a U-Haul trailer behind his Ranchero. "Lookie here!" he hollered. When we'd all gathered around the back of the trailer, he opened the door and a miniature Shetland pony charged out, snorting.

"What did I promise? Huh?" asked my father. "Horses, right?"

His name was Tonka. He was a small blond Shetland with grass-stained buckteeth that he flashed by curling his lip in a way that made him look like my brother Mike. Unlike Mike, however, Tonka was a biter—a fact that was literally impressed upon us within seconds of his arrival. Our new pony may not have been much larger than the Great Pyrenean dogs that would soon join him in the backyard, but he was meaner than cat dirt.

The only thing not tiny about Tonka was his penis. Even under ordinary circumstances, it was outsize—huge and black and reminiscent of an elephant's trunk—and when he was content, it looked like an extra limb. My father tied Tonka to a stake in our front yard to show him off, and it was here that he spent most of his days. When the sun warmed him and the grass pleased his palate, he would extend his fifth leg, lending a tripod appearance to his hindquarters that caused my brothers, the oldest of whom were teetering on the brink of puberty, to gape and elbow each other.

"Jayyyzzz," they screamed, giving the word the same mixture of wonder

and disbelief that they gave to Pat's audacity and balls hit out of the park. Mike, whose modesty was by then renowned, covered his eyes and begged my father to move Tonka to the backyard.

Whether it was to take a second look at the five-legged pony or to consider the great polka dots of shorn grass that Tonka left in his wake, people now slowed down as they drove past. It conveyed a sense of homage being paid. And this, coupled with the fact that Cooke Road was the only fancy and expensive neighborhood in the Brookhaven School District, created the impression that the rich and famous had taken up residence in our new house. Our section of Cooke Road was populated mainly by people who owned small businesses or had made their fortunes working with their hands. The arrival of an "old Columbus family" meant that they themselves had arrived. The awe they accorded us grew with each box piled high with books, each carton labeled, "Fragile: Family China," each velvet-covered antique barrel-back chair that they saw carried into our house. And look! A pony for the children!

On Cooke Road, my father was no longer a ditchdigger and my mother was no longer a shrieking fishwife. "He's an excavating contractor," the neighbors told one another. "Heavy equipment, *expensive* equipment." And, "She's high-class. And what a sense of humor! You should hear her talk about her kids!" Even the teachers and principals in the new schools took a generous view of my brothers. The behavior that had previously been deemed "predelinquent" was suddenly seen as "gifted."

"What moral fiber," said the principal of Clinton Junior High School as he slid the M-80s he'd found in Pat's locker across his desk to my mother. "Your son assumed full responsibility for these. Please accept my apologies. What? Oh, ha ha ha. Your son selling fireworks? No, I'm certainly *not* suggesting that. Clearly, Mrs. O'Neill, this contraband belongs to one of our troublemakers, somebody who thinks he can take advantage of the new boy. Well, he has another think coming, I can promise you!"

"What a fine mind!" said Mike's homeroom teacher. "No, I wouldn't call him hyperactive. I'd instead suggest that he's underchallenged! I'm afraid that perhaps we haven't been doing *our* job, Mrs. O'Neill! But just give us time."

Down the road, at Maize Road Elementary, the idiosyncrasies of each of the three younger brothers were also taken as indications of high IQ. Kevin, who could never keep still, was seen as "high energy." Robert, who pouted constantly in response to being shunned by Kevin, was seen as possessing a great and ponderous intellect. Nor did the school see Paul's constant call for replays in playground games of dodgeball as cause for concern. He was, they said, just like his brothers, "a competitor." Teachers fought for the honor of teaching my brothers.

With their all-star status and new family mystique, my brothers began to think of themselves as a franchise. They needed a ballpark, and shortly after we took up residence in September 1968, Pat announced his plan: "O'Neill-Dome. In the field behind the backyard and the pond. I'm serious. We'll use Tonka's shed for the clubhouse. I have money—never mind where from—and I have the equipment covered. We're player-managers, that's what we'll tell the press." They were also the announcers and the grounds crew. "Forget the Astrodome," said Pat. "We're going to build the *real* Eighth Wonder of the World with *grass,* not Astroturf!"

To the outside world, we were rich! We were talented! We were—finally—the O'Neills! As if unable to accept their good fortune, my parents began telling stories that rendered us deserving of this six-bedroom castle, this social elevation, this dream of a new life.

"Your great-granddad staked over a thousand acres," said my father. This mood to reminisce came over him as he was using a post digger to fence in the half-acre patch of lawn directly behind our house for Nancy, our new dog. But his tone suggested that the family holdings extended well beyond Cooke Road as he stared dreamily over his property—past the apple and pear trees, the ball diamond, the marsh and shallow pond, and another half-acre of grassy fields toward the row of much smaller houses that sat way, way out at the rear of our property line. "By God, he must have fenced half of Nebraska before he was through."

By the fall of 1968, both my grandmother and my aunt Dodo, after a long and painful dwindling, had finally died, leaving my mother freer to reclaim some of her earlier and less-conflicted pride at being a Gwinn. On our family outings to the nearby Northland Mall, my father, true to character, continued to wave at the neighbors ("Grah ha ha. Hey ya, Whatsy!"), but now my mother—buoyed by an unasked-for increase in the credit line of her Lazarus charge card and her family's new and improved image—waved, too. Late at night, she applied terrible chemicals to the mahogany dining room suite that she'd grown up with in the Gwinn house and used first a putty knife and then fine sandpaper to lift layers of old varnish from the wood. She was "antiquing" the furniture, she explained, by applying a bone white pickle and gilt highlights.

"They call it Provençal, but it looks Italian to me," she told me. "Your grandmother was married to the ambassador to Italy—that's the sort of people the Gwinns were, influential—before she lost her mind."

The O'Neills of Cooke Road were too good for ballpoint pens. I took up calligraphy. Sitting at the long table in my art studio in the basement—*my art studio!*—I drafted designs for a sign that might be posted at the end of our long driveway. I was also undergoing a sort of renaissance. My school was the same—I was now commuting back to the old neighborhood to finish up at Whetstone High—but, for the first time in my life, my time was my own. With her youngest child in first grade, my mother had finally allowed me to participate in extracurricular activities at school. I immediately joined the school newspaper, the drama club, and the art club. As if making up for lost time, I drafted and painted and lettered until the wee hours.

"The Kennedys have one in Hyannisport," I explained to my father as I worked on the family sign. "O'Neill," I penned in Gothic letters, and then, "The O'Neills."

But, like every member of my family, I knew we were less than we appeared to be. Tonka told us so.

Although it sprang from the same pretense, the accent I assumed when speaking during this period of time was not as clear as the typeface I chose to master.

"I say, lads!" I might cry, coming upon my brothers as they used a sickle to level the high grass on the proposed site of the O'NeillDome. "Shall I fetch the wickets?" Five minutes later, however, my British affect often gave way to my version of a Beacon Hill brogue as I informed my mother that my father had, in accordance with her wishes, "paahked the caah, raaatheh the Ranchero, *behind* the house and the yaahd."

I understood that The Family That People Thought We Were—The O'Neills!—would sound different from most people in Columbus. I was sure that the O'Neill family would sound like the Kennedys. After all, maybe we could be the Kennedys of Cooke Road, I reasoned, and linguistically I did my best to toe the line. Unfortunately, the accent I deployed when reading Shakespeare in drama club also followed me home on a regular basis.

I did not blame my brothers for widening their eyes and staring at me when I spoke of "dear old Mum." Unlike me, they did not rush to ease my parents' anxiety, nor did they share my urgency to become who others thought we were. How could they have known that in my mind the acres behind our house were the moors, the apple tree was the family orchard, and Tonka was one of a string of polo ponies? In addition, however altered I may have sounded, I did not look any different than I had on Schreyer Place.

At fifteen, I was five feet ten inches tall and weighed 137 pounds, most of which resided between my waist and knees. I continued to ply the swimming pool at the Hospitality Motor Inn, where my family had a membership. Clutching a kickboard, I thrashed out a mile of laps every other day in the name of a perfect size 10. But the god of standard clothes sizes was not appeased. My waist was a size eight and my hips were a twelve, and nothing—not the hours I spent waddling across the floor of my room, my arms extended, not the deep knee bends and leg lifts that I performed, not even the two miles of laps I jogged around the track at lunchtime—resulted in the off-the-rack proportions I aspired toward. My dream of shopping at the Limited and finding a miniskirt that fit was in vain. When my mother had proposed altering a few more outfits from dead Aunt Dodo's wardrobe for me, it didn't seem much more humiliating than the cinching and letting out that was necessary for any garment destined for my closet. As the first tie-dyed T-shirts and peasant skirts appeared on the campus of Ohio State University, I was wearing a wool plaid walking suit by Pendleton, circa 1955, while strolling the family-estate-in-my-mind.

"Talley ho, old chap!" I called out as Kevin flew by, clinging to Tonka's back.

Kevin was the only one of us who regularly rode the pony. They did not share personalities—blond, blue-eyed, agile, and slight, Kevin was as sunny and easygoing as Tonka was miserable and cruel—but both the twenty-year-old pony and the nine-year-old boy loved to fly. Kevin's natural state was motion. When he was very young, his constant, fluttery activity had been similar to a hummingbird's. "Jesus, will you just light someplace?" my mother would say to her third-born son. To me, she would say, "Catch him! Catch him! Jesus! It's like living with a butterfly." As he grew older, my brother's flitting more closely resembled Peter Pan's. In between, there was Tonka. Kevin rode him bareback.

Tonka did not canter, trot, or gallop. Tonka bolted. "Whoa!" Kevin shouted as soon as he mounted. But, unlike Kevin's classmates, Tonka did not swoon for Kevin's smile and sardonic understatement. Instead of yielding, the pony schemed to have Kevin sheared from his back.

"Whoa, boy!" hollered Kevin, pulling the reins and crouching down as Tonka charged under low-hanging branches and then, in hopes of dislodging his rider against a rail, tore up and down along the fence that lined one side of our property.

"Whoaaa," shouted Kevin, clutching the pony's shaggy sides with his knobby knees, shifting his weight away from the fence and yanking the reins ever tighter. Eventually, Tonka would take off for the acres of land that lay behind the houses on Cooke Road. And Kevin would cling to his mane as a drowning man might a life raft, the long tail of his stocking cap streaming behind him as the pony tore out of sight.

Riding Tonka, Kevin adopted his pose for life—he seeks no control, and relaxes into any ride—and often they were gone for hours. Sometimes, for fun, the pony refused to return, and on those evenings my father was forced to give chase. Those observing the pony's rampage swore that the animal smiled broadly as he raced along the suburban road, my father in pursuit. A few times my father was finally forced to tackle the little beast, who weighed about 450 pounds, and wrestle him to the ground. Tonka bit him and laughed. In general, however, the pony returned to our yard when he was through flying and, more often than not, Kevin was still on his back.

Whoever delivered Tonka's meals (he was given leftover oatmeal in the morning; in the evening, he was fed more oats or hay) was rewarded with vicious nips and hideous, bucktoothed leers. The same fate befell any who attempted to pet him or to spoil him with carrots or apples or sugar cubes. The wrath of the little pony was as big and as horrifying as his penis.

"Somebody must have really hurt that little bastard," said my father one winter day. Wielding a two-by-four, he was trying to move Tonka, who had cornered the O'Neill ice hockey team—in uniform—against a wall of our house. But of all the things he detested, nothing was as loathsome to Tonka as a female.

From time to time, he would pull free of his stake in the front yard or slip through a backyard gate left ajar, and Tonka would then spend the day stampeding the lawns and gardens of Cooke Road. Accustomed to receiving treats from our back door, he would clamber onto porches and kick kitchen doors with his hoof. He probably would have bitten whoever responded, but usually, the lady of the house opened the door, and even strangers found it impossible to mistake his malice. "I hope I have not hurt your horse," they would say when they called. "Could you possibly come pick him up so that we can leave the house?" Despite the local largesse regarding all things O'Neill, whispers of Tonka's misogyny spread. I gave him wide berth, and so did my mother.

"I don't know what his problem is," said my mother. "I made him oatmeal! I told him that he was cute!"

Tonka's attitude hurt her feelings. "What more does he want?" she asked me, as we sat in the long, flat living room of our new house, analyzing paint chips and wallpaper samples late into the night.

Wordlessly, we conspired to create the look of a venerable family manor. Unfortunately, our efforts were undeniably inhibited by the modernity of our new house. It was a very large rectangle, with two wings of three bedrooms each, which were separated by a huge kitchen, a breakfast room, a dining room, and a living room. The ceilings were low. The windows were aluminum. The basement was three thousand square feet and included a recreation room, my father's office, a laundry room, a shower, and my art room. It was a house for Eames rather than Empire furnishings and this, along with the varied visions of the males in the household, presented certain challenges.

Our decorating partnership revealed some of the fault lines between my mother and me. True to my generation, I advocated live hanging plants, preferably with macramé holders, rather than silk flower arrangements and plastic philodendron. I opposed the faux-antique finishes that my mother was lavishing on tables and cabinets and chairs. I viewed her efforts to faithfully duplicate the vignettes displayed in the Lazarus furniture department in the same way that the apocryphal Boston Brahmin lady viewed women who buy hats. The O'Neills! shouldn't have to buy furniture; they should *have* furniture. My mother, however, was not moved by my view, and our forays to Lazarus continued on a nearly nightly basis. Construction was flourishing in Columbus; my father's business was doing well. We continued to consider each purchase carefully, if not obsessively, and once we made up our minds, we established a savings plan for every proposed expenditure.

As we turned into the driveway after an evening in the store's furniture department, we noticed that the garage door was closed. Our new house had a double garage connected to it by a breezeway and another garage that was a freestanding building behind the house. My parents parked in the garage nearest the house and whenever they pulled out, they left the door open for their return.

"I'll get it," I said, jumping out of the car.

"Be careful," said my mother, "I don't like the looks of this." And indeed, when I rolled up the door, Tonka came charging out, head down and snorting. He'd been arrested by the local authorities for wandering: they'd taped a threatening note, written on police stationery, to his halter.

"Call the constable!" I shrieked, holding my Jackie O pillbox hat and running away from Tonka with the longest stride that the tapered skirt of Dodo's vintage Chanel suit would allow. "Summon the stable hands!"

My brothers had another technique for dealing with the dissonance between our image and the reality of who we were. They called one another "Inchy." It was a terrible reminder of how their personal plumbing compared with the pony's.

"Inchy!" Mike hissed on opening day of O'NeillDome, the spring after we'd moved to Cooke Road. Kevin was two strikes down in a home-team-versus-everybody-else game. The games became a daily ritual, and so did the way the older brothers disparaged the younger ones.

"Inchy," Mike would say, his voice seething with contempt after Robert, who was only eight years old, dropped a fly ball and allowed the winning run to score. But the younger boys had their revenge. "Inchy," they would say later, if they came upon Mike talking to a girl. "Inchy! Inchy! Inchy!"

It was like a secret handshake. And when distance prohibited a verbal exchange, my brothers used a hand sign. Behavior that was less than competitive, performances that did not yield victories, as well as any sign of vulnerability brought a loose fist held just below eye level with the thumb and index finger posed precisely one inch apart, like a monocle. The sign could be flashed anywhere: behind a parent's back, from the sidelines of a Little League park, while walking past the classroom of another, in the window that was placed high in the door of the examination room at the moment when the pediatrician said to one O'Neill brother or another, "Cough."

Later, the Inchy sign would become an affirmation of their humanity, a reminder of where they came from and what they shared. But in 1968, when it first entered the O'Neill lexicon, Inchy was used almost exclusively to bolster oneself by devastating another. We needed all the reassurance we could get. At the very least, declaring someone else an Inchy meant that, if only for a second, everyone else was Inchy-free. This phenomenon was perhaps best illustrated by the Great Revelation.

In the mornings, before they walked to school, Mike and Pat were charged with delivering water to Tonka, and they hauled the five-gallon bucket in a small cart attached to the riding lawn mower. The task embarrassed Mike, and while Pat steadied the water pail, he nervously scanned Cooke Road lest a car bearing one of the cheerleaders should approach while he was performing menial labor on behalf of the pony with the god-awful dick. The lawn mower, like most O'Neill family vehicles, was prone to mechanical difficulty; on the morning of the Great Revelation, the battery required some work.

Sitting in algebra class an hour after watering the pony, however, Mike didn't connect his morning chore with the curious patch of cold he suddenly felt across the seat of his pants.

It was a shivering feeling, and when he moved in his chair to raise his eyebrows shyly toward the gaggle of girls sitting across the aisle from him, Mike was perplexed to feel his bare skin sucking away from the chair's varnished surface. Looking down he saw a dense map of holes advancing from the outer seam to the inseam of his well-creased bell-bottomed trousers, holes that were growing at a terrible and rapid rate. His pants were dissolving. In horror, Mike watched his flesh emerge in large, chicken-skinned patches. In a frantic calculation, he determined that he had only enough time to make it to the principal's office before his BVDs—and perhaps even more— would be revealed to the coolest girls of Clinton Junior High.

Leaping from his seat, his flayed and tattered britches streaming behind him, Mike raced though the halls of the school. Pat, whose pants were also quickly and mysteriously disappearing, was headed to the same place, only he was walking nonchalantly, watching in fascination—"Jaayyz," he said. "What the heck?"—as his pants began disintegrating before his eyes. In fact, by the time they met, the waistband of Pat's pants was connected to the garment's knees only by several tenuous shreds, the seat of his underpants was gone, and the front portion of his britches resembled a tattered loincloth. It was obvious that he'd taken the lead in the battery repair and wiped his hands more frequently on his britches.

"Hurry!" hissed Mike, whose slacks lacked a significant portion of seat and thigh, and who, in addition, tended to burn red with embarrassment on behalf of any family member who was shamed.

But Pat would not hurry; he would not even move. As the bell rang and fellow students surged through the hallway around the two boys, Pat stood staring at his older brother, shaking his head and solemnly flashing the Inchy sign.

It was generally accepted that Inchy-ness was a male malady. Rooting it out was mainly an intrafraternal pursuit. Only under extreme circumstances— when, for instance, the entire fate of the family seemed to hang in the balance—was the Inchy sign trained on either female member of my family. Mom's new teeth and my kneecaps were two such cases.

My mother's reluctance to smile during our final year on Schreyer Place was not solely a reflection of her state of mind; it was also due to the state of her two upper incisors. Each of the teeth had been in need of a root canal and, as a cost-saving measure, my mother had elected to pursue this treatment at the clinic of the College of Dentistry at Ohio State University. Following several failed attempts to save the teeth, the dentist and patient elected the removal-and-bridge-replacement route. First, the incisors that flanked her four front teeth were removed and then, for months upon months, we waited for Mom's new teeth.

As a family, we were used to waiting for the arrival of significant purchases. Acquiring a new used car, for instance, necessitated months of no "extras," as my mother put it—no restaurant meals, no trips to Knights ice cream—but the slowness of Mom's new teeth tried even our patience.

"What the hell's this quack doing?" asked my father every few months, when he noticed the thin line of my mother's smile. "Is he trying to grow them? Does he have to wait for some poor bastard with teeth your size to die?"

"Honestly, Chick," my mother would reply disdainfully, her voice faintly muffled by her unwillingness to open her mouth, "don't you understand anything? It's an art! He has to *make* my teeth."

From time to time, there would be fittings and, due to the lack of parking near the dental school, I would be called upon to chauffeur my mother there, even though I was fifteen and had to drive with a learner's permit.

"Just circle the block once," my mother would say. "This is only going to take a second." Instead, I would drive my brothers to Pearl Alley to see the black lights in the head shops, the girls with no bras, and the boys with long hair and beards like Jesus. In her excitement, my mother would hardly notice my slow return.

"I mean!" she would say, sliding into the passenger seat of the car. "This guy is unbelievable. I really think he should have majored in sculpture! The detail! The patience! What's that? It smells like incense."

For some months after we moved, the dental resident went missing.

"I think the little shyster skipped with your deposit, Boots," said my father.

"Why, I bet you're right, Chick," said my mother, her sarcasm muted by the resolute crimp of her lips. "With the money we gave that clinic, he could be all the way to Akron by now!"

Finally, after nearly two years of burnishing and refining, the dental resident called to announce the arrival of Mom's new teeth. A reservation for the celebratory restaurant meal was made. Outfits were selected. "Today's the big day!" my mother said as my father left the house before dawn. "Dinner at the Jai Lai! With my new teeth!"

At the appointed hour, I—now sixteen and a licensed driver—backed the station wagon out of the garage and my brothers piled in. "I'm too excited to drive!" my mother giggled. As I slowed near the entrance of the College of Dentistry, my mother applied fresh lipstick.

"Just wait here!" she said. "The artist is meeting me at the door!" and indeed, she entered the building and accepted a small package from a man in a lab jacket that she unwrapped as she ran back out to the car. Normally my mother was a great believer in washing her hands with Phisohex before putting anything in her mouth, but there was no way she could wait to try out her new teeth.

"Well?" she said, flashing a wide, twelve-tooth grin at each of us for the first time in two years. In her excitement, my mother did not think to look in the mirror.

"What do you think?" she beamed, leaning across Paul, who was sitting between us on the front seat, to smile in my face. Only then did I see that my mother was essentially sporting fangs—very long, very white, and alarmingly pointy. Framed by her newly applied red lipstick, Mom's new teeth looked like the wax vampire numbers sold around Halloween.

"Mom," said Paul, "I want to trick-or-treat."

"I have to watch the traffic," I said, making as if to pull away from the curb. Glancing purposefully into the rearview mirror, I did not, however, see oncoming cars. Instead, I saw Mike, Pat, Kevin, and Robert, sitting ramrod straight in the second seat, their eyes like saucers, their upper lips flayed to reveal their teeth, each of their hands opening and closing as they made the Inchy sign, like eight sets of phantom canine teeth, frantically gnashing.

"I want to stop at the dry cleaner's," leered my mother. "And the grocery! And the drugstore!" Not until we reached home did my mother look in the mirror and, seeing the Dracula she'd become, let out a shriek.

There was talk of retribution. "I think we need to have a little chat with Michelangelo," my father said. "Where's the little bastard live?" The possibility of legal action was raised. But, just as they refused to contest Uncle Gwinn's will, my parents would not sue the dental resident for cruel and unusual bridgework. The O'Neills of Cooke Road did not traffic in torts. We did not stoop to litigation. We were The O'Neills! and we were never anybody else's fault.

For this reason, I made no excuses when my brothers turned their attention to the joint between my lower and upper leg.

"Where are your kneecaps?" said Mike, training the Inchy sign on the spot where round, knobby things should have been. I'd only recently convinced my mother that short hemlines were no longer worn only by girls who frequented pool halls and bowling alleys. The sweet taste of this victory soured, however, when my eldest brother said, "Pat, do you see any kneecaps?"

Even before my second-born brother trained his Inchy sign on my hemline, I knew that the people whom our new neighbors thought we were would have knees like my brothers'—bony protuberances free of fleshy padding. I should have had knees like those of a racehorse. Instead, my knees were more like Tonka's: a thickening half point in a sturdy stub. My brothers were right. Fleshiness was my Inchy. Nothing—not my failure to make the cheerleading squad, not my inability to mold my siblings into the Kennedy brothers, not even my difficulty with inorganic chemistry—could compete with the disgrace of subcutaneous padding.

"That would be a negative, Mike," replied Pat. "No kneecaps in sight here."

"No kneecaps!" Kevin and Robert sang the news. Night after night they slid from their seats, crawled under the dinner table, and peered through their own Inchy sign to reconfirm the findings.

"Mom," Paul asked, "do girls have kneecaps?"

"*I* have kneecaps," said my mother, glancing first at my well-polished plate and then at the tidy portions that remained, barely nibbled, on her own.

"Twiggy does!" said Mike. In fact, all my friends had kneecaps. How many afternoons had I coveted the stark hollows and sharp ligaments that appeared when Anne sat down and rested *Teen* magazine on the uncushioned knobs of her knees?

"Do you do any special exercises?" I asked her, lying on my bed and cradling the telephone. The increase in my father's business had, by then, necessitated a second telephone line. My mother referred to it proudly as the "children's telephone," and it was supposed to sit on a bench in the hallway that connected the bedrooms occupied by Mike, Pat, and me with the kitchen. Most of the time, however, the children's telephone lived behind the closed door of my room.

"What's going on?" called my mother when, after talking to Anne, the force of my squat thrusts *boom-boom-boomed* through the house. The thump of my kneecap calisthenics was as steady and determined as the chant of the protestors that had begun to resound on college campuses across the country. "Did somebody call the National Guard?" she said.

"Calling all kneecaps," yelled Mike, pounding on my door as I sweated into the hundred deep knee bends that I began doing after school. "Come out! Come out! Wherever you are!"

"If we could just have a moment of your time, ma'am?" Pat interjected. "We are conducting a national survey of kneecaps." Kevin and Robert each pushed a thumb and an index finger under my door and formed an inch measure between their two digits.

"Philistines," I penned in early Gothic. "Savages. Heathens. Bongo. Tonka. Betty Friedan." But the shame of my missing kneecaps could not be dismissed so easily. Extreme measures were in order. After our summer in Plain City, Bill had become my boyfriend. For weeks, he'd been asking me to accompany him on Friday nights when, instead of football games, he attended the coffeehouse at his church. I finally saw a reason to capitulate.

"I can wear pants, right?" I asked. "I don't have to wear a skirt?" Bill, who had undergone a religious conversion, was deeply moved by my willingness to forgo the homecoming dance in the name of a Christian youth experience and offered complete sartorial accord.

"Pants might be better if you bring your guitar and we play together," he said. He'd given me a guitar for my birthday. We worked on our repertoire and for months, slacks covered my shame on the weekends. Pants were not an option during the week, when the school dress code stipulated skirts or dresses for girls. Tights were some consolation, but as the winter of 1968 gave way to the spring of 1969, I was forced to rely on a system of tying long scarves and huge sweaters around my waist.

To the extent that they obliterated the kneecap issue, peasant skirts were a godsend. They were, however, at odds with my vintage walking-suit image. One would not wear a peasant skirt to park the car in Harvard Yard. Unless, of course, one was the family eccentric, its artist, its beloved bohemian.

My transformation was immediate.

"The answer, my friend, is blowing in the wind," I sang, sitting cross-legged on my bed and strumming my new guitar. I was dressed in a knee-covering peasant dress that was a cross between Haight-Ashbury couture and the attire favored by the Amish of Plain City. I had resigned from my position on the school newspaper in order to edit its literary magazine and to pursue the visual arts. I had left Anne to her kneecaps, her cheers, and her piano playing, and had enrolled in Saturday school at the Columbus College of Art and Design.

"Those slums behind the art museum?" asked my mother. "Why do you want to go all the way down there?"

"We need art," I said, motioning to the bare walls of the Cooke Road house.

"You call this 'art'?" asked my mother, narrowing her eyes at the canvas that I'd first collaged with pictures cut from *Teen* and *Seventeen* magazines and then striped with metallic paint to create jail bars. I was throwing additional paint at this composition as we stood in my art room, talking.

"It looks like something I'm going to have to clean up," said my mother, wrinkling her nose, "and the colors will not work in the living room. Well, maybe you're right. Maybe they *could* help you at the museum school. I guess I can get by without you on Saturday mornings, but you are going to have to be on deck when you get home."

A deal is a deal.

"OK, guys," I said to my three youngest brothers on Saturday afternoon, "this week we are going to begin our life-size Santa Claus. You can see that I've made the chicken-wire form, and in this bucket is wallpaper paste. Now what we need to do is rip all this newspaper in strips."

"OK, guys, today we are going to make fried chicken and mashed pota-toes for dinner. Let's see who can peel the most potatoes! Ready, set—oh, darn it, Kevin. You're just not paying attention. Let me get you a Band-Aid."

"OK, guys, sing after me: 'Puff the Magic Dragon, lived by the sea . . .'"

Bill and I continued to sing together on Friday nights, and in the hours that I should have devoted to chemistry or calculus, I now practiced our duets. By then, we were running the coffeehouse.

"How many years must a mountain exist, before it is washed to the sea," I wailed, strumming on my guitar.

"You better stop howling and start memorizing that periodic table, miss," yelled my mother from the kitchen.

"The answer, my friend, is blowin' in the wind, the answer is blowin' in the wind," I sang.

"Jesus!" said my mother.

"I'm practicing for the Hole," I yelled.

"What hole?" asked my mother. "What are you talking about?"

"The Wholly Holy Hole! That's what we named the coffeehouse at Bill's church! We're performing on Friday night!" I yelled back. "Praise the Lord!"

"Jesus," said my mother. Stung, I stated my position clearly, for the record: "Jesus is my personal savior," I announced. "I've been saved!"

"Saved from what?" she yelled back.

In fact, I was not entirely certain. The Wholly Holy Hole saved me from showing my knees, from worrying about my next date, and—because I ran its food service—the coffeehouse also delivered me from self-conscious-ness and self-doubt: the teenagers who packed the place loved my banana bread, and so they loved me. But the speakers who addressed us on Friday night, of course, had another sort of deliverance in mind. They said that Jesus could save us from eternal damnation. I wanted to believe them—joining Bill on guitar to lead the crowd in a rousing chorus of "Michael, Row Your Boat Ashore"—but, at sixteen years old, I was more interested in knobby kneecaps than I was in eternal life. I prayed to be delivered of adipose tissue. And yet, beneath my peasant skirt, my knees remained wrapped in a cushion of fat.

After locking up the Hole on Friday nights, Bill and I always went park-ing. He would kiss and grope passionately until he touched the source of my Inchiness and then he would stop and insist that we pray together. At first

I assumed that my knees had given him pause, but I quickly realized that it wasn't my knees, it was Jesus.

"Blessed Savior," Bill would intone, "we ask to be saved from the sin of lust." I bowed my head, but my petition was never wholehearted.

"I feel you haven't totally given yourself to the Lord," said Bill, and he was right. I could not surrender my kneecaps to Jesus. Instead, I joined Weight Watchers.

"What others eat is not your concern," said the woman at the front of the class. Weight Watchers met in the basement of a church in Worthington on Tuesday evenings. The leader could have been one of the women who'd given cooking demonstrations at Albers supermarket and mesmerized my brothers and me. She'd aged a little, of course, and there were hints of a deflated balloon about her, little withers of skin that hung from her upper arms, beneath her eyes, and under her chin. It was as if the fervor she'd once had for hamburger-bun pizza had been sucked out of her, and the gratitude she had to the Weight Watchers program could never fully take its place. Nevertheless, her enthusiasm was contagious.

"It's *free!*" she said, describing how to make a vegetable soup from tomato juice—a vegetable soup that could be eaten with no thought of weighing and measuring. "You can have as much as you want, whenever you want!"

"This is the absolute coolest dessert!" she said as she taught us how to make a no-calorie dessert using sugar-free soda pop and Knox gelatin.

I sensed that the Weight Watchers Betty was a shadow of her former self. She smiled like a cheerleader's mother, wide and bright and a little too hard. I had the feeling that she, too, had met her Inchy, a conviction that deepened when she took out a measuring tape and unraveled it to show the class how many inches she'd lost. "Here's for the bust . . . and the waist . . . and the hips. Inch by inch, girls, inch by inch!" I was sold.

"But you are already at your suggested goal, honey," she'd said at first when I tried to join. "I don't see why you are here."

"That's because I am wearing pants."

"Oh, honey! Does your boyfriend hate your legs? Well, my husband was like that, but not anymore!" she said, twirling around like Thumbelina to give me a complete 360-degree view of the slender stalks that emerged from beneath her Marimekko shift. "I guess I showed him!" she added as she handed me my weigh-in card and the mimeographed paper that described the original Weight Watchers diet.

"I have one poached egg, half an English muffin, and one fruit, or four ounces of juice, for breakfast," I informed my mother, sweeping into the kitchen the morning after my first Weight Watchers meeting like a general onto a battlefield.

"Well, I guess that leaves more oatmeal for Tonka," she said. "I cook one meal for everybody, Molly, and if you want something different, you are going to have to make it yourself. Now, I am one hundred percent in favor of this. It would be just wonderful if you could get your figure together! I will buy you whatever you need to make your meals. But I will not cook it. I borrowed that book from your room and I'm with Betty Friedan. I'm a person. I am not a servant. I am *not* a short-order cook!"

Short order—I don't think so! Under the tutelage of the Weight Watchers Betty, whose real name was Kitty, I planned my feedings carefully, prepared them with increasing expertise, and served them with great ceremony. "The better it looks, the better it tastes," said Kitty, and I agreed. I consulted her when, in a departure from her one-meal-for-all policy, my mother prepared two poached eggs for me and served me two white amorphous blobs.

"If you add vinegar to the water, it will help keep the egg white together," said Kitty, and lending me a copy of *Mastering the Art of French Cooking*, she added, "If you read this, she explains how to poach them so that they keep their shape." Thereafter, I brought the water to a boil, added a tiny dash of white vinegar, cracked the eggs into a bowl, and then used a wooden spoon to stir the boiling water until it formed a swirling cyclone. When poured into the vortex created by my stir, the translucent egg white whirled for a second and turned white, the motion creating a plump and perfectly symmetrical pillow completely free of all stringy and unsightly tails. After that we were a team, Kitty, Julia, and I, colleagues in dieting and deliciousness.

When I wearied of the lunch of four ounces of water-packed tuna, two cups of lettuce, one piece of bread, and one piece of fruit, Kitty sounded as if she'd just talked to the other member of our triumvirate when she responded. "Try adding some curry power to the low-calorie mayonnaise!" sang Kitty. "Julia just loves it! Not the low-cal stuff, she makes her own mayonnaise, but she adds different seasonings. Try dill! Try a little fennel and minced onion! It's delish!" And, to my surprise, it was.

Kitty taught me to brush the four ounces of fish allowed at dinner with a mixture of mayonnaise and mustard—"It keeps it so moist and you almost don't taste that old perch," she said—as well as how to reserve my bread from lunch and use it to make a stuffing for my sole fillet at dinner. Julia taught me how to sauté sole à la meunière, to poach cod with shallots and tarragon, and to mince mushrooms and shallots to make duxelles.

"Mushrooms are unlimited!" said Kitty. "Knock yourself out, honey. If you flatten your chicken breast you can put the duxelles in the middle, wrap the meat around it, secure it with toothpicks, and bake it." Kitty told me that I could keep her copy of the French cookbook—"I've moved on!" she said—and suggested marinating the skinless chicken breast—in soy and ginger, or in yogurt and garlic, or in Italian salad dressing—before broiling it.

"The more you feed the eye, the less you have to feed the stomach," counseled Kitty. "Did you know that you can make a rose from a tomato skin? And you can cut cucumbers into daisies, or cut scallions into little brushes. Before you know it, everybody else is going to want your dinner, honey."

Every week, I lost two and a half pounds. Within a month, I was down to 127 pounds. But my kneecaps were still not knobby like my brothers'.

"Where are they?" asked Mike, squatting in front of me as I slid into the oven a water bath containing small Pyrex bowls of pumpkin purée to which I'd added egg, artificial sweetener, and the same sort of spices used in pumpkin pie.

"You'll see," I said, doing my best to sound as if I were in possession of a secret knowledge that was on par with alchemy. And within minutes of closing the oven door the smell of the spices told me that I may well have been: this creation could turn any day into Thanksgiving!

"It's what I don't see that worries me," said Mike. "Pat, we have an emergency situation here. I think we need to call the Bureau of Missing Kneecaps." On cue, Kevin began humming the bass component of the theme song for *Mission: Impossible*. Robert wailed the scary, higher notes.

"Our mission, should we choose to accept it, is to find your kneecaps!" hollered Pat. "Hey, that smells good, can we have some?"

I stopped eating bread at breakfast and lunch. Within another four weeks, I weighed 124 pounds. Yes, my ribs were now clearly articulated, my stomach was concave, and my pelvic bones highly visible, but the cushioning around my kneecaps remained tender and soft. Several weeks later, I fainted at a swimming meet and not long after that, I crumbled during a volleyball game. I decided that athletics were the problem and I retired from the swim team. It gave me more time to plan and prepare my meals. No one noticed that I was disappearing, but everyone noticed my new flair in the kitchen.

"Whatcha cooking, honey?" asked my father, sniffing the mushrooms I'd braised in bouillon to make a sauce for cube steak. "Can I have a little taste?" he asked.

"I don't see why you can't make enough eggplant Parmesan for the rest of us," said Mike.

"I want chicken with artichokes, lemon, and capers," said Paul.

"Perhaps you could prepare that shrimp and broccoli dish for tomorrow's dinner," suggested my mother.

The night of my sixteenth weigh-in at Weight Watchers, I weighed 117 pounds and had dark circles under my eyes. Everything about me was angles and bones, everything but my kneecaps.

"You have to go on maintenance," said Kitty. "You have to stop losing weight, honey. Your knees are just fine! There is nothing the matter with your knees! You have the knees God gave you!"

It was God's fault! I would never have kneecaps! I would never be free of Inchy! Shattered by this realization, I did the only logical thing. I ceased communicating with God's personal representative in my life, my boyfriend of two and a half years.

"Tell him I'm not here," I mouthed when Bill called on the telephone.

"Return to Sender," I wrote in Gothic script on the letters and postcards he sent to our house.

"The answer, my friend," I sang, sitting alone in my room, strumming my guitar, my voice cracking, "is blowin' in the wind."

I eventually realized that I was mad at God, not Bill, but the damage was, by then, done. I tried to patch my broken heart with Reese's Peanut Butter Cups and to fill the hole in my soul with Heath Bars and Mounds bars and Peppermint Patties. It worked. Within weeks, I was tipping the scales at my pre–Weight Watchers level and had come up with a new strategy for foiling the Inchy Inquisition. If I couldn't find my own kneecaps, I reasoned, perhaps over time I could hide my brothers' kneecaps. I stopped formulating diet desserts and started making the recipes from the pastry section of *Mastering the Art of French Cooking*.

"Have another napoleon, Mike," I said.

"Have some chocolate mousse!" I said. "Who wants to try these petits fours? Come on, guys, look how tiny they are—have two!"

O Pioneers!

The pilgrimage to Nebraska came just in time. By the summer of 1969, I was already thinking about college, and as I considered the personal-essay portion of the application forms, I realized that I needed more of a past in order to build the sort of future I pined for.

After Saturday school at the Columbus College of Art and Design and discovering *The Bell Jar,* I saw myself as a young Georgia O'Keeffe with hints of Sylvia Plath, hold the mental institutions. My destiny, bright with artistic accomplishment, also included a litter of boisterous children and a Volvo station wagon like the one driven by my art teacher. As I took up my calligraphy pen to describe my life and goals, I could see it all—the balls and bats and tennis rackets in the cargo area of the car, the bumper stickers that read "Boycott Grapes" and "War Is Not Healthy for Children and Other Living Things."

Within my immediate family, everyone thought of me as a Gwinn, but I wanted to be more than the vessel of an old American dream that, let's face it, had already died. I needed to reconnect with my Nebraskan roots, my history of cows and kolache. The call to an O'Neill family reunion—a week-long party that would coincide not only with Grandma O'Neill's eightieth birthday but also with Annevar, the summer festival in my father's home-town—seemed like Manifest Destiny.

"You'll see where you came from, kids," said my father. "I'm going to take you to the place where I used to move the herd—you stand on a little rise there and turn around and around, and every which way you're looking at O'Neill land. Your great-granddad planted every acre of it. Got rid of the Indians, drove the buffalo off cliffs, built the railroads, and played ball. That's right, kids. And you know what else? We'll have lime rickeys!"

My mother was less enthusiastic.

"What a great idea!" she said, sticking out her lower lip to exhale upward and blow the whitening wave of hair from her damp forehead. "I mean! Four days roasting in the car for a soda pop! I can hardly wait!" My mother hated the heavy, breezeless heat of Midwestern summers. Even in early May, the air was the stuff of her nightmares. The dread of generations of American women—the thousands who'd packed their households, climbed into covered wagons, and set forth for the frontier—could be detected in her voice.

"Ah, come on, Boots," said my father, "I'll put an air conditioner in the car for you."

Like me, my father had a sense of urgency about setting forth to the Great Plains. Shortly after the opening of the O'NeillDome in our backyard, the downside of our move had been revealed. Julian Speer, the local Little League team, could not win for losing. Pat complained that, after his two years of glory with the Frisbee Bears, pitching for Julian Speer was like playing for an expansion team. The other boys were spared this indignity: Mike had already graduated from Little League, and the three younger boys were not yet old enough to play. But in the summer of 1969, Pat was stuck pitching for a team that was light on hitting and heavy on errors, a team whose name my brothers never intoned without flashing the Inchy sign, a team that embarrassed even my mother.

"What in the name of God is the matter with these boys?" she asked as we sat near the first-base line at the round sand lot behind Clinton Junior High watching a 10–2 game limp into the third inning. Other parents shifted uncomfortably in their folding lawn chairs. Pat had hit home runs in each of his two appearances at the plate; the opposing team had scored only on errors. The long, slow unwinding toward an inevitable loss added to my fury. I was sick of sitting at Little League games, and every evening as we packed the car to go, I pleaded to be excused. "I have to work on my personal essay," I argued. "I want to go to Harvard."

"It's family time," my mother replied firmly. "I'm not going to sit there all by myself. Besides, nobody with your math scores is going to get into Harvard, and we couldn't afford it if you did. Why don't you bring that financial aid book your guidance counselor gave you. You can read that."

Instead, I sat sullenly on the sidelines rereading *The Bell Jar* as Julian Speer got creamed. My father leaned on the metal screen behind home plate, expressionless. He'd stopped smoking and he was chewing tobacco. As he studied each of the little boys on the field, he moved the tobacco around the inside of his cheek as if the plug were the player and he was trying him out in different positions.

"Jaayz," whistled Kevin, when a bunt resulted in two runs scored. He was still a year too young to play. "*We* wouldn't have let that happen." Robert, for whom two more years would pass before he qualified for Little League, joined in—"We could do better than these guys, Dad. We look old enough, Dad, we're tall"—and Paul, who was only six years old, echoed them both. "I want to play, Dad," he pleaded. "Dad, I want a glove. Dad, I'm not a scrub. Dad, will you let me play?"

My father said, "Not my decision, guys, I'm not in charge." But as he watched Julian Speer flounder, he realized that he had no choice. He couldn't just stand behind a chain-link backstop and watch his sons be mentored by an amateur. He had to become a Little League coach. In the meantime, he could work on his sons' mental games. He could infuse the ball with the power of destiny. An inspirational trip to Nebraska was just the ticket.

With an excitement stoked by tales of the great John O'Neill—"Did I tell you about the time he played ball with the Indians?" my father would say at dinner, or "Did you know your great-granddad was a newspaper columnist?"— each of us readied ourselves for our return to the source of our greatness.

My father prepared for our odyssey by calling in his receivables. Dollar by dollar, the torturous collecting he did for the trip only served to increase our anticipation. My mother, who was deeply moved by the air-conditioning unit that my father had had installed under the dashboard of the dark green Ford station wagon, prepared for our adventure by pursuing cost-saving measures.

"Chick," she kept saying, "I just can't believe you spent that kind of money to keep me cool." Renting a small trailer for our travels would, she reasoned, offset the air-cooling indulgence by limiting restaurant and motel expenditures. She planned meals and purchased comestibles with a care befitting the Lewis and Clark expedition.

Certain that the dozens of cousins we'd never met would immediately begin choosing sides for a pickup game, Mike oiled his glove. Pat was excited to be headed for a different baseball-card distribution area, and he recruited Robert to help him catalog and pack his collection for transport. Kevin, convinced that Nebraska would feature larger horses to ride, doubled his practice sessions with Tonka. Paul staked his claim on one of the beds in the trailer—"I want the top bunk," he said, looking at the picture of the camper's interior that was taped to the refrigerator. "Can I have it?" At six years old, he was still my shadow, and he reminded me on an hourly basis to pack his markers, his coloring books, the family copy of *Go, Dog. Go!* and manila paper for drawing.

I, in the meantime, had checked most of Willa Cather's books out of the library. Now I could not listen to tales of the great John O'Neill without seeing sod huts, "low, drab buildings huddled on the gray prairie," or imagining a howling wind that "blew under as well as over" the state's fearless inhabitants. I could hear the clatter of my forebear's boots against the wooden sidewalks in Ravenna, smell the damp, sweaty wool of his clothes drying by a cookstove, feel the fatigue in his bones, the fear in his gut, the yearning in his heart, the call of the wild, the tug of settled life, the story of America.

I didn't, of course, have to listen too hard. My father told people the stories they wanted to hear. "What the heck do I know," he would say to me decades later when I asked him specific questions about his childhood. "Just close your eyes and picture how you want it, honey!"

This attitude may explain why I learned early on to believe stories that contradict the facts. Even so, as we prepared to return to the Fatherland, I wondered if our great-grandfather had really left his nine small children alone in a sod hut while he chased baseballs from Nebraska to Montana all summer long. Had he, as our father said, expected them to tend the farm on their own? Left them alone to defend the ever-expanding O'Neill acreage against the Indians, who were increasingly unhappy about the intrusion of his fences, his herds, and the trees he planted? Had he stranded them for months in the middle of nowhere when the closest help was a day's ride away? And if he had, was that heroic behavior?

I asked myself these questions, but I honored my father by dismissing my misgivings. I also refrained from requesting additional detail. As we counted the funds he collected at the kitchen table late at night—the grease-creased checks, the rumpled bills, the envelopes with thin, crisp hundreds—my father and I were becoming partners in reality enhancement.

At first, when he recited the epic of the great John O'Neill, I couldn't see a role for myself—or any female—in the tale. Then I encountered Alexandra Bergson, the heroine of *O Pioneers!* In Cather's book, Alexandra is the eldest and only daughter of a Swedish immigrant who, on his deathbed, recognizes that his sons cannot maintain his legacy and charges his daughter with the stewardship of the family land. Was that so different from being the eldest and only daughter of a ditchdigger who relied on his children to preserve and expand his myth?

"Westward, ho!" I cried as my father, after checking the trailer hitch one last time, backed our wagon train down the driveway before dawn and headed to I-70 West one hot morning in June.

"Roll up the windows!" my mother replied as she turned the knob on the new air conditioner up to high.

Like thousands who set out from the Midwest before us, our mettle was tested by the miles of road that stretched between the Ohio River Valley and Buffalo County in central Nebraska. It was the hottest summer in recent history, and without the air conditioner, my mother would have cracked before Chicago. As we drove across our native state, the AM radio stations regularly issued bulletins about sidewalk egg-frying contests and heatstroke among livestock and the elderly. The power of the new cooling unit—which had one duct aimed at my mother, another aimed at my father, and the other aimed toward the back—did not extend beyond the front seat. My brothers fought over who got to sit between my parents and the other four sat behind them, their sweaty legs sticking to one another as well as to the vinyl seat covering. I curled up with the luggage in the cargo area, battling carsickness and heatstroke, and read passages from Cather for inspiration.

"Air," I croaked weakly.

"We have to keep the windows up or the air conditioner won't work," my mother shouted over the dull roar of its shivery breeze. "Stop reading."

"I want to draw," announced Paul, turning to look at me beseechingly from the front seat. I glanced at him appraisingly and then reread the opening scene of *O Pioneers!*:

He was a little country boy, and this village was to him a very strange and perplexing place, where people wore fine clothes and had hard hearts. He always felt shy and awkward here, and wanted to hide behind things for fear some one might laugh at him.

"I want to draw!" Paul repeated, and he abandoned his position in between my parents, first tumbling into the backseat and then scrambling over his brothers to join me.

"Ouch!" hollered Robert as Paul used the top of his head to help catapult himself into the back. "Baby," hissed Mike, as Paul's knee collided with his shoulder.

At last he seemed to see a ray of hope, his sister was coming, and he got up and ran toward her in his heavy shoes.

"I'm not a baby!" squeaked the baby of the family, as the temperature edged past ninety degrees in the rear of the car. "Did you pack my markers? Can we draw a picture? Where are my markers?"

Without lifting my eyes from Cather's inspiring passage, I reached into my book bag for the new set of sixty-four markers I'd used my baby-sitting money to purchase: *His sister was a tall, strong girl, and she walked rapidly and resolutely, as if she knew exactly where she was going and what she was going to do next*—"Here, honey," I said, "look what I got for you."

The hours crawled by. In the second seat, my brothers kept a tally of license plates from various states. They counted red cars, cars containing fat people, cars in worse shape than our own, and trucks containing agricultural products, particularly livestock. When a brother would holler, "I need to go!" my mother would reach under her seat and pass a sloshing little basin to the requesting party while the others protested ("Don't splash! Mom! Robert splashed!"). If hunger was voiced, sodden sections of peanut butter and honey sandwiches would be proffered in much the same manner. When thirst was mentioned, group pressure was brought to bear on the petitioner: "Wait till we stop! If you drink Kool-Aid now, you'll have to go, and you're such an Inchy that you'll splash it all over." My brothers were glued together with their sweat, Siamese quadruplets. Whenever one of them slid to the floor of the car for a nap, the ripping sound of their separation would be punctuated by a howl.

Still, I reasoned, what were our travails compared with the challenges faced by those who braved the deeply rutted pathways that had etched the Great Prairie prior to the interstate system? Near-delirious from the heat, I raised my head above the suitcases. Glimpsing my father's thick, sunburned neck, I was seized with a rush of admiration and affection—how brave was his effort to carry his family to wider vistas! How stalwart his commitment! Another time, after my father had steered our wagon into a rest area outside South Bend for lunch, my mother's ingenuity after discovering she had no can opener with which to open the tuna fish touched me deeply.

"Somebody else is going to pull in and they'll have one," she said, standing in the open door of the trailer. "And if they don't, we'll just have peanut butter, so all of you go to that shelter over there and wash your hands."

"Fresh and strong the world we seize," I recited. *"Pioneers! O Pioneers."*

We'd planned to make camp that first night about a hundred miles east of Des Moines—"Halfway!" said my father—but after someone threw up in the backseat of the car, the sign for "Lou's Wild West Motel (showers)" had its appeal.

"Just for tonight," my mother called back from her arctic perch. "Every one of you needs a bath after all that splashing and puking. What is the matter with you children? Molly, can you pass my sweater up here?"

Portions of Lou's Wild West Motel had originally been constructed as a movie set. Its rickety stretch of nineteenth-century facade included a general store, a feed store, and a saloon with a creaky swinging door. To this construction, Lou himself had added "Fun House" (with mirrors and a floor built on an angle), a corral, a barbecue truck, a restaurant called Lou's Chat 'n' Chew, a hanging station, and a sheriff's office, which served as Lou's headquarters. He'd also built a line of six motel rooms and fenced in about ten acres. We saw wild horses and several buffalo behind the fence when we drove into the dusty parking lot of Lou's Wild West facility. We were, it seemed, the first customers he'd seen for a while.

"This here's your town for the night," said Lou as my parents signed his guest book. "Breakfast is down to the Chat 'n' Chew, dinner's out at the chuck wagon." Lou wore cowboy boots, a ten-gallon hat, and a leather vest with a sheriff's badge. He was a former rodeo rider who carried a flask in his pocket and rescued large animals that were wounded or insane.

"Don't go inside that fence, those buffalo don't like company," Sheriff Lou told my brothers, and he deputized each of them by pinning small badges on their shirts. "Stay away from that noose out there, we got a hanging scheduled for tomorrow."

The condemned man was soon forgotten, however, as several brothers, having scaled Lou's fence, attempted to play toreador with the buffalo. Paul and I were checking out the vending machines in the Chat 'n' Chew when Sheriff Lou, brandishing a starter's pistol, clumped from his office, jumped on a horse, and took off toward the pasture. From the center of the cloud of dust he created, shots were fired as a frantic and slightly insane Sheriff Lou tried to divert the buffalo, who were, by then, chasing my brothers.

"Just like when you were growing up, huh, Dad?" said Robert.

Certainly Lou's Wild West Motel was right out of the stories my father had told of his youth. Warned of the possibility of an Indian attack, we slept lightly in our roll-away beds that night. Sure that the motel was the final outpost of civilization, I tried to memorize the feel of a modern bed so that I might be able to recall it when braving the roadside frontier in our little trailer. Alas, my preparations were in vain. Six hours after leaving Lou's Wild West Motel, our car blew up. Just as the weight of the load and the rough terrain had cost many a wagon its wheel, the drain of the newly acquired air-conditioning unit combined with the strain of pulling a rented trailer and the terrible heat caused our engine to explode. It happened on Interstate 80.

"Indians!" screamed Paul, when the blast sounded under the hood of the car and smoke billowed up against the windshield. Tired of drawing, he'd been listening to me read aloud.

"What the heck?" hollered my father, slowing the vehicle and steering toward the edge of the highway. "Get down! Everybody! Down on the floor till I tell you to jump out!" The car was towed to Lincoln. We took the bus to Grand Island, Nebraska.

"What's going to happen to our car?" asked Mike from the backseat of the bus, where he sat along with Pat, Kevin, and Robert, all of them still joined at the thigh.

"Our car's in the shop," said my father.

"Mom," piped up another boy behind us, "I'm thirsty, Mom. Can we get a drink the next time the bus stops?"

"Have water," said my mother, who was sharing a seat with Paul and sitting across the aisle from my father and me. "We can't spend money," she added. "Our car's in the shop."

Glancing around to make sure that he was not being observed by a nonfamily member, my father bent to remove his shoe.

"But we're thirsty!" Pat protested. "When can we have a drink? When can we get our car back?"

"You heard your mother, use the drinking fountain," said my father. "The guy in the shop said he'd call tomorrow." Then, after checking once again for prying eyes, he lifted the insole from his wing tip and removed a wad of twenty-dollar bills. Moistening his forefinger and thumb, he counted the money.

"Dad," Paul called across the aisle as my father raised five fingers to signify five hundred dollars to my mother, "why did you put money in your shoe?"

Our bus was met in Grand Island by three of my father's older siblings— uncles Sham and Pat, and Aunt Lucille—and we were driven to the Holiday Inn in Kearney. More than fifty O'Neills had rooms in the place; it was to be the base of operations, the "fort" of the family festivities, and my family had planned to set up camp in the parking lot.

"We tried to drive our room here," Paul explained to the front desk clerk, as my mother arranged for a single room to accommodate the eight of us, "but now our car is in the shop."

"Do you have a drinking fountain?" asked Robert. "We can only drink water. Our car is in the shop."

"Are there toilets in the room?" asked Kevin.

The hotel's cooling system had not been designed for temperatures in excess of a hundred degrees, not to mention the additional heat generated by eight bodies stacked in a room. After the sleeping arrangements had been effected—one adult, one older child, and one younger child were packed into each of the two double beds, and Mike and Pat had been tucked head to toe in a roll-away—our sense of suffocation was complete.

"Chick," gasped my mother through the darkness sometime after midnight, "we've got to open a window."

"It'll mess up their air-conditioning," said my father.

"Imagine a howling wind that blows under as well as over people," I suggested.

"Shut up, Molly," said Mike.

"Imagine a cool sod hut," I countered—and perhaps we did, for somehow we managed to fall asleep in our little Holiday Inn room on the prairie. We slept with no fear of Indian attack, innocent of any intrusion, oblivious to the bandits who must have crept into our camp during the night.

"Very funny!" said my father the next morning. We were sitting with all his brothers and about twenty cousins in the restaurant of the Holiday Inn. We'd finished eating breakfast—"You can order a small orange juice and one bowl of cold cereal," my mother had told us, "remember that our car's in the shop"—and, after reaching for the check, my father had reached into his shoe.

"So funny I forgot to laugh," he said, looking around at his wife and children. "Who took the money?"

When assured that no one was pulling his leg by plucking the wad of cash from his shoe, my father mounted an official, hotel-wide inquiry. Steps were retraced, suitcases were unpacked, the room was taken apart, the mattresses overturned. Hotel management was summoned. The police were called. My father's net worth had been stolen from his shoe. One of my uncles paid the breakfast bill.

The ramparts had been sacked and the descendants of the great John

O'Neill felt as if a part of their spirits had been stolen, too, right out from the shadow of old Fort Kearney.

"His car," my father's brothers said to one another.

"The shop," said his sisters, shaking their heads.

"Did they call?" asked my mother.

"New engine," said my father, "Three hundred fifty dollars." The sum was quickly raised by the uncles. Large bills to cover the cost of the hotel were pressed into my father's hand. Restaurant checks were removed from his reach.

"If somebody can give me a lift to the grocery, we can just eat in our room," said my mother.

"Don't be silly! We'll all eat together," said Aunt Peg.

"My car is your car as long as your car is in the shop," said Aunt Lucille. "Do you need clothes? Do the children need books or toys?" There was much hugging and patting, and while uncles Pat and Russ drove the car-repair money back to Lincoln—"I want to make sure the mechanic's on the up-and-up," said Uncle Pat—the rest of the O'Neills formed a caravan to Ravenna.

"Come on," said Uncle Clark. "It's Annevar!"

Annevar! My brothers and I swooned. For as long as we could remember our father had discussed this glorious event, a three-day festival on the main thoroughfare of his hometown. The rides and the dunking contests! The strong man! The midget! The fortune-teller! The man who boxed with a kangaroo!

"'Annevar' is 'Ravenna' spelled backward," I informed the five cousins who had joined us in Uncle Clark's car to Ravenna. "It's like Disneyland, but with an Old West theme. Right, Dad?"

Acres of corn fringed by sunflowers flew by the car windows as we sped toward our father's heroic past. Signs announced the distance to O'Neill, a town settled by other forebears, and we squealed with delight.

"We have a whole town!" we cried.

"No, that's the other side of the family," said Uncle Clark, adding, as if to assuage this loss, "We have Annevar!"

"Annevar!" we cheered.

"Annevar!" echoed my father.

"Here you go, sweetheart!" said Uncle Clark, winking and handing me a five-dollar bill after pulling into a filling station. My father had leaped from the car to pump the gas and wash the windshield. Uncle Clark put his finger to his nose and shook his head. Later, my brothers reported similar acts of largesse.

The subsidy remained our guilty secret that day as my father led us around Ravenna from one sacred site of O'Neill-ness to the next.

"There's the old farm!" he exclaimed, pointing to a shabby little Victorian house that was situated on a small lot on the outskirts of town. It was the sort of place whose basketball hoop inspired pity from my brothers.

"Where's the barn?" asked Mike.

"Where'd you put the cows?" asked Pat.

"Oh, the barn's gone and we rented fields outside town after we lost the land," said Uncle Clark. "Back in the Dust Bowl and the Depression."

"Half of Oklahoma blew through here!" said my father.

"We used to hold on to the side of the milk truck and ride on the running boards," recalled Uncle Clark. "But if you opened your mouth, all this red dirt would blow in. Jack used to hold your coat, Chick, remember that? Everybody had to make sure you didn't fall down."

"I was always falling on the sidewalks downtown," said my father.

"Wooden! Kids, can you believe that?" said Uncle Clark.

The wooden sidewalks were no longer in evidence by the time we got there, and the sod and clapboard buildings along Grand Street had long since been replaced by low redbrick buildings, the streets were paved, and there was no saloon with a squeaky swinging door. Lou's Wild West Motel was better than Ravenna.

"Where does everybody tie up their horses, Dad?" asked Kevin.

"Where are the rest of the rides, Dad?" asked Robert, when we reached the festival and discovered only a merry-go-round, a Scrambler, and games such as horseshoes and beanbag tosses. There was also a pie-eating contest and a tractor pull.

"Hurry on up!" cried my father. "We can still make the frog hop and the turtle race."

But my brothers did not even consider flashing the Inchy sign. To be effective, after all, the sign must echo a private misgiving, and my father was convinced of the mythological import of his hometown and the supremacy of its summer festival. My brothers could sniff out self-doubt, but they had no mechanism in place with which to address delusion. It made them feel tender and protective.

"Did Annevar used to be as good as the Ohio State Fair, Dad?" asked Robert.

"Maybe we should all give him our money," whispered Pat.

"Maybe we should donate it to the town," whispered Mike. "I think Annevar could use it."

The next day, my father found the slender packet of hundreds, fifties, and twenties in his shoe. The cash had somehow worked its way from under the insole to beneath the tongue of his wing tip; it had been riding beneath my father's laces the whole time, even as the relatives were slipping us cash and buying us presents.

"If we start paying people back now, we won't have enough to get home, Chick!" my mother wailed.

"Don't worry about it, Boots," said my father. Moistening his fingers, he counted and recounted the bills. His lip quivered.

Paul said, "If we give the money to the man in the drugstore, will he make a lime ricky that tastes good, Dad?"

"Write everything down," said my aunt Mike, whose real name was Lucille. The day after our first jaunt to Ravenna, she pushed a small spiral notebook into my hand and said, "We need somebody to write things down for the newspaper, and you are a writer—just like your great-granddad."

I demurred, initially. "I didn't bring my calligraphy pen," I said. But Aunt Mike, who was a retired nurse, stared at me through her rhinestone-studded black-framed cat's-eye glasses as if I were a patient declining medication, handed me a ballpoint pen, and said, "Stop talking, start writing." And I did. Summoning my best Lois Lane imitation, I followed my father and my uncles as they walked the twenty-odd O'Neill male cousins up a ridge on the out-skirts of Ravenna for batting practice and noted each pitch, each swing, and each result. I made notes on the smell of the air—"cow poop, sunflowers, and oil from trucks"—as well as the appearance of the land and sky, the feeling of the tall grass, and the look of the barbed-wire fences beside the rutted roads we were marched along.

"Harder to move these kids than it is the cows," said Uncle Russ.

"Is that one of yours?" Uncle Pat asked my father, pointing to Kevin's small shape as he ducked under a fence and ran across a field toward a wild horse. "That horse ain't broke, son! Gripe's sake, he could kill ya. Get back over here this side of the fence, atta boy."

"Chick, you got a couple boys in the bull's pen over by the barn," yelled Uncle Sham.

"Chick! Your youngest is back up on the ridge trying to hit rocks with sticks," said Uncle Pat. "I better take the truck up, I got cattle up there."

"Stay with me," I said to Paul when he was returned. "I have to take notes, I can't hold your hand." Later, back in town, I lurked in her kitchen as Grandma O'Neill baked kolache and cookies and pie. "Mother was the best baker in Ravenna," Aunt Peg said as she pitted cherries. "She baked cakes and pies for the old Burlington Hotel downtown when we were kids."

"Best in town," I wrote. I was also observing, if not writing down, the number of times that my mother arched her eyebrows, clicked her tongue, or pushed it into the left side of her cheek in order not to laugh. She was impeccably attired in a white linen suit with matching white pumps.

"If you have an apron, I can lend a hand," she said to my grandmother, but an apron was never found.

I, on the other hand, was eager to join in. "Let me help," I said, when my aunts prepared to decorate the church basement for the grand finale of the family gathering, my grandmother's birthday party.

"You make the banners," said Aunt Mike. "Do some cute limericks and poems—you are our wordsmith." Throughout the festivities, I was called upon to write speeches, toasts, and appreciations. While my brothers and the boy cousins played ball with my father and my uncles, I drafted column after column of the story of the family gathering.

"Just like her great-granddad," murmured my aunts and uncles. My cousins were eager to read my words. My grandmother offered me extra kolaches. My immediate family was absorbed by the baseball portion of our legacy, but the other descendants of the great John Hugh O'Neill were fascinated by writing.

"We are so proud!" wrote Aunt Mike in the little note she attached to the newspaper clipping she sent me the next week. Of the twenty-five pages I'd drafted, several lines—in fact, an entire picture caption—had been published in the *Ravenna News*. Based on this debut, my aunt declared me the next executor of the literary estate of the great John Hugh O'Neill. "Someday," she wrote, "I will give you everything your great-granddad published from his travels abroad."

For decades, the "oeuvre" lived in gold-embossed, leather-bound volumes in my imagination. It arrived, finally, when I was forty years old—"old enough to value it," my aunt explained—in a surprisingly thin manila envelope that she sent to my home in New York City after visiting me there in 1992. It consisted of the half dozen pages that he'd penned in 1905 while traveling to Ireland and Scotland. The letters had originally appeared in the *Ravenna News,* and not even the patriarch was impressed by his literary talent. "You know," he writes of Scotland, "the descriptive ability is not in me to describe everything I have seen."

*   *   *

I was not disappointed by the size of my great-grandfather's literary legacy. Reality has always seemed smaller and meaner than the stories our father told about his past, and my brothers and I have long since accepted the dissonance. We blame others when evidence fails to support the expectations our father created with his tales. Only those who refuse to recognize the great swelling of the human spirit, its yearning for deliverance from the ordinary, its straining toward the poetry of universal human experience, could, for instance, fail to appreciate the significance of John Hugh O'Neill's artistic ambitions.

The possibility that evidence proving that our lives are connected to something larger—to something heroic that surfaces and glitters brightly and disappears only to resurface in another hundred years—has been tampered with or lost would not surprise us. But the accidental discovery of such evidence does. Not long ago, as I was sifting through newspaper stories that have been written about my ancestors, I found a mention of my great-grandfather's first season as a paid barnstormer. It stated that he played in Billings, Montana, in the summer of 1881. I immediately reached for the phone.

"When were you in Billings?" I asked when my youngest brother picked up.

"My first year, 1981."

"And wasn't there some sportswriter who said you acted like you were born to play that park?"

"Yeah, I think so," he said, sighing. "You know, *writers*."

The Electric Crock-Pot Curveball Test

The next time my father lost his money he did not notice it right away and he did not find it in his shoe. I discovered the disappearance when I tried to convert my savings account into a cashier's check to pay the tuition for my first semester at Denison University in Granville, Ohio. I was seventeen years old and had long been imagining this moment. Week after week, I had deposited my earnings from baby-sitting and lifeguarding. Sure, I was tempted to buy clothes and makeup and 45 records, but I resisted any incursion against my savings. While my friends purchased tubes of frosted, raspberry-flavored lipstick and records such as "Cherish" by the Association, I fingered the leather-bound savings book I kept in my fringed suede bag and imagined ivy-covered redbrick buildings and late nights in flannel nightgowns by Lanz of Salzburg.

"I'm sorry," said the teller at the Ohio Savings Bank one morning in the summer of 1970, "I can't do this for you." She pushed the withdrawal slip back to me. "There are no funds in your account."

By then I had been watching my deposits grow into funds for five years. One hundred grew to two hundred, and gradually, the fifty cents an hour I made for baby-sitting and the $1.25 an hour I earned working at the swimming pool added up to nearly four thousand dollars.

"Where did they go?" I asked, and I pushed my savings book beneath the grille that covered her window to display the official tally of my funds.

The teller pushed the little book back to me and shook her head. "The government cleaned you out," she said.

My father had always warned me about the government. And yet, as soon as the teller pronounced the word, I remembered the stack of unopened letters from the Internal Revenue Service on his desk. My mother would kill him. I'd have to get a job and support the family. I wouldn't be able to go to college.

"You have got to be kidding me," said my mother when I carried news of the government's seizure, instead of a cashier's check for $3,700, back to our car in the parking lot of the Graceland Shopping Center.

"I warned him! He didn't pay his taxes! Isn't that cute?" said my mother. Sensing that I might have some sympathy for my father, she added, "He's a cosigner on your savings account, you know. You can thank him for this one."

We drove across the street to Jerry's Drive-In and ordered hot fudge sundaes. I was worried that this could well be the last sundae moment that my mother and I would share before my entire family was taken to debtor's prison, and I ordered accordingly.

"Extra-large," I said to the waitress, "extra fudge, no whipped cream, no cherry." My mother ordered a regular size with extra whipped cream, no cherry.

"My God, Molly, they'll take the house," she said, curling her nose at the maraschino cherry that had been placed on the igloo of whipped cream that topped the tall, tulip-shaped soda glass full of vanilla ice cream and hot fudge sauce.

"What in the name of God is the matter with these people? Do they not listen? Do they not care?" she said, using a long-handled spoon to lift the offending red ball. "Look!" she said. "Red stuff all over the cream! Isn't that enough to rot your socks! Jesus, Molly! The electric! The gas! Lazarus! All the bills are due!"

I had hoped for the hot-fudge-sundae cure. And happily, the efficacy of excessive calories was once again demonstrated. Over the next hour, a program of economic recovery took shape in the circular booth at Jerry's Drive-In at the intersection of Morse Road and High Street.

"I'll have to go back to the hospital," said my mother. Her announcement elicited a sympathetic glance from the waitress who had failed to hold the cherry. Although I understood that my mother meant to return to the hospital as an employee, not a patient, I moved quickly to give the waitress an opportunity to display her compassion.

"Would you mind bringing me a little more fudge sauce?" I asked.

"You can take this," said my mother pointedly, indicating the bread plate where she'd placed the candied cherry. And then, as if reluctantly accepting assistance from a wealthy relative, she said, "I guess we'll have to let Nancy pay your tuition."

Nancy was our dog. For months before moving into our new house, my mother had researched dogs and had determined that a Great Pyrenean—a white mountain of a dog, considered to be the aristocratic cousin of the St. Bernard and known for its protectiveness—was the breed for us. Nancy, a twelve-week-old puppy, had arrived soon after Tonka, and within a year, when viewed from a distance, the pony and the dog looked to be about the same size. Even as the Internal Revenue Service was drafting orders to seize my baby-sitting money, Nancy was lying in a pen in our basement suckling eight well-bred puppies.

"We can get three hundred fifty dollars for each of them," said my mother, "and you can get a job to pay for the second semester. And you know what else? I'm going to buy a Crock-Pot! I can't work all day long and go home and cook dinner. Come on! Let's go. We have to get a Crock-Pot before the IRS comes to take my wallet."

"What'd I tell you about the government!" my father fumed. In the months following the levy on our bank accounts, he regularly sought like-minded individuals at the dinner table. I'd gone away to college but returned home to work as a lifeguard and a cook on the weekends. The question my father posed was similar to ones raised by my fellow students. "Hell, no, we won't go," they chanted at antiwar rallies. "Can you believe this government?" they asked, shaking their heads and sucking on cigarettes. My father, however, was looking for a different sort of reassurance. At the dinner table, he searched first my mother's face and then my own for indications of empathy. Then he turned to Mike and Pat.

"What'd I tell you about banks?" he said. Still no one grunted or shook his head, and after moving his fork through the thick puddle of ground beef and mushrooms on his dinner plate, my father leaned toward his three youngest sons.

"What'd I tell you about curveballs, huh?" he said.

"Stop talking, start hitting," said Robert. He was ten years old and he spoke without affect, as if he were a contestant on *Hollywood Squares* and was bored by his habit of getting the correct answer every time.

"Hit it right back up the line," said Paul, who was seven years old and eager to be noticed. "Right, Dad? Huh? Out of the park!"

"Got that right!" said my father. "Life throws you a curve, you don't just hit it. By gum, you hit that sucker out of the park, that's right, uhh, Mike, er, no, Pat, er, no, Kev, er, Rob, er, no, I mean Paul."

My father had trouble remembering his sons' names and this difficulty seemed to increase, rather than diminish, as the older boys graduated from Little League and junior high and moved into high school sports. No matter which one he meant to address, my father began by saying "Mike," and then moved through the birth order several times before landing on the name that matched the boy he had in mind. Beginning with the name of his first-born son was logical and may even have helped orient my father. "Mike!" he said, as if cheering. But his point of departure was also his first and surest hope for athletic supremacy. Mike was a natural. Pat was not, and when my father pronounced his name, "er, no, Pat," his voice was lower and dismissive, as if he knew before he even said it that the name was not one he needed to remember. He proceeded to "Kev, er, Rob"—the sons born only seventeen months apart were, in his mind, a single unit. My father always sounded surprised when he said "Paul," and he paused for a moment as if to say, "What do you make of that? I have a kid named Paul!" before returning to the top of the birth order. In the long run-on sentence that preceded my father's pronouncement of any son's name came, also, his correction and dismissal of the previous name he'd mentioned. Pat was, therefore, "Mike, er, no, Pat," or "Mike, er, no, I mean Pat." We learned a lot about anticipation by listening to my father call his sons.

"Darn tooting, Kev, er, Rob, no, Paul," he said, "somebody throws a curve, you hit it back."

"Unfortunately," said my mother, "your daughter was not eligible for a baseball scholarship."

"What the heck is this?" my father said, once again prodding the carnivorous mush on his plate.

"Crock-Pot chili," said my mother. "I hope you enjoy it."

The demise of distinct dishes in our home had been sudden and final. In the predawn hours, my mother would pile meat and potatoes and vegetables, along with seasoning and water, in her slow cooker and turn it on.

Twelve hours later, she returned home from her job at the hospital and ladled the brown amalgam into bowls or over mashed potatoes or rice. For recipes requiring less cooking time, she sometimes called from work after my brothers returned from school.

Robert usually answered the telephone. He delighted in the rare quiet of the house at this hour, and used the time to read history books alone in the room he shared with Kevin. He carried his book with him to the kitchen and continued to read it as he answered the telephone, listened to my mother, replaced the receiver, opened the back door, and yelled, "Mike! Mom said turn on the Crotch-Pot."

Book in hand, buck-toothed, and always dressed in the clothes that Kevin had rejected—bell bottoms that flared at the knee and ended midshin, for instance—Robert looked a little like Elmer Fudd. Nevertheless, his message initiated a three-way relay that circulated the acre behind our house. Kevin, who took advantage of our mother's absence by practicing the forbidden game of football, was the next point of communication. After Robert's voice issued from the house, Kevin would punt over an imaginary field goal and holler toward the closed doors of the second garage, "Mom said turn on the Crotch-Pot!"

Paul, who spent his afterschool hours pestering Kevin and Robert to play Twenty-one while shooting baskets on the half-court in front of the second garage, was the final broadcast station. First he taunted Robert—"Come on, Rob! You scared I'll win? Huh? I'll get twenty-one before you. Come on!"— and then he walked to the garage door and kicked it.

"Turn on the Crotch-Pot," yelled Paul. "Mike! Mom said!"

The effect of these directives was immediate, but generally unrelated to plugging in the slow cooker. After a brief and failed incarnation as an antiques-and-crafts shop, the second garage had, thanks to Pat's entrepreneurial spirit and my parents' naivete, become home to a very large waterbed, a stereo, and a collection of eight-track tapes, and—under the aegis of Mike and Pat—it had become a mecca for high school girls.

"Turn on what?" a girl would gasp.

"Jaaayz," Pat would bellow.

"Mom said!" Paul would say again. "You better turn on the Crotch-Pot! Are you coming?"

"I hope so, Junior," Mike would say pointedly.

At fifteen years old, Mike had developed a dry, mocking humor that often drove his younger brothers to tears. Mike was tall—he stood six feet four inches—he was dark, and he was handsome. He was a basketball and a base-

ball star, although shortly after my mother returned to work, his athletic ener-
gies were diverted by the activities in the second garage. In the era of the
Crock-Pot on Cooke Road, Mike's goal-oriented, dad-pleasing, laser-sharp
vision was blurring as certainly as the boundaries between food groups. The
same was true of Pat. As a small businessman, Pat had long since diversified
and expanded beyond fireworks. Instead of counting baseball cards, he'd
begun counting the days until he could get his driver's license, get a legitimate
job, and get a car.

"You're not going to have to worry about the Crotch-Pot once I get my
wheels, honey," he would yell to Paul when his youngest brother stood outside the door of the waterbed palace repeating messages. "I'll drive you over
and get you pizza for dinner!"

"Want to play ball?" Paul would ask hopefully.

"As a matter of fact, Junior, I do," Mike would say from inside the
garage, "but not with you."

The shift in the attitudes of his two top prospects was not lost upon my
father. The fear he'd felt before Little League had saved his sons returned
almost as soon as the first two became too old to play Little League and old
enough to question haircuts and coaching directives. Indications that Mike or
Pat thought about anything other than the Hall of Fame made him spiteful.

"Rise and shine!" he bellowed before six o'clock on the Sunday mornings
following his older sons' late nights. He turned on the lights in their rooms,
opened the shades, and said, "Gee! I wonder how my truck got parked in the
middle of the front yard!" He tossed off their covers and pulled them from bed.

"Breakfast!" shouted my father. "Wait till you see the pancakes your
brother has for you!"

As part of his bid for recognition, Paul now apprenticed himself to my
father on Sunday mornings. After years of making art with me, the little boy
determined that by adding food coloring to the pancake batter and strategically drizzling the batter onto the hot griddle, he could pioneer brave new
shapes in pancakes. I applauded his creativity, and when I was home, served
as his sous chef. Mike and Pat were less enthusiastic when, roused from bed,
heads spinning and stomachs churning, they stumbled into the kitchen table
to face amoebic blue and green blobs with Mesozoic pretensions.

"The green one is triceratops," said Paul.

"No way," said Robert, for the moment a patient paleontologist. "It's
walking on two legs. Triceratops walks on all four, Paul. That's stegosaurus."

"No, it's not! The green one is triceratops and the blue one is bron-
tosaurus!" cried the cook.

"Looks more like Barf-o-saurus to me," said Mike. Sunday after Sunday, he managed to eat the pancakes that would be dinosaurs, but swallowing the rules of baseball proved more difficult. When colleges began to romance him with athletics scholarships, Mike began saying things like, "The coach acts like it's the army. Why should I give *him* fifty push-ups?" And: "Can somebody tell me what the length of your hair has to do with the way you hit a baseball?"

"You want to look like a ballplayer or some dope fiend?" countered my father. Soon after Mike accepted an offer from a small liberal arts college instead of a Big Ten school, Pat announced his intention to quit the high school baseball team in order to work in a grocery store, and my father went berserk: his efforts to bust my brothers and save the younger children knew no bounds.

"What's this!" he thundered, taking one of the red and white tins from the spice cupboard and shaking it. Thinking that his father was, perhaps, testing his qualification for grocery store work, Pat responded quickly.

"Oregano," he said. "You use it to make pizza."

"Origanum vulgare," said Robert flatly. "Wild marjoram."

"Don't give me that!" bellowed my father. "You think I don't know what's going on around here?"

"What do you think is going on, Chick?" asked my mother. "Hormones?"

"We'll see what the lab says!" yelled my father.

"Origanum vulgare," read Robert several weeks later when the report arrived from the lab to which my father had delivered the suspicious can for analysis. It was a Friday night and I'd gotten home in time to save my family from the Crock-Pot and demonstrate my growing expertise with a wok. Arranged on heaps of rice at each place at the table was a medley of previously frozen broccoli and peas, canned water chestnuts, and chopped celery and carrots that I had stir-fried with sliced ham and tossed in a sweet-and-sour sauce. Made from a can of pineapple chunks, half a cup of brown sugar, two tablespoons of soy sauce, one bouillon cube, two cups of water, and two teaspoons of cornstarch, the sweet-and-sour sauce was my personal invention as well as my reigning masterpiece. Robert glanced up from the letter to reach for a pair of the chopsticks that I had also brought home from college.

"Origanum vulgare," he said again and then, as if addressing a seminar in classics rather than eight members of an all-American family whose identity was being rocked by the winds of Woodstock Nation, he added, "from the Greek *oros,* meaning 'mountain,' and *ganos,* meaning 'joy.'"

"What's the vulgar part?" yelled my father, glaring at my mother, then me, then Mike, and then Pat. "I know what you're up to! Vulgar! Mary Jane! Woodstock! Kent State! I read *Newsweek* magazine! I know what's going on!"

"Yes, you certainly do seem to know what's going on, Chick," said my mother. "Let me see, we have dope in the spice tin and condoms in their pockets and a communist conspiracy in the kitchen, right?"

"Who do you think eats like this!" my father said. "The Viet Cong, that's who! Where do you think it starts, Boots? Right here! Right under our own noses. Right at our own table, that's where."

Then, pointing his middle finger at me while glancing toward his three youngest children, he said, "I'm not going to sit here and let you pervert the rest of them, young lady. Boys your age are over there dying so we can eat steak. If you think I'm going to sit here and let you dish up gook food, you have another think coming."

Denison University was only thirty-five miles east of Columbus, but to me and to my family Denison was the East. Most of us liked it when people called Denison the "Harvard of the Midwest." In his junior year of high school, Mike bragged about his sister, the almost Ivy Leaguer, and came to visit along with Pat, who sensed business opportunities in Granville. Kevin and Robert wrote me letters every week. Paul drew me pictures and begged me to come home, and, most weekends, I did.

My father was the only member of our family who was not impressed by the Harvard of the Midwest. He watched me through the same narrowed eyes with which he observed girls at the Little League park, women in miniskirts, and young ladies who did not wear bras. My father had a certain tone that he reserved for "coeds," a term he used to signify girls who slept with boys before marriage, as well as girls who tricked boys into marriage and girls who had no interest in marriage. This inflection crept into his voice when he talked about me.

"Boots, what's with Pocahontas?" he asked my mother when I began parting my hair in the middle, braiding it, and wearing a leather headband wrapped around my forehead.

"What's that smell?" he asked, catching a whiff of my Herbal Essence shampoo.

"What sort of trash do you call this?" he yelled, storming into the kitchen carrying a pile of the books he'd found in my car. After the government took my college savings, my father had promised to buy me a car to drive between college and work and, after months of covert harassment—"Hey,

Molly," my brothers would say at dinner, "is your car still in the shop?"—he'd purchased a 1967 Le Mans convertible from one of his employees. Along with candy bar wrappers, dirty laundry, empty Tab cans, and empty packets of the Marlboros I'd begun to smoke, I left volumes from my growing library in the car.

"You think I collected good money to buy a commie bookmobile?" yelled my father, slamming the incriminating books down on the kitchen table like a prosecutor in a courtroom.

Thwack! *The Autobiography of Malcolm X.* Thunk! Thunk! *The Communist Manifesto, Small Is Beautiful.* He held the final volumes up to my mother and brothers as if they were the jury in the Rosenberg spy case.

"*Sexual Politics?*" my father said, witheringly. "*Our Bodies, Ourselves? The Whole Earth Catalog? The Tassajara Bread Book?* Not in this house!" he yelled.

"Not in front of your mother!" he fumed.

My mother was, in fact, far less worried about my reading material than she was about her own. She was reading my diary. For months, she'd wrestled with the moral implications of reading her daughter's private pages. But the appearance of the leather headband, the Earth Shoes, the love beads, and the paint-splattered overalls that I'd begun wearing all concerned my mother. She was disgusted when I had my ears pierced and nervous about the boys in wire-rimmed glasses with whom I now consorted. Her darkest fears sprouted in the growing silence between us.

"Is he your boyfriend?" she would ask.

"Not exactly," I would say and then, echoing the debates from my world religion and philosophy course, I would add, "At least, he is not *only* my boyfriend and he is not *my only* boyfriend."

"Jesus," said my mother, and shortly thereafter, Ann Landers gave her the go-ahead. She advised parents who were concerned about their children to listen to their phone conversations, check their stories, open their mail, and read their diaries. My mother had strong feelings about the sanctity of a closed door or a sealed envelope, but she respected Ann Landers. As if serving notice, she clipped the column and tacked it to the small corkboard in the kitchen where she kept other snippets of inspiration. A week later, she began reading.

How could my mother have known that my diary had never been an account of my life, but instead had been a narrative of whatever life I happened to be imagining for myself? Reading one entry, she would learn that I was pledging a sorority and trying to decide between opal and diamond chips in the straight gold-arrow pins that the sisterhood wore. In the next entry, I'd be formulating plans to take over the college's administration building with the black students' league. Still later, my mother would have read about how I accompanied my high school boyfriend, who attended Denison and whom I now called "Bible Bill," to a religious happening in which people sang "Up, Up with People" and spoke in tongues. Bible Bill told me that he was waiting for a sign from God to determine the course of our relationship.

On other pages, I had a boyfriend named Ned, an artist whose commitment to Transcendental Meditation as well as to my best friend made it difficult for him to commit to me. Unbeknown to anyone, presumably least of all my imagined companion, I drove the back roads of Licking County with my painting professor, discussing abstract impressionism, Camus, and Mao's Little Red Book. There was just enough reality in the words I formed with my calligraphy pen to keep my mother's head reeling.

In the pages of my diary, I mooned over soccer players, served tea and crumpets at my sorority house, and planned a wedding in Greenwich. I also shacked up with a former mental patient who was now in a rock band, hitchhiked to San Francisco, and dropped LSD on a regular basis. College was a busy time for me.

"I want to talk to you," said my mother when I arrived home one weekend. Our house was, by then, completely decorated, and when waiting for her teenage children to come home, my mother would sit in a large upholstered chair covered in dusty-rose velvet, knitting sweaters and ponchos and ornate angora scarves for my wardrobe.

"I don't have time," I said. This, unlike my diary, was a statement of fact. In addition to a full academic load, I was painting until dawn at least three nights a week and working a full-time job. I had no time for any culture, be it the counterculture or the conventional one. I was treading the perilous edge between the two only in my mind—usually on Saturday and Sunday mornings, while washing lettuce and making tomato-skin roses and scallion brushes on the 7 a.m. to 3 p.m. shift in the kitchen of the Hospitality Motor Inn. Later, on the 3-to-11 shift, when I sat in a chair high above the hotel's indoor swimming pool, I caught up on my journal entries. It was never easy to remember all I'd imagined.

"Ned giving me shit about sorority," I scribbled. "Told him it means nothing to me, something I do for my mother, maintaining family tradition. Etc."

"Dr. J. invited me to spend the summer with him in Provincetown," I wrote. "Told him I had to work, don't want to take money from trust fund."

"Get pregnancy test," I scrawled.

"Went to sit-in," I wrote.

"Bad trip," I noted.

Ann Landers had advised discretion in dealing with ill-gotten information and so, at the dinner table on Friday nights, my mother wove her concerns into conversation and held forth on certain moral imperatives.

"I went to a girls' school," she said.

"St. Mary's of the Springs," said Robert, who in my absence had become my mother's best friend, interpreter, and conciliator. "Dominican. Liberal arts. Founded 1911."

"There *were* no sororities," said my mother. She held forth on the irrelevance of college sports, how it was more important to study than to date, the danger of illicit substances, how girls always paid the price for boys' sex drive, and how any idiot would pay for college with her trust fund, if she had one.

"Unfortunately," said Mike, "Molly's trust fund is in the shop."

"We might be able to sell the bookmobile," said Pat.

As soon as I finished committing one soap opera to the pages of my diary, I immediately began to inhabit a new one. Therefore, my mother's digressions at the dinner table had nothing more than a strange, déjà vu quality to my ears, not unlike the sound of the waiters and waitresses in the kitchen of the Hospitality Motor Inn.

"I need more lettuce!" In a fuguelike state, I raced from my cutting board to the service counter filling the orders, over and over and over again.

"I need parsley garnish for this omelet!" hollered a waitress. "Why should my party sit around waiting when they can go to Bob Evans and eat in ten minutes?"

"I need sliced berries for this waffle!" screamed another.

"I need a broiled tomato for this steak and egg!" yet another cried. I leaped as I might to the sound of a starter's gun from a starting block over a swimming pool. And, perhaps because of my athletic approach, I was soon plucked from the prep kitchen and given a kingdom of burners and grills and toasters to work on the weekend mornings. Armed with the poached egg expertise I'd gathered from Weight Watchers and the pancake technique I'd picked up from my father, I immediately distinguished myself. Soon, I could make eggs in more positions than the Kama Sutra—over hard, over easy, basted, broken, steamed, scrambled light, scrambled, sunny-side up. With *Mastering the Art of French Cooking* opened to the omelet page, I practiced ladling in beaten egg, stirring it, and holding my breath until the membrane reached the moment of truth, the moment when it is strong enough to be folded but still exquisitely tender. In short order I was a legend of break-fast cookery. I'd achieved synchronicity between toast and egg. My butter-milk and blueberry pancakes were better even than my father's. My Monte Cristo—a ham-and-cheese sandwich that was dipped in French toast batter, deep-fried, cut into quarters, and served awash with maple syrup and gar-nished with an exotic-looking bird that I carved from an apple—was often imitated but never duplicated. No one else thought of using stale bread and adding brandy to the batter.

Management at the Hospitality Motor Inn was relieved to have found a more suitable deployment for my natural efficiency. Initially they'd imagined that, like every girl they hired, my future lay in waitressing. They'd quickly reconsidered. On my first day, when serving shish kebab to a party of ten, I'd decided it was more efficient to flambé all the plates simultaneously rather than flame each individually. This innovation triggered the fire sprinklers, emptied the dining room, brought fire trucks to the door of the Hospitality Motor Inn, and made me a legend among the wiry ex-con from Appalachia and the gargantuan black man from Georgia and all the other men with red faces and shaky hands who cooked for the elite Four Winds restaurant at the Hospitality Motor Inn.

"Light my fire, baby," they hooted. "You got them good, girl! What can I make you for dinner? You want shrimp? You want lobster? You want steak?"

They called me "Flamer," "Little Match Girl," and "Three Alarm." After I joined their ranks, I wore clogs along with my new white chef's uniform, and they called me "Clomp, Clomp." I was not allowed to light my own ciga-rettes—"Jesus, baby, put that match down! We don't want no sprinkler action today, girl"—and I was discouraged from sharpening my own knives, carry-ing heavy pots, or cutting meat.

"You want to handle meat, you come talk to Papa," the chef said, grin-ning toothlessly and winking at his parole officer, who came by for weekly visits. I was the first female to work in the kitchen.

"You take care of them early morning egg calls on the weekends, baby, and Papa's gonna take care of you," said the chef. He was from New Orleans and he taught me how to cook gumbo, jambalaya, and dirty rice. When he asked me to quit lifeguarding in order to work double shifts on Saturday and Sun-day, I asked him to give Mike and Pat jobs as busboys and dishwashers. It was not unusual for me to arrive at work late Friday night and cook for forty of the next forty-eight hours. I earned $1.65 an hour and rarely had time to shower.

"$200!" I scribbled in my diary, and I continued to detail the lives I heard about while smoking at the employee table near the time clock in the kitchen. "All in quarters! And you meet so many interesting people, too! Just tonight, Johnny Cash (he's staying at the hotel!) asked me to join him in the bar after work! Yesterday it was Sonny and Cher!"

"Why you taking notes, Clomp-Clomp?" purred the chef. "Cooking's a thing you learn by doing, and, baby, I do you any time."

He taught me how to use a knife and made me practice until the blade was like a long, sharp sixth digit in my hand; taught me to chop, mince, and slice; demonstrated the difference between the give and spring in steak cooked rare and one cooked medium rare, and one cooked medium, and tutored me in the smells associated with each stage of doneness. Perhaps most important, he taught me to read the waiters' tickets—or "dupes," as they were called—to organize the work that was called for and to sound the cry like a tobacco auctioneer.

"An' we got two tenders going medium, medium, going with the fillet on the rare, drop four broccoli, four, four, give me eight lyonaisse, on the side, eight on the side, going on table twenty-three, table twenty-three going, going, you're picking up now, now, give me a busboy, bus, bus, two trays, in a hurry, hot plate, hot plate, what's your problem use a rag get this kid out of here where's twenty-three, twenty-three, twenty-three, hot plate, drop four green beans, need the potato garni here, here, béarnaise on the side, table twenty-three, in order, medium, mister, mister, mister, and rare, your chicken, your sole, your chop, you're gone don't forget your hollandaise and we're dropping carrots and three chops going under every one a mister, four kebabs behind them, fire two scallopini, going out on table fifty-one, fifty-one, fifty-one, going, going, three prime rib going now, where's my broccoli, four broccoli, four, hot plate, hot plate, are you deaf? Get out of here. Behind you, setting up your two scallopini, running low on parsley, new tray of stuffed tomatoes, back up, rotate out to prep, I've got your broiler, picking up table thirty-five, thirty-five, thirty-five, who's got thirty-five?"

On weekends I swore like a sailor, smoked like a fiend, lived on coffee, and learned to cook. On weekdays, on the other hand, I argued modernism, discussed Herbert Marcuse, and consulted with my academic advisor on the meals that I would cook for visiting literati.

"Denise Levertov likes French food," said my advisor.

"Quiche!" I countered. "Chicken divan, turned carrots, and green beans!"

"Gary Snyder said nothing fancy."

"Gumbo!" I said. "With cornbread."

"Allen Ginsberg wants toe food and brown rice," said my advisor.

"No problem!" I sang. Neither ingredient, however, was familiar to the owners of Fuller's Market and Baskets from Around the World in Granville, Ohio. Undaunted—and unwilling to reveal even a hairline fissure in my epicurean facade—I studied every package in the rice section of the store and, after holding various packages up to the brightest light, decided that Rice-a-Roni appeared to be brownest of all the available choices.

"We have about thirty people," I said to Mr. Fuller. "Can you get me a case?" I made a cauldron of my famous sweet-and-sour stir-fries to accompany the rice.

"Ommmm," intoned the poet when this special banquet was laid forth for his delectation.

"I'm sorry I wasn't able to find any toe food in town," I said, "and this was the brownest of the rices."

"Ommmmm," said the poet, lingering on the "mmmm" sound long enough to convince me that he liked what he smelled, loved what he saw, and couldn't wait to dig in. The book that he sent, along with a thank-you note, a few weeks later confirmed my feeling that we shared a common mission.

"Finished *Diet for a Small Planet*," I noted in my diary. "Tofu, not toe food."

Cooking keeps one in the present. It is a thing that has a beginning, a middle, and an end. If you don't pay attention you cut off your finger, burn yourself or your meal. You can't lie about cooking. You either do it well or you don't. You are fast or you are slow. You are neat or you are sloppy. You have taste or you don't. It's only dinner, but cooking makes honest people of liars, realists of dreamers, and well-ordered minds out of chaotic and impulsive ones. Baseball saved my brothers but cooking saved me.

By the end of my second year of college, I no longer used my diaries to write about lives that could have been. I ruminated on real events, recorded tastes, and made shopping lists.

"Fuller's Market: tamari? millet? bulgur wheat? alfalfa sprouts? aduki beans?" I printed neatly in the margin.

"Buy a wok," I wrote on another page. "Get Henkel chef knife."

Of course my mother had been praying for a change, but as my diary began to read more and more like a home ec textbook, she got a little bored. At some level, I must have figured out what my mother was up to, but I couldn't admit to myself that she was doing something that she herself disdained: invading her daughter's privacy. Instead, I explained the overlap between the pages of my diary and her speeches at the dinner table as evidence that we were still close.

One Friday night at dinner she held forth on the fact that cooking was really a blue-collar profession; another time, she talked about how happy she was that society had "moved past the barefoot-in-the-kitchen crap." But it wasn't until I ridiculed the family knives—dull and flimsy things that had been given away for free one Saturday at Albers supermarket years before—that my mother could voice her real concerns.

"Who cares about the knives?" she said. "Molly, what's happened to you? You used to be so interesting! You used to be fun!"

You're It

M y mother was right. I was no fun. Fun was no longer on my list of things to do. Halfway through college, I was eager to get my finances in order, my social conscience cleared, and my identity as an artsy intellectual articulated. I worked two jobs and spent four hours a week restocking the grain bins at the food co-op. I volunteered at Planned Parenthood and attended antiwar rallies. It was important to my self-image to keep up with both *Dialectics,* the Marxist literary journal, and *Aphra,* the feminist literary journal. It was critical to my body image that I ride ten miles a day on my ten-speed racing bike—how else could I inhale quiche and hash brownies with impunity?

To save money I'd moved from the college dormitory to a small apartment with two other girls, and to ensure their affection, I cooked every night. It was not unusual for a dozen people to drop by for dinner on our living room floor. Balancing plates on their crossed legs, they would nod along with Joan

Baez, who was always playing on the stereo, and talk about the future. Most had trust funds or promises of support from their parents for graduate school or a year of foreign travel. I had about twenty thousand dollars' worth of college loans and a recurring fantasy of sipping café filtre in the shade of a Pernot umbrella, preferably with Jean-Paul Sartre.

"Just wait for your opening," my father counseled my brothers when they were on base, burning to be heroes, hungry to get home. My opening was yogurt. In the spring of my sophomore year of college, I overheard the writer Gary Snyder bemoaning the lack of thick, European-style yogurt in central Ohio. I didn't hesitate. I bought a Salton Yogurt Maker. With the help of the instruction booklet that accompanied the little incubator, I mastered the art of inoculating warm milk with enough *streptococcus thermophilus* and *lacto-bacillus bulgaricus* bacteria to begin a fermentation. Days later, I opened little pots of creamy yogurt and my future was secure. The yogurt alone earned me entry into the Pernod umbrella society in Granville, the dinner parties given by professors for visiting artists and poets, the salonlike evenings in the homes of people boycotting the war and reading *Small Is Beautiful.* The cold cucumber soup that I made from the yogurt, on the other hand, guaranteed that a line of bowl-bearing supplicants—any of whom might possibly hold the key to my future—would stretch before me. I spent the summer in Granville. It was very hot.

"And now, if only we get the bitter winter," said Jean Carlos one evening in July when the sky was yellow and the air was still. A bacteriologist who was born in Milan, was raised in Argentina, and was now a lecturer at Ohio State University, Jean Carlos Cristi would have been rubbing his hands in anticipation of extreme meteorological fluctuation had he not, at that moment, been holding a pottery bowl. "Very hot, very cold, this is the best circumstance for my childrens," he said, nodding excitedly as the thick white soup poured from my ladle into his bowl.

"You will perhaps come to my attic where I keep them all," he said, and for the next several months I pedaled the five miles to his home late at night and climbed to the fourth floor of his Victorian farmhouse. There I sat near the casks of vinegar that he called his children and received instruction in alcoholic and acetic fermentation and wood aging. Beginning with the largest and stepping down to the smallest, a row of wooden barrels rested on a shelf that was about waist high and ran the entire width of his attic. The largest was approximately the size of the kegs featured at fraternity parties, and every fall Jean Carlos bought grapes from an Italian man near Lake Erie, ground them up, simmered the juice in a huge pot set over a fire behind his barn, and transferred the resulting liquid into his keg-size barrel. After a year, he said, it had evaporated enough to be transferred to the adjoining barrel. Jean Carlos had first come to Ohio State in 1962; in the summer of 1972, he bottled his first aged vinegar.

As it turned out, Jean Carlos's ancestors had been making vinegar even before my forefathers had taken bat to ball. When pressed, he admitted that the quantity of that ancestral vinegar used in his own production was minuscule, but he still called the collection of acetic bacteria "Mother," likened it to DNA, and felt a grave responsibility for the quality and character of its offspring. Aging, he said, is the only way to ensure a lush and deeply complex vinegar. But so much can go wrong, he muttered, shaking his head whenever he titrated vinegar to test its pH or decanted samples into Mateus bottles. The type and quality of the cask were also vital.

"It's been in cherrywood, the fruit is a parody, I must transfer into juniper," he would say, handing me one such bottle. Or, bemoaning the spiciness of another sample, "I left it in the mulberry too long."

Sometimes in the morning he stood on a small stool, gently lifted one of the blankets of cheesecloth that rested across the hole in the top of each barrel, and peered in to gauge how much had evaporated during the night.

"It becomes more of itself," said Jean Carlos, who was a self-described anarchist and a member of Students for a Democratic Society, "which may be better or may be worse."

At that moment I saw my future and it was as Mrs. Jean Carlos. I, too, understood how the raw propensities in a bloodline can be shaped by time and environment, by luck, and by lessons learned. How else could the essential similarities between my brothers be explained? Both Jean Carlos and I were caretakers of a thing too large to hold, a thing that needed us and had no use for us, a thing whose failure would always be our fault but whose success could only be a result of fate. We were Dionysian! We were Apollonian! We were Siamese!

"Someday we will travel to Reggio Emilia!" cried Jean Carlos. "We will meet my family!"

For the rest of the summer, AM radio orchestrated my romance. "Last night, I didn't get to sleep at all," I sang along with the Fifth Dimension while inoculating warm milk with bacteria in my kitchen.

"You!" I crooned with the Stylistics as I drove to work. "You make me feel brand new!"

"To us!" sang Jean Carlos, raising a small glass of vinegar high in the air and studying its color in the column of light that fell through his attic window.

"Let's stay together," I sang along with Al Green. I did not, however, invite Jean Carlos to accompany me on the weekends when I visited my family. How could I take him to Plain City when he'd offered me Italy? But how could I resist my brothers' pleas that I witness their games or my mother's accounts of just how awful it was to sit in the bleachers without me?

My father was less bothered by my absence. We'd been missing from each other's life, after all, for quite some time, and he didn't notice the lack of me as much as he noticed—with surprise—something about me that he liked a lot whenever I reappeared.

"She's got gumption," he said approvingly, when my mother complained of my work-obsessed life. Gumption, he thought, could trump pinko leanings, loose morals, and commie cooking. In my father's flossy-fee, gumption was the key to eternal happiness, and by 1972, he suspected that his top prospects lacked the very particular form of gumption that he'd sought to instill in them. In fact, he'd begun to run their names together. "Mike-Pat," he said, quickly and dismissively. His oldest sons were, after all, not simply disregarding baseball, they were also defying his rules about hair.

"Charlie Finley wouldn't even take you," he said, referring to the owner of the Oakland A's, who'd shocked the baseball world by allowing his players to wear their hair so long that it stuck out under their caps and even hung below the collars of their uniforms. He was unaware of the degree to which my own activities might have worried Charlie Finley.

"You're my little coed," my father told me in order to remind himself, "and you've got drive." His smile, however, was a little rueful. At fifty years old, my father's life of hard labor showed. His sons were stretching past six feet tall, but he was shrinking. His weathered, Apache-looking skin now had cancerous patches, and his lower lip trembled more frequently. My father was tired. He was not, however, beaten.

"Kev-er-Rob?" he said hopefully.

"Er-ah-Paul?" he added.

At first glance, it appeared that the O'Neill mania to be number one had dissipated as it moved through the birth order. Neither Kev-er-Rob nor er-Paul had their older brothers' brash dominance or swagger. They were less likely to assume victory, more likely to notice their competition. Far from being diluted, however, the need to prevail had gathered depth and complexity in the younger children.

For the older boys, winning was a powerful preference, even an entitlement, but it had never been a life-and-death matter. For the younger boys,

winning was a prerequisite for their next breath, an entrance into the fraternal order of O'Neill, the only way to be noticed by my father, Mike, and Pat.
Winning was as essential as oxygen to my three youngest brothers. Losing was
unimaginable to them. They defied it, they bargained with it, and from a very
early age, they refused to accept it. They were bad sports.

Kevin was just two years old the first time he declined second place. He
was watching my mother diaper Robert when the baby uttered his first
word.

"Dada Dada Da," said Robert, who was about a year old.

"Oh, Kevin," said my mother, "did you hear that? The baby can say
'Dada.'"

Kevin stared at his little brother for several moments before leveling his
gaze on my mother.

"Can he say 'hardware store'?" Kevin asked.

Kevin was a catcher. Choosing this position may have been an extension
of his sense of cool and of the pleasure he took in dressing up. It also could
have been self-protective. After all, Kevin had caught for Mike at the
O'NeillDome; before he was old enough for Little League, he'd developed an
appreciation for chest and shin guards as well as the habit of donning a helmet and pulling a wire cage over his face before he crouched down behind
home plate.

Kevin would flash signals against his inner thigh, but only for show. There
was no relationship between what was known of the batter—his strengths,
his weaknesses, his past performances—and the pitches Kevin called for. He
was not the sort of player who remembered such things and it wouldn't have
mattered at the O'NeillDome, anyway. Mike did not accept signals; the
pitches that exploded from his wind-up were always a surprise. Kevin's
speed, agility, and catcher's armor were the only things that delivered him
from bodily harm.

Kevin couldn't wait to get rid of the ball. It would still be vibrating as he
snatched it from his catcher's mitt and hurled it back to Mike. He hated to
pause, even to spook a runner back from a long lead or to slow the game.
Like the hundred deep knee bends that I performed daily in the name of thin
thighs, Kevin's rising-and-crouching behind the plate was quick and dutiful.
It was as if he'd calculated the number of balls he'd have to catch before he
could retire, and wanted to get it over with as quickly as possible.

"Come on," Kevin would growl at his older brother. Later, after Robert
began pitching, he said derisively, "Hurry up!" Robert did not, after all, have
the same power that Mike had had when my father decided to send him to the

mound in Plain City. He was a year too young for Little League—"He's ten!" bellowed my father, adding under his breath, "*almost,* grah ha ha ha!"—old enough to know what to throw, but not old enough to be able to control the ball. "Hurry up," hissed Kevin.

Awkward and shy, Robert also lacked his brother's popularity—fans packed the stands to scream Kevin's name, girls waited for him to throw off his catcher's mask and chase pop flies, boys waited to congratulate him after games. It was true that Kevin had a significant case of O'Neill: he hurled helmets and even bats when he failed to be a superstar. But his frustrations on the field didn't affect his image as the sweetheart of Clinton Junior High. Robert's case of O'Neill, on the other hand, was cause for concern. At first, trying to pitch his way into both Kevin's social circle and my father's affection, he crumbled under the pressure.

"Jesus Christ," said my mother one night in 1971, when Robert was on the mound in Plain City. Down three runs, with the bases loaded and having thrown three balls and no strikes to the batter he was facing, Robert was sobbing into the glove on his left hand while seeking to comfort himself by slipping his right hand down the front of his green pinstriped baseball pants.

"Molly!" whispered my mother frantically. "Run down there and tell your father to pull him out before somebody else sees him. Hurry up!"

But Robert would never leave the mound. Instead he learned to pitch through his tears and his boners and soon he had the fine motor skills to control the curveball, the fastball, and the slider that my father taught him. Robert also remembered which pitches each player couldn't hit in June and July, and then replicated them during the tournaments in August. He quickly understood Kevin's limits behind the plate. Soon he'd pegged my father as a remarkable teacher and motivator—and a lousy field manager. He was too eager to please and was loath to bench faltering players, and he was not capable of strategic thinking. But Robert was; and by the time he turned eleven, he was running the game from the mound.

Pat, who'd begun helping out in the dugout as soon as he himself retired from Little League, was Robert's mentor. "Watch the batter's feet," he counseled. "Sell him what he wants to see with your motion, then throw him exactly what he's not lined up for.

"Concentrate on the ones that are willing to face you straight-up and honest. The ones that stand by the plate and put their energy into knowing you and knowing the game. Memorize what they do with every single pitch," said Pat. "Those are the ones you are going to see again in junior high and high school."

Few could hit Robert. If they succeeded, and his work was not backed up by his teammates with swift and certain outs, Robert took it personally.

"Did you see where his feet were?" he spat at his brother when, after losing a slider in the dirt, Kevin ran from behind the plate and out to the mound for a conference. "He was behind the plate! He was looking for a fastball and I sold him one but if I threw him one, he was going to park it. Now, thanks to you, we got him on base!" Kevin, his mask in hand, shook his head in disbelief.

"Jaaayze," he said, laughing and turning to wave at his fans.

"You can't remember shit!" persisted Robert. "Are you incapable of strategic thinking?"

"Take 'er easy," said my father, joining the two on the mound.

"Where were you?" screamed Robert another evening, taking a swing at the first baseman who had botched a bunt.

"I'll kill you," he roared, charging from the mound to left field where an outfielder had dropped a routine fly ball.

"Take 'er easy," said my father, giving chase.

"No way!" bellowed Robert at the plate when an umpire had the temerity to give him a called strike. Whereupon my father, leaping first over his son's hurled bat and then over his batting helmet, ran up behind Robert, enfolded him in his arms, and dragged him back to the dugout.

"It was in the dirt!" screamed Robert, his arms and legs flailing like a protester's caught in a cross-chest carry by a member of the Ohio National Guard. "The guy's blind! Check the ball! The guy's a thief!" Kevin's bad sportsmanship could cause a titter in the stands and cost the occasional batting helmet. Robert's objections, on the other hand, stopped games, made a serious dent in the team's equipment budget, and got him thrown off the field.

"Chick!" my mother said after the games. "You've got to do something! People are simply appalled!"

"You don't want to break a kid's spirit, Boots," he'd reply, rubbing a dab of snuff into his gums above the gold-tipped molars in the upper-left side of his mouth. Unbeknown to those of us seated directly above the Julian Speer dugout, however, my father routinely slammed both his bad-sport sons into its walls and pinned them down until they returned from their altered state.

Kevin was not difficult to subdue, and from this my father knew that his third-born son, although a superb player, was only a tourist on the baseball field. Robert was a different story. When a game served his second-to-youngest son an opportunity for recrimination, my father moved quickly to contain the boy's predictable frustration and fury. He met force with force and threatened to bench him. After the game, however, if the team won, my father would smile as he tended the gashes bored into his shins from his son's furious cleats and the bruises left on his forearms by the boy's fists. He also remembered his name.

"Nice game, Rob," he said.

My father wasn't the only adult who rewarded Robert's mania for victory. In 1973, Paul Kaiser, the tournament director at Plain City, gave him the Most Valuable Player award. "You're a wonderful ballplayer, young man," said the white-haired patriarch. "Don't let that famous temper of yours take away something from you that most people never get." Robert nodded obediently and went home with his gold trophy: within a week, he was once again excoriating himself and everybody else on the field.

"Cheater!" At ten years old, Paul's voice had lost some of its squeak. When threatened—and he was threatened by Robert on the basketball court after school—he was capable of summoning a prosecutor's timbre, an outrage that banished any thought of mercy, a thunder that demanded swift and certain justice. Every day, he challenged Robert to twenty-one-point games of one-on-one hoops. Every day, Robert allowed Paul to score twenty points and then, as effortlessly as a serial killer ending a life, Robert clicked off seven or eight baskets in a row.

"Cheater!" Paul's response to losing caused the dogs to whine and the pony to whinny.

"Cheater!" he would roar, hurling the basketball at Robert—who routinely took off running as soon as the winning shot left his fingertips.

"Cheater!" howled the younger boy, kicking, screaming, giving chase, and finally hurling anything he could toward the departing back of his brother. "I'm telling Mom!" Then Paul would call the hospital and have her paged.

"Mom!" he would sob into the telephone. "Robert cheated!"

"Why do you do it?" my mother asked Robert one evening after dinner. This was their special time together, when they would sit in the living room debating who was to blame for the incidents of the day, parsing her marriage, and discussing the Vietnam War and existentialism.

"It's more fun to give him some hope," said Robert, adding, in his level and philosophical voice, "It's also better for him. You win by getting bad at losing."

"Well, I think you could let him win once in a while," said my mother.

"That would be immoral," replied Robert. After winning the Most Valuable Player award at Plain City, Robert had begun to see himself as an intellectual, an educator, and a beacon of ethical living.

Thoughtfulness had indeed led him to victory over a better team in his final game of his Little League career. In that game Robert, who was playing for Julian Speer and being coached by my father, faced the indomitable Frisbee Bears, whose star was a boy named Bear Nespeca. Bear pitched for the Bears, and Bear was indomitable. For weeks before the tournament even started, Robert studied Bear and the Bears. He analyzed pitch rotation and discussed game strategies and contingencies with Pat. Robert understood that the only chance he had of beating Bear Nespeca was to rattle his confidence and, in the first inning of the big game, he did just that. At his first at-bat, Robert took Bear to a full count. Then he stepped out of the batter's box and raised his hand to slow the contest and to allow himself to savor his imminent triumph. Bear was nervous and when Bear got nervous, he threw the pitch he relied upon most: his fastball. Moving back into the batter's box, Robert crowded the plate to encourage an inside pitch. Then he parked the ball for a three-run homer. A major league veteran could not have had a more professional appearance at the plate. Bear never recovered and Julian Speer swept through the tournament.

Robert's interest in the game, however, immediately began to wane. He continued to play through his adolescence, easily making the all-city teams in junior high, but he was a player in an empty uniform. His passion had migrated to tennis, which he taught himself.

"We can't afford to get you a racquet, Rob," said my mother, "but if we have enough Green Stamps you can get one of those Spaldings that are in the S & H catalog."

My father was less supportive. "If you think I'm paying some little country club snot for tennis lessons, you're wrong, er, ah, Buster," he said. "You think I'm going to *help* you throw it all away? Turn into some little, uh, unhappy person? Huh? Huh? Hey, I have an idea! Why don't you just take up badminton, huh? Or shuffleboard! There you go! THuffleboard! TenniTH!"

"I'll hit with you, Rob," Paul would say every afternoon, thirty minutes after his daily humiliation on the basketball court. "If you play one more game of twenty-one, I'll hit tennis with you. Huh? Huh?" Initially rebuffed, but nevertheless undaunted, Paul followed Robert around and issued other challenges.

"You afraid I'll win, huh?" Paul would taunt, standing in the kitchen as Robert plugged in the Crock-Pot and set the table for dinner.

"What's the matter, cheater?" he would ask, dribbling a basketball on the floor outside the door of Kevin and Robert's room while, on the other side of the door, Robert read *The Rise and Fall of Civilizations.*

"Huh?" said Paul, stalking Robert as his brother pushed the mower along the edges of the vast lawns up and down Cooke Road. By this time Pat was not only coaching Little League and working in a grocery store but also running a lawn-care company, and Robert, who was saving to buy an aluminum tennis racket, was his star employee.

"I'll help you mow if you'll play Twenty-one again," said Paul.

"You're too little to mow," said Robert.

"I am not!" insisted Paul.

"You can't keep a straight line. It's too dangerous. I won't allow it," said Robert. In addition to plugging in the Crock-Pot and setting the table, he was responsible for Paul's welfare until my mother returned from work. Robert took his responsibilities very seriously.

"Pat!" wailed Paul, trotting alongside his older brother as he steered the riding lawn mower. "Robert's lying! Robert cheated!"

It was not clear to Paul exactly how Robert had played foul during Twenty-one. He could not articulate the terrible unfairness of being smaller and weaker, the agony of not yet being capable of swooshing every single free throw through the family's professional-grade basketball hoop. Every day when he was unable to procure an instant rematch, Paul's only option was to play himself, shooting basket after basket, chasing the Holy Grail of twenty-one consecutive points.

As a student of Nietzsche, Robert understood that "strong hope is a much greater stimulant of life" than any single realized ambition could be. "A little anticlimatic, isn't it?" he said several years later, when Paul finally beat him at the one-on-one game.

"I'll play you again," offered Paul. "Come on! Huh? I'll spot you three points."

"Come on, Rob," wheedled Paul one afternoon in August 1974. I'd come home for the Plain City tournament. I was making dinner, watching my two youngest brothers through the kitchen window, and hoping that WCOL would play a song that could explain the lump in my throat and the chlorinated-pool feeling in my eyes.

After many months, my relationship with Jean Carlos had come to resemble the sophisticated liaisons I'd formerly written about in my diary. He'd taken me to fancy dinner parties and wine tastings at Ohio State, taught me about the importance of grains in Parmesan cheese, and introduced me to opera. That summer, he'd not only invited me to accompany him on his August pilgrimage to Reggio Emilia, he'd also bought me the necessary plane ticket. But as soon as my fantasy love affair became reality, I developed migraine headaches. My parents, who believed that much depended on a girl's virginity, would certainly commit me to the state mental institution if they discovered that I had left the country with an anarchist who made vinegar. Three days before, I'd packed peppers and eggplants from his garden and a few Mateus bottles full of his balsamico in my convertible and had driven home for the Plain City tournament.

"My brother broke his ankle," I wrote in the note that I left, along with my plane ticket, on Jean Carlos's kitchen table. "I have to go home."

In fact, Paul had, a week before, broken his ankle while sliding into second base. But my family assumed that I'd returned to witness the final O'Neill appearance in Plain City. Paul—who, despite his plaster cast, had every intention of being the winning pitcher—was twelve. The next year, he'd be too old for Little League. My eyes burned as I stared at my brothers in the backyard.

Robert was dressed in his white tennis shorts and a belt that his girlfriend had macraméed for him. His hair, which was lank and damp with sweat, fell over the collar of his white shirt, and he was standing, knees slightly bent, in the middle of the basketball court. Sweeping his new aluminum tennis racquet back and forth, he was hitting a tennis ball against the second garage. Forehand. Backhand. Backhand. Forehand. Easy, steady, and deliberate. Robert, his brow knit, exhaled into each ball, stroked it, and made it spin like a small planet on an invisible axis.

"Topspin," he said, without taking his eye off his green Day-Glo tennis ball, and sounding as if he were delivering a lecture on the subject. "That's what you want. You don't hit it, you stroke it."

Robert loved the bounce and lightness of tennis balls, how unfreighted they were by dreams and family history and expectation. He also loved not having to depend on a team. In fact, Robert savored the solitary contest of tennis almost as much as he relished my father's dismay at his growing dominance on the court.

"Please," begged Paul, who was windmilling huge circles in the air with the blue aluminum baseball bat that he was grasping with both of his hands, "just a few. I *need* BP."

"I'm retired," said Robert, rotating to return a backhand shot. In the two years since he'd taken up tennis, the pleasure he found in having a racquet between himself and the ball was undiminished. Nevertheless, he remained

Paul's best hope for a pitching, catching, batting, and fielding partner. After all, if Robert deigned to pick up a baseball, he did so with unrivaled skill.

Unfortunately for Paul, the team he'd spent his childhood scrambling toward—the Big O'Neill Machine—was all but defunct by then. Kevin—who'd always rid himself of any baseball as quickly as possible—had left baseball for varsity football and believed that pitching or catching might harm his quarterbacking. Mike's relationship with the sphere of O'Neill destiny had always been a powerful mixture of desire and rejection.

"If you don't SHUT UP *I'll* come out and throw you BP," he often bellowed from the second garage in the afternoons. Home from college, Mike worked nights and slept during the day. In order not to be disturbed by the sounds inside the house, he'd moved into the second garage. If he had not arisen by the time Robert began stroking his tennis ball and Paul began lobbying for a baseball buddy, Mike greeted the disturbance in a manner that might have given Bongo pause.

Pat's interest in baseball was undiminished. Unfortunately, however, between his business ventures and his car—he'd bought a 1963 Ford Galaxy, painted it baby blue, carpeted it with a thick, navy blue shag, installed an eight-track tape deck, and christened it the Luv Mobile—he was not often home when Paul was seized by the spirit of baseball. And Paul was seized by the spirit of baseball with a worrying frequency. When his badgering failed to produce a partner for playing catch, he sometimes retired to the house to mend baseball socks, darning the stirrups as if they were a family dream only temporarily frayed, one that he could make whole again.

"What the hell?" asked my father, returning home late from work. "Who taught you how to sew? Huh? Huh?" His tone suggested that retribution was in order. "Boots! Who taught, uh, uh, the darned baby how to sew socks? Huh?"

More often, however, Paul took his bat and a bucket of baseballs to the field behind the second garage and there, in the overgrown grass of the O'NeillDome, he popped ball after ball at the sky.

"Now will you play?" he would yell at Robert after lofting a hit long and hard.

"Now do you like my hat?" Robert would ask derisively, fanning his tennis racquet, his gaze unwavering.

"COME ON!" bellowed Paul as I watched them.

"Rob," I yelled through the window, "throw him a few. Come on, have some mercy. The poor kid looks like a peg leg."

The white cast covered Paul's foot and rose nearly to his knee. When my youngest brother dragged this heavy club to complete his swing, his game against the sky seemed especially poignant. Tears began to slide from my eyes as I wheedled a cork from a green, heart-shaped bottle that had formerly contained Mateus wine.

"Never can say good-bye," I sang along with Gloria Gaynor on WCOL. Through the open window, the metallic *pong* of ball against aluminum bat and the steady bounce of Robert's tennis balls were my backup band.

"Never can say good-bye!" I repeated, standing in my mother's kitchen and cutting the eggplant into thin slices to make eggplant Parmesan for my family. "No, no, no! No, no, no! No, no, no!"

"Mike!" yelled Paul from the back field when his oldest brother emerged from his lair in the second garage, followed by the Eagles singing "Already Gone" from his tape deck.

"You should see what I have to do to get around on the ball with this sucker on," yelled Paul, thumping his cast. "Come here! Just throw me a few."

"I have to go to work," said Mike.

"Pat!" cheered Paul a few minutes later when the Luv Mobile roared up the driveway, windows down, Cat Stevens blasting. "Wait till you see what I had to do to my stance because of this cast!"

"I have to load the equipment in the car for tonight's game," said Pat, opening the trunk of the Luv Mobile and beginning to bring barrels of bats and gear out of the garage while humming, "Oh very young, what will you leave us this time?"

"Kev!" Paul called out when his brother walked up the driveway from a football workout. "You should see my delivery with this cast on! Come on!"

"I have to take a shower," said Kevin.

A few hours later, in Plain City, Paul pitched the winning game of the championship series while wearing a plaster cast. He also hit the winning run, and as he hobbled around third base, his brow furrowed and dragging his cast behind him, my father, standing outside the dugout, clapped once and said, "Paul!"

It was a statement of fact, the right name for the right son with no warm-up or misstated monikers preceding it, and no one was more surprised than my father.

"Go, Paul," he said a little while later, when his youngest son was awarded the Most Valuable Pitcher award and the fans at Plain City went wild.

Like players finally freed of a hot potato, Mike, Kevin, Robert, and even

Pat seemed lighter and happier as they leaped up to join the cheer. We stood in the stands—a row of teenagers and young adults who had better places to be—sounding the way we used to on Schreyer Place playing tag in the back-yard. We cheered, "Go, Paul!" But like our father, my brothers and I were really saying: "You're It."

A Fish Without a Bicycle

"I guess the cheerleaders get the doctors," sighed my mother. We were sitting in the living room discussing my plans for the future. I wanted to be a poet and a painter and now, several months before I was to graduate from college, my mother was questioning this plan.

A snafu with my financial aid had caused me to take a semester off of school to work. I graduated the December following my last summer with Jean Carlos and used much of my additional time writing and publishing a book of poems about missing him. He was on sabbatical and had remained in Italy.

"I just don't get it, Molly," said my mother, leaning forward from her pink velvet chair to unwind a length of fuzzy white yarn from a canvas bag on the floor near her feet. "You didn't think you could make a living painting pictures or writing poems now, did you?"

For several years, my mother had been collecting dog hair. Big, white puffy clouds of fur blew off our dogs in the summer, and the bags of hair had quickly turned into bales of Great Pyrenean wool. My mother had arranged to have it spun into yarn, and now she was using the yarn to knit herself a coat, an undertaking that had our dogs barking, sniffing, and whining nervously. They followed the bag of yarn around the house whenever they could.

"They think I'm knitting one of their friends," she said when the two Great Pyreneans bounded into the living room, causing her collection of miniature glass dishes to rattle on the étagère at her elbow. "Put them back in the basement. You have to lean a kitchen chair under the doorknob, or they'll just stand on their legs and open it again. Won't you?" she added, pausing to compliment our pets. "You are so smart! Now get out of here."

In addition to working at the hospital, my mother frequently attempted to leverage her domestic skills into cash. She'd written a book on miniature Sandwich glass, and was supplementing my college financial aid package by breeding dogs. She'd also tried her hand at rental property, refinishing furniture, making needlepoint pillows, knitting afghans, and decoupage. It is unclear whether her industriousness was solely aimed at making money or also at reducing the time she had available to spend it. Like my father—whose attempts to create a sideline for his ditchdigging business had included the marketing and sale of fiberglass steam-bath cabinets—my mother was incapable of being idle.

"Maybe I shouldn't have made fun of you when you practiced Two Bits, Four Bits, Six Bits, a Dollar," she said, staring down at the pattern of X's and dashes that she was following as her needles *click-click-clicked*. "I'm telling you, this dog hair is as soft as angora, Molly. I think I could *sell* these coats."

"You hate cheerleaders," I reminded her. "You think they're trashy, remember?"

"Trashy" was my mother's word for girls who wore bikini panties instead of cotton underpants, girls who took typing and home ec, girls who were, in my mother's opinion, at risk for teen pregnancy and suited for nothing more than becoming somebody's secretary or somebody's wife. Had she forgotten the hours she'd spent hammering these precepts into my young mind? Had she forgotten all she'd prohibited so that I might be saved from trashiness?

"I guess I was wrong," said my mother, without looking up from her pattern. "I mean, I would have thought a doctor or even a lawyer would want someone interesting. Well, you could never have been a cheerleader, anyway, not the way you're built. But now what are you going to do? Who's going to marry you if you won't wear makeup?"

"I'm moving to Massachusetts," I said, quickly and firmly. Unlike my plan to be a poet and a painter, my plan to move was not something I'd had time to develop in detail. Massachusetts was mentioned frequently in the pages of *Ms.* magazine, and Massachusetts was simply the first distant location that came to mind when my mother reversed her stance on cheerleaders.

"What's in Massachusetts?" asked my mother.

"*Our Bodies, Ourselves!*" I replied with the sort of prim triumph that trashy girls cannot muster.

"What are you talking about?"

"The Boston Women's Health Collective!"

In my last year at college, I'd taken a women's studies course and begun to read feminist publications as others read *Travel Holiday* and *Gourmet* magazine—with dreams of deliverance. Now my unpremeditated declaration helped me understand my destiny: Massachusetts. In a mere four syllables, the Kennedy ambitions of my early adolescence merged with my hope of finding a place where girls mattered as much as boys.

In the absence of a plan, I looked for signs. Suddenly they were everywhere. One friend had been accepted at the Smith School of Social Work, another at the University of Massachusetts, and yet another was to begin teaching at Deerfield Academy. Then Aedan, a poet with whom I'd studied at Denison, took a job at Amherst College. I renewed our friendly acquaintance via telephone, and soon had convinced myself that the poet needed a muse. What did my mother know about the desires of cultured, literary men and what they looked for in a mate? After that, the frequency with which WCOL played the old Bee Gees' song about Massachusetts seemed cosmic.

"Feel I'm goin' back to Massachusetts," I sang. "Something's telling me I must go home!"

"What are you going to *do* in Massachusetts?" asked my mother after several months of this.

"You don't have to be a cheerleader to make it in Massachusetts," I informed her as I slapped letters inviting me for job interviews on top of her knitting pattern. One of the colleges in western Massachusetts had offered me a position as a dormitory counselor; another had invited me to teach a poetry course at its women's center.

"But they don't want to pay you," said my mother, frowning, raising her brow, and curling her lip as she scanned the letters. "You'd be better off working in Columbus, living at home, and saving up for graduate school." Pausing then to hold both knitting needles in one hand, she used the other hand to lift the wide wave of white hair that framed the left corner of her forehead. Against the rest of her dark hair, this patch rose up, up, up, like a large white question mark. In her periods of fierce conviction, her white patch provided a note of levity. In her moments of self-examination, on the other hand, the question mark of my mother's white hair seemed to underscore her self-doubt, the if-only-ness that had always haunted her.

"Maybe I should have let you wear panty hose in seventh grade and have slumber parties," she said with a tiny shake of her head that caused her white S-shaped wave of hair to jiggle like a wagging finger. "Maybe I should have let you pierce your ears and wear blue eye shadow. Jesus! Will you get this dog out of here? He's humping the sleeve of my coat! I'm telling you, the male of the species have one thing and one thing only on their minds."

I did not mention to my mother that I had flooded the Pioneer Valley with my résumé, as well as with slides of my paintings and copies of my book of poems. I wanted her to believe that my talents had spontaneously come to the attention of Massachusetts and that Massachusetts wanted me. I was equally subtle with Aedan.

"Hampshire College invited me for an interview," I said casually. "Isn't that close to where you are?"

"Near enough," said Aedan, inhaling deeply and then holding his breath into the telephone. "Maybe a bit too lunatic for the likes of you, though," he rasped. As he held the smoke in his lungs, his voice squeaked and rushed with deathbed urgency. He said that he'd seen signs for a women's writing group, a film co-op, and a crisis center.

"It could be like you got to go to Smith, after all," he said. "Hold on. I've got to find my lighter."

For the seminar Aedan had taught at Denison, I'd written a poem about my mother's refusal to allow me to leave Ohio to attend a girls' school. Aedan had spent an entire class analyzing the poem, which was titled "The Ohio State Penitentiary," and pushing for additional information. "What was the mother's motivation?" he'd asked the class. "We know that a girls' school saved her life but we do not know what she had to gain from denying her daughter the same experience. What was she protecting? Herself? A fault line in the life she's made?" Aedan, a Jungian, was extremely interested in confessional poetry.

Aedan's descriptions of Northampton made it sound alluringly highbrow. "If you stand on the street in that town and call 'Sappho,' you'll end up surrounded by dozens of golden retrievers," he said. "I wouldn't advise calling for Virginia, Anaïs, or Djuna, either." The idea of leaving a state where people named their dogs Rover and Woody Hayes and venturing to the land of the literary pet was irresistible to me. So were Aedan's persuasive techniques. "My apartment is right across the street from Emily Dickinson's house," he added. I interpreted this as a romantic overture and decided to move in with him.

"Jesus, I got the munchies," he coughed into the telephone. "I really miss those brownies of yours."

I began to arrange my trousseau accordingly.

"Where can I find Izod shirts?" I asked a salesperson at the shop in downtown Granville where the rich students from the East Coast bought their clothes. Fingering my final paycheck from the Hospitality Motor Inn, I decided to pay full price for the first time in my life. It was an investment in my future, I told myself.

At home, when I announced my plan, my father said, "Did they ever catch that Boston Strangler?" Paul had also objected, "Massachusetts is too far! How can you be my sister if you live all the way in Massachusetts?" It broke my heart, but I remained stalwart.

"Do you carry Sperry Top-Siders?" I asked the salesman.

"Lose the boat shoes," said Aedan.

We were sitting at Amherst Chinese Food. After a month of living with Aedan, Amherst Chinese Food still felt racy, daring, and exotic. Its egg rolls were far, far from Ohio, and its chicken with cashew nuts made me feel even more cosmopolitan. Other aspects of my new life were not, however, conforming to my imagined scenarios.

"The feminists act like I have cooties," I complained as we waited for dinner.

"You might stop ironing those creases in the legs of your chinos," Aedan suggested, adding, "Give it time; once they get to know you, they'll love you."

Was my boyfriend setting the stage for a declaration of his own undying love? I stopped breathing for a moment. But like all the men who were discussed in my women's consciousness-raising group, Aedan was not able to articulate his feelings, and this had been another disappointment. As I drifted from faculty dinner parties to poetry readings, from job interviews to my women's group, I tried to imagine that I was playing Simone to his Jean-Paul, but from the start of our life together he'd been more interested in honing my image than discussing our future as a bohemian couple.

Aedan had been neither surprised nor gratified by my arrival. "Oh," he'd said when he opened his front door to find me posed—TWA bag over my shoulder and suitcase in hand—near the bamboo wind chimes on his front porch. "Wow."

"Will you be staying?" he asked later as I unpacked my suitcase into one of the milk crates on the floor of his room. "Here?" he added. "Staying here?"

Aedan also seemed incapable of imagining the sort of domestic bliss that I had in mind. Once, when he'd handed me a package from a lingerie store, I had imagined unwrapping it to discover a diaphanous little je ne sais quoi. Instead I found a T-shirt that read: "A Woman Needs a Man Like a Fish Needs a Bicycle."

"I don't get it," I'd said.

"Lose the bra," he'd suggested.

My vision of our future had been shaken by the incident, but not shattered. Aedan's appetite for my cooking was compelling evidence of his devotion to me. And who else would read and comment on his poems, sweep up the marijuana seeds that he let roll to the floor, cover him with an Indian-print quilt night after night when he passed out on the couch?

In the other part of my life, however, Aedan's inability to commit to a life-long partnership after a month of eating my brownies proved to be unexpectedly useful. As our relationship deteriorated, I discovered that I was no longer suspect among my fellow feminists: instead, I was some boy's victim, and I quickly became the darling of my consciousness-raising group. All those sisters-in-struggle who'd previously ignored the gangly, well-creased preppie from Ohio now nodded their heads softly whenever I spoke. Those who'd previously given me wide berth suddenly opened their arms to offer me empathetic hugs. After our meetings they would pull out the academic Day Planners to "make a time" to meet over a cup of Red Zinger tea.

"No way!" they cried when I related how Aedan had given me a new pair of Frye boots and then suggested that I wear only them and nothing else (except, perhaps, an apron) around the house.

"Loser!" they shrieked when I confessed that Aedan had asked that I give him a lesbian for his birthday.

"Finally!" they exclaimed. "Now you understand the patriarchy on a personal level! The personal is political!"

After a month of this support, I felt that I had no choice. I accepted my new friends' offer to move me out of Aedan's house. I took a job as a nanny.

"Want me to take care of that prick for you, sis?" asked Amazonia, who had a black belt in karate as well as a Harley.

"Want a ride home?" she asked.

*   *   *

"My mother!"

Most intimate conversations in the women's community began with this phrase. It was generally pronounced with a bitter groan and greeted with a returned groan and sympathetic nods. With all its lowing, and groaning, and my-mothering, a roomful of feminists getting to know one another— at an encounter session, for instance, or at the first meeting of a political group, a support group, or a therapy group—often ended up sounding like a calving barn.

Mothers were demanding, insufferable, and insatiable. Mothers were passive, competitive, or overbearing. They were clueless and deluded, controlling and in denial. Mothers hated their husbands or loved them too much. Every mother was different, but all mothers abandoned their daughters. There was nothing worse than having a mother for a feminist's mental health. At least not in Northampton in the mid-1970s.

"My mother."

I said the words tentatively at first, sitting cross-legged in the circle that my women's group formed on the wide-plank floor of the Valley Women's Center on Tuesday evenings.

"Five sons!" cried Roxanne. The daughter of a dentist from New York City, Roxanne was a social worker and a hippie who could not control her response to injustice in matters of class, race, and gender. She was perpetually outraged, and she organized boycotts and demonstrations, printed and distributed posters, and collected signatures on petitions whenever inequity reared its loathsome head. "Too *much!*" she declared when she was displeased. "Too *much!*" she squealed when she was delighted—which, with the exception of her despair at the suffering in the world, was most of the time.

"Too *much!*" she cried at the spectre of my male-dominated past. Shaking her head, Roxanne leaned forward over her crossed legs from her position several women down from me in our circle. Under her tank top, her small, unfettered breasts trembled indignantly as her fingers played with the drawstring of her loose, gauzy pants. "How did you survive?" she asked, shaking her long, brown Gloria Steinem hair.

On the other side of the circle, Alezzie Womynstein clucked sadly and this immediately commanded the attention of the entire room. The former Elise Weinstein had grown up in New Haven, Connecticut. The daughter of a labor lawyer and a biochemist, Alezzie was also an incest survivor, and when still a student at Radcliffe, she had written a book about that experience. Alezzie was a folk hero of the Northampton women's community, as well as its literary star. When she held forth, she spoke so softly that everyone else had to lean forward to hear her. Now she crossed her arms over her chest, partially obscuring the Michigan Women's Music Festival logo on her lavender T-shirt.

"Think of what your mother might have been if she hadn't been turned into a breeder," she said softly, and every young, girlish body in the room swayed toward her like flowers toward their sun.

Alezzie—who generally refused to eat anything that had been touched by male hands at any point in its growth, harvesting, distribution, or cooking—was built like a scrawny adolescent boy. Under the shelf of thick dark hair that she cut herself, she had large, hungry brown eyes. When she lowered her head, stuck out her lower lip, and shook her head slowly from side to side, she bore a startling resemblance to my brother Robert when he was on the mound, shaking off a catcher's signal.

"It wasn't really my mother's fault," I tried to explain. "She was trying to have another girl."

"Another girl to wait on her husband and sons," said Alezzie gently, rising to walk across the circle and crouch in front of me.

"Another girl to cook and clean. I know this is painful for you to hear," she whispered, "but deep down inside, you already know it. I can feel your anger."

Alezzie returned to her place, picked up the can of Tab she'd left on the floor next to her journal, and took a sip. Tab and cheeseburgers were the only exception she made to her woman-only food plan. Putting down the pink can, she regarded me as one might a small, wounded animal. "Your mother," said Alezzie firmly—and, for once, clearly—"is an agent of the patriarchy."

An Agent of the Patriarchy. As suddenly as my destiny in Massachusetts had been revealed, so was my past reinterpreted. My mother's slights—the way she squinted her eyes and curled her lip and said "What *is* it, Molly?" when she looked at my paintings, the tentative way she used her fork to explore my sweet-and-sour tofu, the way she railed against the mess of my room and questioned my fashion sense—were no longer simply one woman's bias, bad mood, or exhaustion. They were part of a patriarchal plot to squelch the female spirit. Just like my mother's revisionist cheerleader theory, and the way she always rubbed her temples and swallowed Bufferin when I sang along with the radio. How could I have missed the prejudice? The baseball chauvinism? The sex-role stereotyping?

"My whole life she made fun of cheerleaders and then she *blamed me* for not being a cheerleader!" I said, and I began to cry. "She blamed me for not marrying a doctor!"

"Oh, for fuck's sake!" said Amazonia. "You could never have made cheerleading. Not with that ass." Amazonia had been the captain of the cheerleading squad at her high school in Jackson, Mississippi.

"Too *much!*" cried Roxanne. "Amazonia! You're too much, already."

But I didn't care: I'd burst from the shackles of a lifelong collusion with the patriarchy, and I was flying far too high to feel hurt by Amazonia's comment. Suddenly I had no regrets about my lack of cheerleading skills, no longings for an attentive boyfriend, no worries about my future career. I was being lifted up, up, up, along with my consciousness. I was weightless, buffeted by a wind that was as loud and strong as the one that raked my hair and rippled my T-shirt when I rode behind Amazonia on her bike. Burdens I'd assumed to be eternal—doing dishes, ironing shirts, and changing diapers—floated from my consciousness like fur from the backs of my family's dogs. I had glimpsed a life that did not include coddling, cooking, or caring for boys— a life that did not, in fact, include any boys at all. It took my breath away.

Several days later, when the plans for the Miss World USA pageant were announced, I had the chance to put my new insights into action. The beauty pageant was scheduled for mid-August. It was to be held at the Springfield Civic Center in Springfield, Massachusetts, and the Northampton women's community was outraged.

"Bunch of patriarchal pets prancing around!" hissed Amazonia, and to demonstrate her disgust, she gathered her shaggy Farrah Fawcett hair into a ponytail, cut it off, and then shaved her head into a fine, military bristle.

"The embodiment of what boys call female," murmured Alezzie. "Designed and executed to make real women feel less-than." But she did not cut her hair.

"What if we make a *real* woman," I said from the lofty heights of my raised consciousness. "We could make an Amazon out of papier-mâché."

My experience of making life-size Santas with my brothers served me well in the design and construction of Wanda, a twelve-foot-tall Wonder Woman. Two women carpenters built the infrastructure from two-by-fours and chicken wire; my support group helped with mixing the wallpaper paste, shredding hundreds of pounds of newspaper, and blowing up balloons to use as various prosthetic devices. Wanda's breasts resembled basketballs, her calves were boulders, and her thighs were the size of a horse's flank—a Clydesdale's, to be exact. After plaster and base coats of paint were applied, artists in the community with tiny sable brushes joined me for hundreds of hours to render each of Wanda's muscle groups anatomically correct.

"Do the hair under her arm," one artist directed another.

"No, use this!" yelled Amazonia, swinging the long, shaggy ponytail that had formerly been attached to her head.

"We could glue it," I said thoughtfully. "It might be nice to have some movement. I mean, if the wind blows."

"Under her arms!" cried Roxanne.

The idea caught on, and before long seven other women had cut off their ponytails and given their hair to Wanda. I'd constructed Wanda on a dolly that was used to move pianos, and as I inspected her in the final hours before she was rolled into the back of a flatbed truck for transport down the Massachusetts Turnpike to Springfield, I suffered some misgiving: these donations lent a hirsute aspect to the goddess-warrior that grossed me out. I'd been proud of the meticulous rendering of her pores and hair follicles, proud of the way the short leather skirt I'd painted beneath her ornate bronze breastplate had flapped to reveal a creamy inner thigh with no need of bikini waxing. But feminism was a consensual process and I had neither the standing nor the self-confidence to object.

"Don't forget her sign," I said. In addition to the bow and quiver that was slung over her shoulder, I'd built Wanda's hands to support two poles that, in turn, would support a billboard.

"Be careful!" I yelled forty minutes later, when I jumped out of the back of the truck at Bradley Airport in West Springfield. I wasn't going to the demonstration. Before my epiphany—before Wanda had even been a twinkle in my eye—I'd planned my vacation. I was going to Ohio for a week with my politically benighted family.

"I'll call tonight!" I yelled, waving to Wanda as Amazonia pulled the truck away. Roxie and Alezzie and all the other women supporting Wanda waved from the flatbed. But Wanda could not. She was, by then, holding her sign, which read, in huge lavender letters: "STOP MISS WORLD I WANT TO GET OFF."

"What the heck is that?" asked my father two nights later, as my mother and I sat watching the evening news.

"Annelise Ilschenko!" said my mother, without dropping a stitch of her knitting. "Miss Ohio won the Miss World pageant. Isn't she darling?"

"No, I mean that thing in the background there," said my dad. "Looks like Colo. Or maybe Paul Bunyan's wife."

"Oh, that's some women's libber stuff," said my mother, glancing down at my unshaven legs. "Not pretty enough to compete so they have to ruin it for everyone else. They drove Sammy Davis, Junior, away. That's right. He was supposed to host the event and he changed his mind and left. Well, Bob Hope and George Hamilton stayed right there, and good for them."

"I don't know about that," said my father. "I'd a run the other way, too, if I'd a come face-to-face with ole Mrs. Bunyan there."

Wanda was our Eve and soon we built our Eden. Shortly after our warrior made the national nightly news, Amazonia, Roxie, Alezzie, and I, along with four other feminists, made a pact to stop reacting against the male-dominated culture and start creating something for women. Our solution was the Ain't I a Wommon Club—a women's restaurant that served nonviolent cuisine.

The club was located in a building on Center Street in Northampton that had previously served as a halfway house for the mentally challenged. We purchased the building, gutted it, and made it into a restaurant. It had an open kitchen, pink walls, tables made out of two-by-fours and pine planks, and a stained-glass window that featured a goddess reigning over a forest primeval. A long length of butcher block separated the kitchen from the dining room, and that is where customers placed their orders and sliced bread from big, heavy multigrain loaves. There were no waitresses at Ain't I a Wommon because waitressing and tipping were considered demeaning to women. The sound system lived in the shelves behind the counter and featured only women's music. The donation can lived on the counter. The club had a sliding-scale menu—one made a donation according to one's means. The club also provided child care (for any boys and girls under the age of two, and women children of any age) and had a sunporch where dogs could stay while their mistresses dined.

The feasibility of Ain't I a Wommon may in part have been testimony to the grace of the Goddess, but it was also undeniably a direct result of the forgiving nature of the food service industry. In 1977, it was still possible to learn how to run a little café by opening one, and that is exactly what we did. Nine of us built and operated the Ain't I a Wommon Club. We made every decision collectively and we considered, debated, and struggled with the political implications of every move that we made.

It began with our name: "If we are saying that we won't serve men, then we can't have the word 'man' in our name," reasoned Roxanne.

"My problem with 'wommon' is the womb implication," mulled Alezzie. "I don't want us to be seen as promoting the tyranny of breeding."

"Barefoot and pregnant," said Sky contemplatively. Sky, whose full name was Blue Sky Mulvaney, had ridden on Ken Kesey's bus. In addition to baking the club's bread and overseeing its group process, Sky was the local feminist therapist. She was fond of quoting Marshall McLuhan. "We look at the present through the rearview mirror," she said, lifting her long blond hair from her face and shaking her head. "We march backwards into the future."

Our debates often continued for days. Granny glasses would fog in the heat of these discussions, voices would be raised, doors would sometimes be slammed. Experts would be consulted—the woman who'd developed a feminist vegetarian theory, the woman who lectured on Marxist food-delivery systems, and, when we were formulating our child-care policy, the woman who had studied aggressiveness in male toddlers were all tapped.

At first I was in awe of my colleagues' erudition as well as their ability to dissect and debate issues. I was eager to do the cooking so that those better qualified might have more time to talk about the cooking.

"Does anyone find it necessary for me to explain the violence and maleness inherent in meat eating?" asked Alezzie rhetorically. No one did. To be free of meat was to be free of murder, males, and mayhem—anyone could see that.

"What about stock?" I asked. "I don't know how to make soup and sauces without a little chicken stock or demi-glace."

"We don't want blood on your hands," said Alezzie protectively.

I was the youngest member of our collective, but I was the only member who had worked in restaurants; I took it as my duty to liberate the group from its lack of experience, and regularly swept into the kitchen like the marines on a rescue mission. For months, I worked to develop a broth that could be used in place of beef stock: roasted mushroom stems and onions simmered together and then thickened slightly with a slurry made of tamari sauce, arrowroot, and roasted and puréed eggplant.

"We could open a Chinese restaurant," marveled Alezzie, when tasting the hot-and-sour soup that I made from this concoction. From the tall pot on the giant Garland stove in the back of our kitchen, she ladled herself a large bowl, sniffing it—"Rox! You've got to try this! It's better than Chinatown!"—and parsing the ingredients that I'd added to the black broth of the soup. Slivers of cured tofu, fresh pickled ginger, and salted chili peppers floated beneath its surface. I also shaved dry Oriental mushrooms and added them, along with minced scallions and a tangle of fresh mung bean sprouts, to each serving.

When Alezzie hunkered into something I'd cooked, I was as thrilled as if the great writer had complimented one of my poems. I continued to write verse and to show these creations, shyly and with great trepidation, to Alezzie. "This sounds like Adrienne Rich," she cautioned one time. "This sounds like Audre Lord," she said another time. "Maybe you should stick closer to your own experience." I began filling my journal with recipes and notes from the kitchen.

"Do you want rice?" I asked, bending close to Alezzie as she settled into her first bowl of hot-and-sour soup.

"Is it brown rice?" she asked suspiciously. Ain't I a Wommon served only fully intact whole grains, preferably brown ones.

"It *looks* brown," said Alezzie doubtfully, "but it doesn't *smell* brown."

"I pan-toasted the rice in sesame oil and then cooked it like risotto," I explained eagerly, "adding the broth little by little. Then I added toasted sesame seeds and dark mushroom soy, but I had to offset that with a speck of rice vinegar."

While the women of the collective debated the use of egg-roll wrappers on the Chinese Evenings that resulted from my hot-and-sour soup—"They're made from white rice," worried Alezzie. "I'm worried about what sort of message that sends"—I figured out how to make a whole-wheat-and-seed crust for the daily quiche. While the morality of white sugar was measured against that of honey, maple syrup, and molasses, I invented a roasted vegetable broth to use in making French onion soup. As my colleagues struggled with the question of what music should be played on our tape deck, I made mushroom bisque.

"We're in agreement that we only play women," said Roxanne, "but what do we do about the male-identified girl bands?"

"It's better to leave them on the tape deck, because you can only take so much Holly Near and *Lavender Jane Loves Women*," said Amazonia, unwrapping one of the cheeseburgers that she'd bought at Friendly's and passing it to Alezzie. Alezzie liked her double cheeseburgers served on toasted English muffins with mayonnaise, lettuce, and tomato, and so the rest of us, giggling at the outrageousness of it—cheeseburgers in the club!—all followed suit.

Amazonia and I both thought that mayonnaise on cheeseburgers was disgusting, but we kept this opinion to ourselves. We were the only members of the collective who had not grown up on the East Coast and gone to Ivy League colleges, and we were best friends. Amazonia said the things that I thought but was too intimidated to voice. Many members of the women's community regarded her with horror—in addition to her motorcycle and black belt, she had begun amassing outlandish tattoos in obvious places—but I was her Boswell and I never failed to laugh at her jokes. Everyone thought we were lovers, but we each had clandestine boyfriends, and we each had unrequited longings; I was enamored of Alezzie, and Amazonia was hot for Roxanne. We were actually a perfect foursome for a while.

"You've got to taste this, Alezzie," I said, carrying a spoonful of soup into the music debate. "Green minestrone with roasted garlic and toasted pine nuts."

"Wanna ride to the bank, Rox?" asked Amazonia. Standing up from the discussion, she crumpled the paper from her cheeseburger into a wad and, supporting her right hand with her left, aimed it at the garbage can. Then she slipped the fat envelope of the day's deposit into the back pocket of her Levi's and strapped on her motorcycle helmet.

"Let's not legislate the music," said Alezzie quietly as Roxy rose to follow Amazonia. "Let's leave it up to whichever woman is working the counter."

As the club became the cultural and social center for the huge feminist community that was clustered on the floor of the Pioneer Valley and scattered throughout the surrounding hills, the donation can filled again and again. We couldn't empty it often enough, couldn't donate the profits to other worthy causes fast enough. The Ain't I a Wommon Club was a hit.

As if fearing that only constant and ever-increasing vigilance could ensure its continued success, our focus became sharper, more finely honed—all but molecular—in our second year of operation. We held the strings to one of the few purses in the women's community, and we held ourselves and one another to ever-more-exacting standards.

"Are you *sure* that you did not put dairy in it?" asked Alezzie when, one winter day about a year and a half after we'd opened, I offered her a bowl of my butternut squash soup.

By this point, after heated debate, the use of dairy products had been banned at the club. A researcher had described to us the process through which female cows are kept in a state of perpetual lactation and the collective had immediately agreed to boycott this cruel practice. Emboldened by my growing acclaim as a cook, however, I had taken exception to the dairy vote, and the points I raised were argued for weeks.

"I don't know how you expect me to make quiche," I had said, "or bisques or soups, really. I mean, what do I use, soy milk instead of cream? And pie crusts with no butter? How am I supposed to make the crust for the honey-yogurt pie—which is, in case you haven't noticed, our top seller? And forget the crust—what am I supposed to fill it with?"

Realizing that eggs could not be far behind milk products, my arguments escalated. "What happens to the customer who comes here expecting honey-yogurt pie and gets served tofu-oat buckle?" I asked. "Some of them drive all the way from Boston and Brattleboro." And: "Is it cost-effective for me to spend hours and hours developing all new recipes every time we change some policy?"

Everyone was surprised by my vehemence. "You really feel strongly about the dairy issue," Alezzie had said one evening after the club had closed and we were cleaning the kitchen. "You can still have dairy, just not in the club," she said appeasingly, as we each grasped a handle and lifted a fifty-gallon stockpot off the stove.

"That's not the point," I said curtly.

"No?" Alezzie asked, widening her eyes and smiling up at me as a mother might at an obstreperous adolescent.

"The point is taking responsibility," I said. "We are human. We are omnivores. We have breasts, we do not have udders. We have a business, not a toy. At least some of us do. Some of us have to make a living, OK? And that means making the work we do count and add up to something. It means not being some Wanda-Sisyphus, rolling the rock, rolling the rock, and then, whoops, we gotta start all over again because the patriarchy owns the peanut industry or because sprouts are part of the male military-industrial complex!"

"Wow," said Alezzie.

After the identification with aching udders prevailed, I resolutely if grimly searched for alternatives to dairy. I developed techniques for purée-ing, frothing, and stabilizing tofu cheeses and using them instead of cream in some of my soups. In the months that I'd fine-tuned the butternut squash soup, I regularly regaled the women of the collective with the technical and aesthetic challenges I faced.

"Soy milk and cheese is like custard. If you heat it too fast or too long it will separate, so you have to heat it gently and slowly, which is a big hassle. Then you have to find a way to disguise that sort of tofu-y flavor.

"Since we can't use sugar, I first roasted the butternut squash. This caused it to caramelize, but once you've brought out all the sweetness you need a counterpoint," I continued. "I put the squash through the food mill along with vegetable stock. I used fresh rosemary but it was still like, I don't know, Thanksgiving, OK? Like a patriarchal holiday. And so I added minced-up orange peel and black pepper and some roasted poblano. And that did it!"

"Mazel tov," Roxie said absentmindedly.

"Only puny secrets need protection," Sky said, quoting her personal philosopher. "Big discoveries are protected by public incredulity."

Alezzie was not impressed by food science and she was not reassured. "Are you absolutely positive that you didn't put in any dairy?" she asked again.

Several months later, I was riding behind Amazonia on her Harley and we were zooming down Route 6 on Cape Cod. We were moving to Provincetown. Amazonia had broken up with Roxie and taken up with Sky. Sky had driven ahead in a U-Haul. Rebecca, the collective's bookkeeper, was also moving to Provincetown. She was ahead of us, in her Saab 96, our four Motobecane bicycles precariously mounted on the sloped back of her car.

"Put your arms under my jacket," screamed Amazonia. "The leather gets slippery. I don't want you to fall off." I was scared of motorcycles—especially when the driver had downed several pints of Guinness. I squeezed Amazonia's waist, closed my eyes, and in the terrifying four-hour trip heard nothing but the sound of my own heart as I felt my future rushing toward me.

My decision to leave Northampton was abrupt and occurred several days after Alezzie detailed her plans for the revolution. "If every woman killed one man in one night, that would be the revolution," she said. "I could kill two, because I have a car."

Like most feminists in the Pioneer Valley, I had a Saab 96 and I tried to imagine aiming it at any two of my brothers and pressing the gas. I thought of the pictures that Paul regularly sent me from Columbus.

"Tonka kicks the back door and Dad feeds him oatmeal," my youngest brother lettered across the top of one picture, of the mean little pony standing on the back porch. "Come home!"

"Pat says my fastball is deadly and so does Dad," Paul printed on a drawing of a pitcher. "P.S. Come home soon!" scrawled Robert.

"Don't tell Mom," Paul wrote across the top of a portrait of Pat's baby blue Luv Mobile, stuffed with boys and smoke. "You better come back!"

I was not, I realized, cut out for vehicular homicide. And neither were my fellow feminists.

Decades would pass before I understood that none of the members of our collective was who we'd appeared to be, before I understood how we'd shaped one another and made one another possible, before I got over being embarrassed for all of us and began to grasp the enormity of our good fortune. Back then, I didn't know that I'd found my voice in Northampton; I thought instead that I was leaving to look for it. Flying blind toward Provincetown, all I felt was free.

"Fuck feminism!" Amazonia hollered into the wind.

"Screw soy milk!" I screamed back.

An Encyclopedia of Seafood Cookery

The kitchen of Ciro & Sal's, an Italian eatery in Provincetown, bore little resemblance to the vegetarian convent in which I embarked on my career in the food service industry. Ciro & Sal's did not operate on a consensual model. It was a totalitarian state and the chef, Gunnar Erikson, was its reigning despot. When he began a sentence with "Fire!" the four cooks would freeze, tongs in one hand, cocktail or Marlboro in the other, waiting for the order that inevitably followed. Blue-collar workers with jailhouse biceps, they were the sort of man my mother had married, the sort of man she was terrified her sons might become. Certainly, they had a lot of bad habits, and I immediately started worrying about my new colleagues' well-being. In fact, soon after I signed on as the restaurant's salad girl, I proposed the one-cigarette-at-a-time convention be adopted by the kitchen corps.

"Only one person can smoke at a time," I explained. "It worked at Ain't I a Wommon, and the feminists smoke even more than you guys!"

My suggestion was met with the same disbelieving stare that had greeted me when I first clomped down the basement stairs to report for work early in April. I was, by then, twenty-five years old, buff, buxom, and bra-free. I had more hair on my legs than I did on my head, and I was wearing baby blue satin basketball shorts, a shirt with spaghetti straps and a rainbow across the front, red-framed Annie Hall glasses, and a pair of clogs.

"Fire one veal Parmesan, two *sole simplice,* and a side of balls," the chef had shouted in the silence that followed my entrance, adding for clarification, "meatballs in red sauce." He ended the stillness that followed my smoking proposal in a similar way: "Fire two saltimbocca, a veal picatta, three lasagna, one carbonara."

Like a general directing an execution squad, the chef used the word "Fire!" to activate the four men who worked the kitchen's twenty-five-foot line of stoves and broilers. From 5:30 p.m. until past midnight, six nights a week, he cooked alongside them; his orders rang out above the clatter of pots, the crash of dishes, the sizzle of the Frialator, the cursing of the cooks, and the sound of the Red Sox game on the radio that blasted on the shelf above the twelve-burner sauté stove.

"Fire one bass no sauce, two pesto, one carbonara, two marsala!" Chef Gun called to the cooks.

To the waiters, on the other hand, the chef said, "Go!"

"Go!" he would hiss through the stacks of plates and the clothesline of little yellow tickets that separated him from the dining room staff.

"Go, you little faggot twat," he sneered as the waiters loaded their big oval trays. "If that food comes back here cold I'll take this knife and carve you a new asshole," he promised. "Go!"

Gun, whose name was pronounced "goon," began most of the orders he gave me the same way. "Go," he'd say, jerking his head toward me in the salad station. "Not you," he'd bark at the waiters. *"Her."* Walking around the corner from his post he'd snap his tongs at the opal studs that now lined my right earlobe.

"Go grate that wheel of Parmesan," he'd say. I knew that the cooks used an attachment to the Hobart mixer to grate cheese. "Do it by hand," the chef would add.

He refused to say my name at first, and when he referred to me he curled his lip in a manner that reminded me of my brother Mike.

"Go make marinades," he'd say when there was a lull in service and the cooks ran upstairs to replenish their cocktails or snort a line of coke or meth.

Or, if he spotted me wielding chopsticks over my dinner of tofu and seaweed, "Go learn how to cut a leg of veal."

Gunnar had been ruling the kitchen for over a decade when, without consulting him, the restaurant's founder and owner hired me. Hiring a woman probably wouldn't have occurred to Gunnar, and if it had, he certainly wouldn't have selected a feminist vegetarian. The chef, who was tall and craggy and bitter enough for a Bergman movie, hired men like himself, men who fished and hunted and drank a lot, men who wore boots with steel-reinforced toes, men too ungovernable to work corporate jobs, men full of pathos, unrealized ambition, and rage—just the sort of men I'd spent my feminist years objecting to. In other words, for me, going to work at Ciro & Sal's was sort of like going home.

I understood my colleagues and believed myself superior to them. They were carnivores and drunks; I was, at the time, a model of moderation and a health-food devotee. They'd barely graduated from high school and would probably be cooks forever. I was an artist and a writer, and I was just passing through—headed, I thought, back to the mainstream from the radical fringe and destined for something greater.

In 1977, few college graduates worked in kitchens for minimum wage, and those who did were generally unprepared for the factory aspects of food production and the physical demands of the job. I was an athlete and an O'Neill, and I'd begun working at the Hospitality Motor Inn when I was fifteen years old. I understood the importance of readiness, and I responded to any challenge with a blind will to win.

Within days of my arrival, I was determined to move from the salad station to the line of stoves where the food was cooked. I'd sworn to myself, as well as to Amazonia, Sky, and Rebecca, that I would become a keeper of the flame. The first woman to man the broiler and Frialator, to mind the pasta pots, to effortlessly flip and flame shingles of veal in the sauté pans at Ciro & Sal's restaurant. My resolve had emerged much as my youngest brother's determination to beat Robert in games of one-on-one basketball: in response to humiliation.

"Go bleach down the trash area," said Gun. "Get down on your hands and knees."

"Go," he'd say, nodding to one of the gigantic stockpots in which ten gallons of marinara sauce simmered on the stove. Two cooks routinely lifted these pots; each would grasp a handle with both his hands, and the muscles in their arms would flinch and flair. "Flex your stuff," Gun would jeer. And flex it I did.

From my first day as salad girl, I had six five-gallon plastic buckets of lettuce cleaned and twelve gallons of vinaigrette on hand at all times. I also had a gallon of each of the marinated vegetables—mushrooms in lemon, parsley, and oil; artichokes in olive oil with sliced garlic and black pepper; and a vegetable medley of carrots and cauliflower and peppers in a vinaigrette—waiting to be spooned into a cup of iceberg lettuce and served. Cantaloupes were cleaned and at least a hundred wafers of proscuitto were laid neatly on parchment paper, ready to be draped over fanned slices of melon. Every day I made two pint-size containers of the pesto sauce needed to prepare oysters Gianinni, as well as a quart of the bread crumbs that were sprinkled on top of the oysters before I passed them to Gunnar to be broiled. I was, in other words, always prepared to serve far more food than I'd ever be asked for on those spring evenings. I could afford to greet each rush with a song.

If the cooks noted my readiness, speed, and efficiency, the waiters complimented my presentation and humor. My colleagues tended to summon a waiter the same way Gun did. I summoned the same waiter to the tune of "Johnny Angel": "How I love you," I sang, "how I'd love for you to come pick up." The chef was not amused.

"Wait till Memorial Day," Gun would say ominously.

Before my arrival, Gun had always assigned two strapping dishwashers to carry cases of supplies up the stairs to the storeroom. Now he directed me to perform the task alone. "Go," he'd say, nodding toward twenty cases of canned tomatoes. Each case weighed approximately fifty pounds, and when I finished the job and returned, flushed and sweating, to the kitchen, the chef said, "I order twice that many for Memorial Day."

I began to lift weights at the community center every morning. My coach also trained Marvin Hagler, so I worked out with the boxer and started to learn the difference between brute force and its strategic application. Soon my colleagues were bringing me stubborn jars to open. It was not, however, until Memorial Day weekend that I applied this lesson to oysters.

I'd been told that it was not uncommon to serve five hundred guests on the weekends during the high season that began on Memorial Day weekend and ran through Labor Day. By mid-May, the only question I had about my ability to meet this volume was oysters. I couldn't open them. Oysters, I believed, were all that stood between me and the inner sanctum of the kitchen.

At the Hospitality Motor Inn in Columbus, Ohio, oysters had come in a can. Serving them had been a matter of plucking the slimy blob of gray meat from the oyster juice and positioning it in the center of a porcelain shell. In Provincetown, oysters came in a shell and, lo! though I went to the kitchen and, without punching the time clock, practiced opening oysters every morning for a month, I'd developed neither speed nor finesse. Serious shuckers can open 250 oysters an hour. It took me ten minutes to open the six oysters that were required to fill an order at Ciro & Sals.

When a waiter shouted an order, I would wrap one of the rocky-shelled creatures inside several layers of towel and, leaning on the center of the shell with the palm of my left hand, I would grasp a small, thick-bladed knife in my right hand and begin ravaging the narrow back end of the oyster. One of the cooks had recommended this technique—"Think of it as foreplay," he'd advised, "rub her tits, rock her, and stick it to her"—and I'd assumed that this technique was designed to supply the best leverage for boring down and brutalizing the bivalve. My colleagues could pop open an oyster in less time than it took me to swaddle one in protective layers of towel. My self-taught, shell-shattering technique left much to be desired.

"Picking up?" the waiter would ask, glancing nervously at the hot appetizers that were cooling as he waited for the oysters needed to complete his order. In my panic, I dug deeper and pushed the knife harder. Shell crumbled and the blunt tip of the oyster knife sank into the mound of flesh beneath my left thumb. "Oh, Christ," the waiters would say as my blood spurted over the shellfish.

As Memorial Day neared, I doubled my early-morning practice sessions. My left forearm ached from the hours of push-ups it performed on top of the oyster shells. A new set of sinewy muscles appeared above my right wrist and a significant collection of white, crescent-shaped scars accumulated on the heel of my left hand. The increase in my shucking speed was negligible and complaints of shell shards continued to issue from the dining room.

"Wait till Memorial Day," yelled the chef.

"Fie, thix, theven hundrwed weservations," leered James A. Madison, who worked the broiler, ovens, and Frialator alongside Chef Gun. James A. Madison was an African-American teamster from Memphis who had a speech defect, anger management issues, and the ability to broil fish perfectly.

"Oh, you'll be popping bushels of oysters, dah-lin," said Petey Boy Costa. The son of a Portuguese fisherman, Petey Boy suffered seasickness and worked the pasta section. For nearly a decade, he'd minded pots of salted boiling water and pursued the al dente state of noodles just as his forebears, presumably, had chased the great white whale.

"Go, you Red Sox!" roared Alex. Alex's parents had immigrated from Russia when Alex was an infant. I was told that he spoke four languages, but for the first month I knew him I never heard Alex say anything other than those four words.

"Go, you Red Sox!" he bellowed at regular though unpredictable intervals throughout the evening. He would stop cooking and lean toward his radio. Then, pointing his right finger up to the exhaust, Alex howled like an Old Testament character railing against his God. No one could work until he finished. Following a moment of absolute silence, each cook would drain his own glass of cranberry juice and vodka and go back to work.

"Go on two lasagna, drop the zucchini, TWO GIANINNI!" Gun would say. The chef wanted every serving of oysters opened to order, but I quickly learned to open a dozen or so ahead of time.

"Memorial Day," he would say to me when I instantly passed him two impeccably prepared orders of pesto-topped oysters for broiling. I knew that drastic action was called for.

At five a.m. on the Friday of Memorial Day weekend, I went to the kitchen and began opening oysters. There were two bushel containers in the walk-in cooler. For the next four hours, I stood in the cool, dark kitchen and jabbed and shattered the eight hundred or so individual Wellfleet oysters they contained. I then replaced the top shell on each, arranged them on baking trays, wrapped them in plastic, and concealed them among the trays of minced parsley and breaded zucchini and cut veal on a rack in the walk-in cooler.

At three p.m., when I returned to the kitchen to set up for the evening, I discovered that another bushel of oysters had been delivered and was waiting in the walk-in. Grimly, I pulled the sack to a counter around the corner from the cooks and, as everyone else prepared for the evening, I shattered another four hundred oysters. Shortly after I'd stored this batch on the rack in the walk-in, I noticed Gun storm out of the cooler and, the muscles in his jaw twitching, rush to the telephone. An hour later, in the quiet between the first and second rush, a fisherman dragged two more burlap bags of oysters down the stairs into the kitchen.

It was war! Throughout the evening I filled orders at my counter and then rushed around the corner to shatter a few more oysters. Back and forth I trotted. Faster and faster I jabbed. Weaker and weaker my forearm became. The number of orders I'd actually served—four or five—failed to mitigate my frenzy to pass the oyster test.

By the third rush, at nine-thirty, I was ankle-deep in oyster shells and working my way through a fourth bushel. I had more than two hundred orders of oysters on hand. Still I hacked with hatred in my heart, determined to shut out the clatter and crash of the kitchen, where, on Friday of the holiday weekend, both the volume of business and the rate of vodka consumption had more than doubled.

It was a hot night. I'd sweated through my T-shirt and basketball shorts. Little bits of oyster shell spackled my Annie Hall glasses. A stream of oyster liquor and my own blood *drip-drip-dripped* from the aluminum counter and onto my clogs. I licked the salty sweat from my upper lip and gritted my teeth.

"Memorial Day." My physical force dwindled. My resolve increased. And in this confluence, I suddenly—and without even realizing it—began to open oysters deftly, painlessly, and without shattering the shells. The tip of my knife found the sweet spot that controlled the hinge and released the oyster's own vacuum seal. It was as easy as unlocking a door, and my hand suddenly knew the precise flourish required to loosen the meat from the top shell while leaving it perfectly intact. *Click, click.* From one oyster to another, my shucking time went from two minutes to under twenty seconds. *Click, click, click.*

By the time the last order was sent from the kitchen that evening I'd served 6 orders of oysters and had 244 orders on hand.

"Will it be busier tomorrow?" I asked the chef, brushing aside the cooks' offers to help and heaving the stockpots effortlessly off the stove.

"Just you wait," he growled.

The next day, a new bushel of oysters awaited my knife when I arrived to set up my station at three p.m. I opened them all in under an hour, and, having run out of storage space in the walk-in, I secreted trays of opened oysters behind the trays of *coeur à la crème* and cassata in the dessert refrigerator and iced them in bus tubs that I stored in the trash area.

"Is Sunday the big oyster night?" I asked when Saturday's five hundred meals included only fourteen orders of oysters.

It was past midnight. The rims around the chef's eyes were as red as the cranberry juice he'd been drinking for eight hours and his breath was 100 percent Stolichnaya as he rocked over me, scowling. And suddenly I realized that he had no idea how many opened oysters were stashed in his walk-in and his reach-ins, or hidden in bus tubs full of ice outside the back door. Throughout the weekend, when the chef had failed to find a bag of oysters in the walk-in, he'd simply panicked and ordered more. I also understood that my brother Robert had been right: victory can be a letdown.

Years later, when I was a restaurant critic and Alex was finishing graduate school at Columbia University, he told me that Gun had called all the cooks into the walk-in that night. They'd voted me onto the line and had agreed to a moratorium on words such as "cunt" and "twat."

"This is your uniform," said Gun, handing me two pairs of folded white pants and two white jackets when he informed me of my promotion and ten-cents-an-hour raise.

"You are going to have to eat meat, too," he added. "Now go figure out what the fuck to do with all those oysters you opened."

Within weeks of our arrival in Provincetown, Amazonia, Sky, Rebecca, and I had discarded our Susan B. Anthony posters. Without consulting one another, we all traded in our four-poster bedsteads and vintage quilts for futons and duvets, and hung dragon kites from the ceilings. Each of us had acquired secret new lovers and had additional holes punched in our ears. The transition from being feminists in a patriarchy to being locals in a tourist town couldn't have been easier if Betty Friedan herself had been the president of the Provincetown Board of Selectmen.

The stiff, white-tipped waves of winter had just begun to relax in the bay. Like bees stirring in a hive, the sound of saws and hammers buzzed along the tip of Cape Cod as loose shutters and roof tiles were replaced, cheap walls were erected to form rental units, and new signs were hung above storefronts. The sense of baiting and waiting was as palpable along Commercial Street as it was in the waters off Herring Cove, where lobstermen were beginning to set their traps. We immediately aligned ourselves with those who'd weathered the dark days and cold winds of winter, those who'd spent the last six months collecting unemployment and working off the books. Within weeks we had joined the ranks of the three thousand locals who sustained the onslaught of thirty thousand tourists and seasonal residents every summer.

Possession of a year-round rental, a ten-speed racing bike, a post office box, and a taste for linguica sausage more or less guaranteed admittance to the town's exclusive, almost-local club. And Blue Sky Mulvaney was quick to assert our entitlement to the townie discount. The white paint was not even dry on our walls when Sky began demanding the insider price on vintage pleated linen trousers from Uptown Strutters Ball and blousy camp shirts from Jimmy Whalen, not to mention the henna and streaking services from Wave's hair salon. Before I'd mastered the art of oysters, the four of us had acquired the androgynous glamour of longtime residents, and we wore our white, flowing garments lightly. We did not flinch when confronted with women who chose their lovers for erotic rather than political purposes. We did not gawk at the man dressed like Alice in Wonderland, or the one who looked like the original Barbie doll, or the one wearing the hair curlers, furry mules, and housecoat of a 1950s housewife.

"Camp is popular because it gives people a sense of reality to see a replay of their lives," said Sky knowingly. In addition to feminist sex therapy, Sky had recently announced that she was also qualified to treat drag queens.

"Hmmmph," said Amazonia, who was working as a bartender and teaching karate. She was not pleased by the parade of Marilyn Monroes, Eleanor Roosevelts, and Garbos who now teetered through the apartment that she shared with Sky.

Removed from Northampton, flashes of doubt now glittered among us like the lights across the harbor. We wondered if Sky's therapeutic training extended beyond McLuhanisms and whispered that Amazonia might need Alcoholics Anonymous. Rebecca had taken a job as a bookkeeper; her full-frontal embrace of capitalism was cause for concern. My voracious disregard for the precepts of nonviolent cuisine, along with my interest in somebody else's husband, also gave pause. Still, we maintained a united front when Sky demanded the townie discount and bemoaned the onslaught of summer. By mid-June, Commercial Street was a permanent traffic jam, the wait for driers at the Laundromat interminable, and the risk for being busted for nude sunbathing, even on isolated patches of beach, had exponentially increased.

"Labor Day," said Amazonia, echoing the hope of all good townies.

"Tomorrow," said Sky sagely, "is our permanent address."

But I gave more than lip service to achieving insider status in Provincetown. After my trial by oyster, I gave myself to seafood.

Like most people who grew up landlocked in America during the 1950s, I was deeply suspicious of any piece of fish that was not rectangular, boned, breaded, and deep-fried. Unlike most Midwesterners, however, I'd spent my toddler years confiding in a mermaid named Karen, and the briny, fishy smell of my new hometown moved me. In the fog before dawn, I pedaled my racing bike down the pier to watch the day boats, the scallopers, and the draggers leave the harbor. Whenever I could, I also rode back for their return, an empty pail swinging from my handlebars.

The fishermen gave away "trash fish"—the monkfish, goosefish, and dogfish, the eel and squid, the tinkers and herring and occasional "cull," or one-clawed lobster, that they couldn't sell. I had no idea what to do with any of it. In my kitchen in the west end, the writhing contents of the pail made me gag. Determined to be a local, I resolutely studied A. J. McClane's *Field Guide to Saltwater Fishes of North America* and his *Encyclopedia of Fish Cookery*. I spent hours imagining recipes that would conceal the flavor of the often hideous, slimy, and flopping fish I was given.

I shared the basic misconception of many young would-be Escoffiers. I thought cooks were conquistadors: I thought that my mission was to triumph over my ingredients. My coworkers, however, did not share this vision of our vocation. They didn't lie in bed at night imagining what an ingredient could become; they just tried to cook their dishes fast and well and to do no harm. Alex appointed himself my teacher, countering each of my gourmet innovations with lessons in the anatomy of seafood and drills in the simplest cooking technique appropriate for any given species.

When, for instance, I presented my colleagues with fluke poached in tomato sauce with anchovy and olives and enough garlic to frighten a vampire, Alex countered, "I can't taste the fish." He used his fork to unravel the tomato skin that I'd formed into a rose garnish, and said, "Let me show you how to clean a sea urchin."

"What do you think?" I asked when, after weeks of reading and recipe development, I served him gray sole fillets stuffed with shrimp and crabmeat and blanketed with a champagne cream sauce.

"Shrimp are not local," he said. "Have you ever had bone squid? The size of a thumb, so tender, too good for customers. Let me show you how to fry them, *fritto misto*."

In the face of flounder in dill cream sauce on a bed of cucumbers, Alex offered a lesson in sautéing scallops with roe. My flounder with Nantua sauce brought a lesson in steaming clams the size of a quarter, and my flounder Florentine with spinach and béchamel earned me a lesson in deep-frying whitebait and serving it—to cooks only—with homemade tartar sauce.

"Too good for customers," said James A. Madison, dipping a tiny fried fish into the pickle-spiked mayonnaise.

"Did you use olive oil in the tartar sauce?" asked Petey Boy approvingly.

One night, Alex decided to teach me how to make a perfect pan-fried sole and, for the duration of the Red Sox pregame show, we made sole à la meunière again and again. I learned to season milk lightly with a fleck of Tabasco sauce, to soak the flounder fillets for two minutes, to season flour with salt and pepper, to dust the fish with the flour and to shake it off. I learned the sight and sound and smell of the moment when a slick of butter is hot enough to seal the fish, and the sound and smell of the instant the fillet needs to be turned over. The staff ate well that night.

"Do it with your eyes closed," said Alex, and then, handing me tiny wads of paper towel, "OK, now put these in your ears, close your eyes, and do it again."

I obeyed. "Out, out, out," he cried less than a minute after I flipped the fish. "Get it out of the pan! Now hit the pan with lemon, OK. A chunk of fresh butter. No! Not on the fish, not yet. Now the secret! Open your eyes," he said, and when I did, I saw that his fingers were poised twelve inches above the fish fillets. He released a delicate rain of sea salt.

"It brings the flavor of the fish and the flavor of the sauce together in the mouth," he said. "Call the waiter before you put the fillet in the pan. Hold the salt and the sauce until he's standing in front of you. OK. Now you do it again. Close your eyes."

As I learned from my colleagues to cook by my senses, I also absorbed their antipathy for the clientele. These attitudes and habits seeped into my pores and lived in my body, just beneath my rational mind: I began preferring the company of cooks. After all, customers were the other—the tourists, the day-trippers, the Philistines, the rubes. Cooks were us. We worked harder and we knew more. We had substance and we had moral fiber. This lesson was brought home to me on the night of the full moon in June, when the striped bass were running.

As the moon waxed, the bass had begun to run, and commercial and sport fishermen alike brought their catch to the restaurant. The fishermen wore shorts and tall black boots and they bargained with Chef Gun for cash, drinks, and dinner. Using shiny metal hooks, they lugged their fish in heavy wooden boxes behind them. Sometimes they were iced; more often, the creatures were still flopping and writhing. One or two would regularly escape the boxes, which were deposited in the trash area outside the kitchen door.

During lulls in the kitchen, Gun would send me out to clean and steak the fish. He wanted enough bass in the freezer to last the entire summer. I still had the lowest rank in the kitchen and, having mastered flatfish, I was ready to learn about the oily species. The lesson was hideous. But rather than blame the chef, I blamed the patrons for my assignment. If there weren't so many of them, after all, I wouldn't have to clean so many fish.

"Customers," I huffed as I arranged two garbage cans four feet apart and heaved a length of butcher block between them to form a counter.

"Customers," I groused as I reached into the gills of one of the bass and heaved the huge fish onto this counter.

I stared at the big, beautiful fish and the fish stared back at me. I memorized its head, the shape and size of it, and its relationship to the butcher block counter. Then, grasping the wooden handle of the cleaver with both hands, I raised it above my head and slammed it into the sloping indentation between the fish's skull and the first vertebra of the spine. Its glistening blade whistled in the cleaver's terrible descent. I made a noise that was part scream and part grunt. I sounded like Amazonia teaching karate.

"*Ay!*" I gasped.

I blamed the customers for making me murder the fish and I blamed them, too, when my aim was imperfect. When I hit the right spot, the cleaver met the table with a dead and final thunk. If I missed the mark, there was a slushy, splintery sound followed by a splatter of fish blood across my white apron. The fish's body jumped a little and then flattened against the wooden plank. I used the back side of the cleaver to push the fish's head into the five-gallon bucket that I'd placed near one end of the execution table.

I then exchanged the heavy cleaver for a fillet knife to gut the fish and cut out the fins after removing the head and tail. Then, taking an aluminum scraper, I scraped the scales from the bodies. The bass ranged in weight from five to thirty pounds and were, at this point, sometimes still moving.

After scaling the fish, I used the tip of a chef's knife to locate the sweet spot between each vertebra then, using a rubber mallet, I cut the body into a series of steaks. There were nearly a hundred steaks that night. Later I would wrap each in plastic and freeze it. Later still, the bass steaks would be thawed, marinated in Italian vinaigrette, broiled, and served with a lemon crown.

"Their fish is always soooo fresh!" I could hear one customer tell another as a group of them crunched the shells in the alleyway that ran past the trash area and led to the restaurant's front door.

How stupid they were! Naugahyde palates! Beneath the stockade fence that shielded them from my murderous activities in the trash area, I could see the tiny rounded toes of their Pappagallo shoes, the errant ties of their Top-Siders. I was close enough to smell the balsam from their shampoo, while my own hair was caked with fish blood and scales. But at least my coworkers and I could tell the difference between fresh and frozen.

We knew the sweet, briny flavor of a fish that had still been alive when a serving was cut from its frame. We knew the faintly acrid flavor of fish that had died after writhing frantically on dry ground before being butchered. Our tongues could tell what a fish had fed on, whether it was male or female, and whether it was young and lean, or older, fatter, and spent. We knew good from bad. We knew everything. We had taste.

After the first rush, the cooks joined me in the killing area to smoke. "So fresh," said Alex with the sort of reverence he normally reserved for his Red Sox. Taking my fillet knife, he cut bites from the center of the bass on my counter. He balanced the small triangle of meat on the tip of his knife and squeezed a single drop of lemon on it. Standing around the execution table, my colleagues and I watched silently as the flesh winced under this acid. Closing our eyes and opening our mouths, one by one we each accepted the tip of the knife. The cold weight of it against our tongues was metallic. The still-warm flesh was sweet and faintly briny. It quivered and winced in my mouth.

Seafood was my tabula rasa, the medium on which I honed basic cooking techniques, the food that taught me about the symmetry between the nature of the ingredient and the feel of the day. The bass, I soon learned, were followed by the bluefish that swam in their wake, mouths wide open, eating indiscriminately, which made their oily flesh taste disturbingly unpredictable, fish to fish. A brutally quick cooking and an acidic accompaniment—mustard, lemon, vinegar, or tomato—was the answer. These bold dishes were also an antidote to the swath of rainy days that often followed these fish. The swordfish of July was a different lesson, a simpler fish. Cut into steaks, the fish was as firm as the pectorals of the young men who danced bare-chested to Gloria Gaynor late at night, their T-shirts bobbing from their back pockets like tails. The fish steaks needed a dose of olive oil or compound butter and a quick turn on the grill. Likewise, the tuna of August wanted nothing more than a fast, hot romp.

It made sense that the mackerel came when the tourists left and life turned inward. Mackerel was harder to handle than the big, easy boys of summer. It needed more fussing—a slow, cool smoke, for instance, a light pickle, or, like the cod and other fish that appeared in the fall, a pungent poaching, a simmer or slow bake. I walked the breakwater and picked mussels in September. I played God, experimenting to see which aromatic improved and which detracted, honing my timing as I steamed the mollusks to capture the moment between a juicy life and a dry, tough death.

In October, there was a scallop bonanza on George's Banks. I got scallops in forty-pound muslin sacks and cooked them until they were gone. After a year, I could pick up a piece of seafood and know whether it wanted to be cooked fast or slow, if it wanted liquid or oil or to be cooked dry. The taste of my fingers after touching its flesh told me whether to underscore its richness, it herbaciousness, its sweetness or its brine, and how to offset these flavors. One can build a life around knowing one thing well.

By my second summer on Cape Cod, no one would have suspected that I grew up in the test-market capital of America. Then my brothers moved to town.

The Rescuers

"Can you get me a job?" Robert asked. He'd arrived, unannounced, after his freshman year of college. It was June of 1978.

We were sitting at the wooden spool that served as the dining table on the cloistered brick mews outside my apartment. I had moved out of my rented room and now lived in the street-side portion of an old wharf that was tucked behind a rose-covered white picket fence. Wet-headed and well-pressed vacationers strolled past us on their way to dinner, fresh from their after-beach showers. Often they walked hand in hand—men and women, men and men, women and women. Some minced, others jogged, still others shrieked and shared joints. The smell of pot and the coconut scent of after-sun lotion joined the rosy, briny perfume that drifted onto my patio.

"This place is loose," said Robert, inhaling. "Can I stay with you?"

Divine, the male actor who played beehive-sporting women in John Waters's films, lived behind my apartment in the bay-side portion of the wharf house. In a local bar, on most evenings, he and his entourage were working on the piece that would become the movie *Polyester*. When they were not rehearsing, they joined the painters and writers and cooks who hung around my outdoor kitchen on my night off.

"Are we dining before my curtain call, Julia?" called the star from his bathroom window, where, at five p.m., he was in the process of becoming a she.

"Ten minutes!" I called back.

I'd pounded almonds, stale bread, garlic, and olive oil together and added tomatoes, cucumbers, and chilies to make gazpacho. I'd also wrapped corn, clams, lobster, chorizo, and potatoes in twelve individual foil packets and buried them in the coals of my hibachi. Robert was mincing bell peppers to add to the cold soup. Above us, like a very large link of linguica stuffed into a hot-pink tube dress, Divine appeared in the bathroom window. Her platinum wig secure, she was now fine-tuning the immense quantity of adipose tissue that she'd shaped into two huge breasts.

"Is this your brother?" she shouted, lifting and jiggling the flesh to realign her cleavage.

"Jayzzz," said Robert.

At seventeen years old, Robert was tall and thin and moved like an Afghan hound. He looked pensively out at the world through long, light brown bangs and had a habit of flinching at unexpected noises. It was easy to feel protective of Robert, except on the tennis court, when he pushed his hair back with a yellow bandanna and displayed neither hesitation nor mercy. By the time he was sixteen years old, he'd opted not to go pro, deciding instead to become a poet. Robert was drawn to the Hemingway potential of Provincetown. Hitchhiking down the Cape, he'd felt an immediate affinity for this stretch of land, a fragile arm of sand curving into the Atlantic. He'd also sensed the abandon that comes from having gone as far as possible.

"Goodbye, Columbus," he'd said that afternoon, when we'd been sitting on the beach and some topless girls had called him to join their Frisbee game.

"I guess this isn't Ohio," he muttered, sotto voce, when boys in muscle shirts beckoned him toward the dunes behind the beach.

The bikers who subsequently flirted with Robert, the woman whose old Huffy bicycle was festooned with plastic poinsettia, the aging hippie who looked like Walt Whitman and recited a sonnet to us—they all elicited the same sort of refrain from my brother. He sounded a little like Dorothy after she landed in Oz. I was eager to lend him my ruby slippers, and began his cooking lessons that very evening.

"Slice the pepper into a small julienne," I said after we'd returned to my apartment to prepare dinner. I showed him how to hold a chef's knife in his right hand, how to use the bent knuckles of his left hand to guide it. Then, leaning into a fistful of bell pepper strips, I demonstrated the rocking motion—the light, tip-to-shank seesaw of the knife—that, with enough practice, yields perfectly uniform squares.

"Every cooking technique was invented for safety, speed, and symmetry," I informed my brother. "It's like hitting tennis balls. You do it until you don't have to think about it, until it is automatic and absolutely consistent, until you can write stanzas in your mind while you are chopping," I said.

Looking up from his cutting board, Robert regarded me through his curtain of stringy hair. "That's loose," he said, casting his eyes back down to the red pepper beneath his chef's knife. Eager to prove his mettle as a houseguest, Robert was also—like any O'Neill—easily animated by the spirit of competition.

A half hour later, when Divine teetered across the bricks to join us at the table, Robert was still cutting thin strips of bell pepper into minuscule squares. He was so intent that he did not even look up when two more friends strolled in, followed by three others who hopped off their bicycles to join us for dinner. I set pottery plates on the table, poured slushy margaritas into glasses, and unleashed a cascade of spiced tomato ice cubes into the tureen of cold soup. Still, Robert's attention did not waver. Using tongs, I pulled the steaming foil packets containing individual clambakes from the coals and piled them on a platter in the middle of the table. Even as dinner was being served, Robert remained on task.

"She just pulled into town and she's already mincing," said Divine, watching the quick rise and fall of my brother's knife. "It must be genetic— look at that girl go!"

When he was two or three years old, Pat established the theme song for one of the ways that my brothers and I express our love for one another. Instead of a tricycle, Pat had a red fire truck. In bad weather, when we could not play outside, he would pedal it furiously around the basement, bellowing the song from the Mighty Mouse cartoon.

"*Here I come to save the day!*" Pat would yell, careening around the jack poles, the furnace, and the hot-water tank, ringing the bell on his truck against the tedium of a rainy afternoon.

We've always tried to save one another—from mean teachers, bad lovers, and oncoming traffic. But we've also always tried to save ourselves from being embarrassed by one another. The urge flares up like weather, imperious and impossible not to heed. I'd been seized by the mania to save Robert from being ordinary before he'd even unpacked his knapsack in my Provincetown apartment. I had also immediately recognized that if I didn't remake my sibling in my own new-and-improved gourmet image, he might reveal that I myself had once, in Columbus, ordered steak tartare, medium-rare.

"Use the back of the knife to scoop the peppers into the tureen," I murmured discreetly as I ladled the gazpacho into bowls. I leaned in close to him, admiring his work and sniffing the Cheer laundry detergent, our mother's brand, that lingered in the collar of his polo shirt. "You'll hold your edge longer if you never use your blade for anything but cutting."

I was working as a chef in the stylish Café at the Mews by then, but the day after he arrived, I helped Robert get a job on the salad station at Ciro & Sal's. A month later, when Kevin showed up, he endured the same trial-by-oyster and soon both my brothers had joined my staff at the Mews. Their ambitions ranged well beyond the culinary, however—primarily toward tennis matches, nude races along the bike trails through the dunes, and late nights with as many different girls as possible. As the chef of one of the most popular restaurants in town, I worked sixteen hours a day and I was blessedly oblivious to my brothers' extracurricular activities. I was, however, acutely aware of what each did well in the kitchen.

Robert did swordfish. He grilled and broiled everything the menu required, but swordfish was his specialty. After first searing it, he would, with a worried and deliberate intensity, move a fish steak from the hottest spot on the grill to its cooler regions. He moved fish, in fact, with the same furtive glance up through his bangs that he exhibited when tinkering with words on the page.

"Yes?" he would ask, raising a grilled swordfish steak on a spatula near my face and waiting for my approval before lowering it onto a plate, garnishing it, and calling the waiter to serve it. "Huh?" he would ask, anxiously watching me as I read one of his poems. "Huh?"

Kevin, on the other hand, did salad. Unlike his younger brother, Kevin hadn't exactly planned to stay in Provincetown; he just didn't get around to leaving. Kevin was comfortable wherever he was admired, and around town he was known as "Redford." In the past, Kevin's eyes had wandered constantly; determined, now, to "grow up," he practiced keeping his gaze downcast and flashing his movie-star smile up at the world as our father did—as if surprised to be so sought-after, so beloved. He worked hard at being modest, mellow, and cool; the salad station supported his efforts. Fortunately, Kevin had a special relationship with cold food.

He'd been allowed to spend several summers working with my father's brothers on the farm in Nebraska, and he appreciated lettuce, herbs, and other things from the garden. In addition, pounding anchovies and garlic together with lemon, black pepper, and the yolk of a barely coddled egg in a wooden bowl to make Caesar salad made Kevin feel useful. He had a similar response when he worked milk into balls of the fresh mozzarella that we served with roasted eggplant and tomatoes, or when he mixed cream and lemon and sugar together and churned it to make the ice cream that we served in almond tuiles.

In my mind, the three of us could go anywhere. We were a team—chef, sous chef, and garde-manger—and, in fact, we would work seasonal restaurants together for the next four years. We were the Gastronomical O'Neills. Between turning out orders of grilled swordfish *au beurre maître d'hôte* and lobster succotash *en croute,* we stood together in front of the stoves and strummed our stainless-steel spatulas as if they were small guitars.

"I'll be your savior steadfast and true," we sang above the sizzle of *medallions de veau aux champignons* in my sauté pan and the thunk of a lobster's tail against the lid of a pot as an order of cioppino was warmed. "I want to come to your emotional rescue!"

Our mouths were open. Our stardom was imminent. We knew what everybody ate.

By my third summer on the Cape, I'd mastered the art of counterculture chic. It was a pared and casual style that demanded bamboo place mats instead of table linen, votive candles instead of tapers in silver, and little bundles of wild flowers and herbs instead of formal floral arrangements. Keith Jarrett took the place of Pachelbel in the casual-chic idiom, and French classics were replaced by a combination of nouvelle improvisations and classic American dishes rendered in the new French style.

Suddenly, requests for my assistance—to design wedding and party menus, to collaborate on new restaurant concepts and food businesses— abounded. I began receiving glamorous invitations for the off-season: this writer's château in Provence, or that wine merchant's villa in Tuscany. In the meantime, there was a bidding war for my professional services in Provincetown. When I cooked, customers followed. I was hot.

The O'Neills who stayed in Columbus, however, were unconvinced of my new importance and success. Cooking was no way to make the fans go wild. They suspected that I was squandering my gumption and were concerned about how this might affect Kevin and Robert.

Not that I hadn't attempted to share with my family the power and poetry of my cuisine. Returning home for Thanksgiving and Christmas, I would bring anything I knew I couldn't find at home, which was pretty much everything: good wine, fresh herbs, sherry vinegar, cartons of iced seafood. To help my family appreciate my elevated culinary status, I also packed my chef's whites.

"Jesus," said my mother, arriving at the baggage claim area of Port Columbus Airport one November to find me standing among leaking cardboard cases and overstuffed canvas bags. "Did you come steerage?"

"Miss O'Neill," said the loudspeaker overhead, "Miss Molly O'Neill. You may claim your weapons with the baggage claim representative behind carousel three."

"Your *weapons?* My Gawd, Molly," said my mother, who had never fully recovered from the texturized-soy-protein turkey I'd made for Thanksgiving in my feminist-vegetarian phase. "What now?"

"It's just my knives." I sighed, adding, "And I wouldn't have to bring them if you had any decent blades in the house."

"Jesus! Am I going to be safe in the car? Should I call the police?"

My family was concerned that my culinary mania might derail us all. And so in the summer of 1979 they journeyed, one by one, to the tip of Cape Cod to rescue us. Visitor by visitor, I tried to cook away their fears and wow them with my sensitivity and savvy. I recalled each one's favorite dish and used its elements to create recipes that seemed familiar but that opened a window onto a wider world. My world. Sitting on the wharf behind my apartment, I would scribble these recipes in the small leather-bound notebook that I used to record my taste impressions, my recipe ideas, and my thoughts on cuisine. Drawing sketches of the dishes I planned, I pictured each member of my family in the throes of a culinary epiphany: the gasp of recognition as they fully understood the embarrassing limits of their own taste, the plea for help in their eyes. I would smile beneficently, part Jesus, part Madonna. "Don't worry," I whispered as I tested my custom-tailored recipes.

Kevin and Robert assisted me during the weeks of recipe development, and several nights after Mike blew into town, they exchanged nervous glances on the patio as we cooked one of the meals I'd planned. Kevin was rubbing garlic into a wooden salad bowl and Robert was tending the coals beneath his grill and worrying three thick slices of center-cut tuna when

Mike, who was positioned inside in the living room, called, "Exactly where do you think this cooking is going to *lead*?"

Mike had left college abruptly several years earlier. At six feet four inches, he was powerfully built, and he had the habit of getting a little too close and holding eye contact a little too long. For years, he'd butted heads with teachers and coaches and had believed that his talent—and their tolerance—had no limit. No one was more surprised than Mike when he was thrown off his college baseball team. He left the school. His native imperiousness had been further rearranged when he was able to secure nothing more than menial jobs. He'd been raised to believe that failure was not possible, and having found that victory was not always assured, Mike was suddenly and profoundly interested in health benefits and retirement plans. Now he was living at home and working nights for United Parcel Service.

"I mean, *really*," he yelled from his spot in my living room in Provincetown. The first day of his vacation, after a night of partying with Robert, he'd borrowed my bicycle, raced through the dunes, and collided with a tree. Now enthroned in my green leather club chair—his dislocated shoulder taped, his leg elevated—he was battered but undaunted as he questioned my future in food.

"What do you think?" Robert said, directing my attention to the grilling fish.

I was standing next to him, whisking chunks of cold butter and dabs of crème fraîche into the purée of roasted tomatoes and red peppers that was simmering in a copper pot on the grill next to him. I'd envisioned the mixture as a ketchup substitute. "This is going to be amazing," I said, dumping the shoestring potatoes that I'd cut by hand into the extra-virgin olive oil that was bubbling in a small electric Frialator nearby. I'd already grilled slices of brioche for Mike's "tuna sandwich" and had long since minced celery and capers and stirred them into a homemade remoulade to create the "mayonnaise" that would, after the tuna was grilled and sliced, be piped between the pieces of rosy fish.

"Light on the garlic," I reminded Kevin. "And don't tear the lettuce leaves—we want them intact so they look like part of a sandwich."

Along with hamburgers, Mike loved tuna fish sandwiches. He also shared our mother's urgency for truth-telling.

"It looks awful *dark*, Doober," he said, curling his lip slightly when Robert presented him with the grilled brioche topped with grilled sliced tuna and surrounded by a confetti of fried potatoes. Kevin was behind Robert, carrying a small pot of "ketchup."

Kevin, Robert, and I shot one another the kind of glances that cooks exchange when a customer orders meat medium-well. When they thought I wasn't looking, however, they shook their heads at Mike and frantically mouthed, "Shut up!"

"I'm not trying to be a *rube*," he insisted loudly, ignoring my brothers, "but I have never seen tuna this *dark*. I'm serious. I like solid white, not chunk light."

"Oh, no," groaned Robert.

"*Canned* tuna?" I said, my voice quivering in disbelief.

Mike winced as the "tuna sandwich" was lowered to his lap. "I thought you were going to law school or grad school or something." He shifted to steady his dinner plate on his left leg, which was splinted, heavily bandaged, and propped on the ottoman. "You got any beer?"

"You want *wine*, Mike," said Kevin. "We have a nice California chardonnay selected for you."

But Mike was undeterred. "Do they give you health insurance? How about disability? How much vacation do you get?" he asked me.

For the next week, although he was situated next to the black shelves and gray plastic milk crates that housed my cookbook collection, Mike did not use his convalescence to elevate his taste or to delve into my world. As if ruined for tuna, he became obsessed with hamburgers—"There's got to be someplace in this town that serves them," he'd say every morning as I left for work. "Can't you bring me one?"—and finally he had a revelation.

"I'm going to go back and get a business degree," he announced one evening after I'd pedaled home to deliver the Chateaubriand that I'd broiled between rushes in the kitchen. "Dad needs help and I'm going to try to give it to him. Do you realize that our parents have no retirement plan?

"Look, I'm not trying to embarrass you, but are you sure this hunk of meat is cooked enough? What's with the mayonnaisey-looking stuff? And how'd you get the carrots to look like little footballs?"

Pat, who had married shortly after graduating from high school and was supporting his bride and infant son by selling waterbeds in Columbus, showed up a few weeks after Mike had departed. He, too, had arrived unannounced, and so I had not had time to deconstruct and reimagine his favorite dishes, which included Kentucky Fried Chicken, Krispy Kreme doughnuts, and pizza.

"Jaayze," he bellowed, roaring into the kitchen of the café one night and greeting us with the same voice he used to summon his Little League team from the outfield back in Ohio. "So did you hear I was coming?"

The waiter picking up hot food, Amy Rosenzweig, puckered her lips and shook her head no. Amy was a cross-dressing dentist named Murray Moskovitz from New York City who desperately wanted to become a restaurant critic; tonight she was dressed in a burgundy-colored jumper, high-heeled Mary Janes, and a hedge-size wig of cascading black curls.

"No?" hollered Pat. Lowering his voice then, he lurched across the kitchen to shake Amy's hand—"Hey, uh, hello. I'm Pat O'Neill, how ya doing? Ma'am, mister, hey, what the heck are you, anyway?"—before continuing his story. "One of my waterbed customers was moving to Boston, so I said, 'Rent me a truck, man, I'll move you, I've never been to Fenway! And I got brothers and a sister down there just dying to cook me dinner!' Aren't you? Look at my sister. Why, she looks like Annie Hall! Are you the chef, honey? Why didn't they give you one of those tall hats? Discrimination! I want to speak to the manager! Grah-ha-ha."

"Pat, you got to keep it down," said Robert, walking out from behind the stainless-steel shelves and counter that separated the stoves, grills, and broilers from the rest of the kitchen to greet our brother.

"Jesus," said Kevin from the salad station.

"Shhhh," I said.

"Hey!" said Pat, nodding toward the dining room door. "They got nothing on me! I'm going out there, sitting down, and ordering the biggest lobster you got. That's the most expensive thing? Right? Look at this!"

Pulling a thick wad of bills from the pocket of his cutoffs and thumbing the bills like a picture book, Pat said, "This guy paid me cash! See that? Huh?"

"Not tonight, honey," said Amy Rosenzweig, sashaying past him, a little tin tray of escargot in one hand and a bowl of bourride in the other. "I've got my period."

An hour later, dressed in a tennis shirt and borrowed pants, Pat was sitting behind the five-pound lobster we'd steamed and split and reassembled for him. Posed upright, with a lemon crown stuck into the tip of its carapace, the creature looked almost like a seal balancing a beach ball. Its playful presentation, along with the champagne flush in Pat's cheeks and the plastic bib that was tied around his neck, gave my brother an infantile aspect.

"What the heck am I supposed to do with this guy?" he whispered, after asking Amy Rosenzweig to get me from the kitchen. "You're going to have to feed me," he declared, leaning across the table and opening his mouth expectantly. I hesitated, glancing around the dining room.

"Come on!" said Pat, beginning to regain his normal timbre. "You need the practice! You're going to have a baby soon! You got to! I swear, you have not *lived* until you start having kids. But I have to tell you something, honey, you are going to have to come home."

I used a nutcracker to break one of the lobster's claws and offered my brother the meat. I saw winters in Paris, not children in Columbus, in my immediate future. "I'm not ready for a family yet," I said.

"Sure you are, honey," he said, leaning forward as if to tell me a secret. "There's just not much fatherhood material around this town, no offense."

A month later, when my parents arrived with sixteen-year-old Paul in tow, we called at their hotel to escort them back to my apartment for dinner.

"Hey ya, Whatsy, grahh-ha-ha!" my father yelled, waving and beaming his crooked, iridescent smile up from under his downcast eyes at the two men in flowered housecoats and hair rollers who waved at him from the other side of the street. "How ya doing?"

My mother pursed her lips, arched her brows, and stared ahead. She was, by then, taller than my father. Her high-heeled sandals and her hairdo, which was all white and very big, emphasized the discrepancy between their heights, but my mother provided few opportunities for comparison. She stayed as far away from my father as possible.

"You walk with me," she said, adjusting the rope belt on her blue, tie-dyed pantsuit by Halston.

"Come on, little buddy," Paul said to my father in response.

Paul had grown, and the high-rise Afro of his curly hair made him seem even taller than his six feet four inches. My father, in contrast, had begun to shrink, but he still stood out. His lime green polyester slacks, matching striped shirt, and white patent-leather shoes had caught the eyes of the two would-be housewives who'd greeted him, and, like Pat, his voice had a foghorn quality in the seaside resort.

As we made our way along Commercial Street, Robert strode ahead. Like a security expert working a VIP detail, he scanned the block for anything unusual and did his best to shield our guests from potentially disturbing sights. I walked next to my mother, one step ahead of my father and Paul, and provided additional diversion.

"Look at the boat!" I cried, directing their attention to the huge sails of the *Hindu* on the bay as a man wearing a studded leather strap-on approached us on the sidewalk.

"Look at the hydrangea!" I cried as we drew close to the guesthouse whose front yard had been transformed into an S and M playground for Barbie dolls.

"Look at your arm," said my mother, stopping to gape at the red, lash-shaped burns that scored my right forearm. "What are you *doing* to yourself?"

"Oh, steam burns," I said. "From the lobster pot."

"You've got to stop this, Molly," said my mother. "You could be marked for life! What will people think?"

"They're doing Cinderella at the playhouse!" Robert called loudly over his shoulder from his position a few steps ahead.

"*Jaayze!*" my father bellowed as an elderly man wearing a Cinderella costume pushed by on a scooter.

"This is a big arts center," I said quickly. "Eugene O'Neill lived here."

"That's your cousin! Eugene O'Neill!" yelled my father, and then he lowered his voice to ask me, "Is that it, honey? Family tradition? You writing a play?"

"Just visiting," said Kevin, who walked behind the rest of us in order to soothe any ruffled feelings. "From Ohio," he said, shrugging his shoulders and beaming his version of our father's smile.

Before setting out to get our family, I'd draped my picnic table in white damask and arranged vases stuffed with hydrangeas and roses and trailing sweet peas in its center. Robert and I finished the cooking as soon as we returned, arranging the dishes I'd made for each family member on a platter and setting them, along with the turned zucchini that we'd sautéed in butter and tossed in chervil, on the table. The recipes were formal; we'd decided that the service should be casual. We'd put a bowl of cold cucumber soup at each place, but once we'd cleared that course everything else would be passed family-style.

"Now *this* is what my life was supposed to be like," said my mother, surveying the tumble of blue and pink and white flowers, the sea-foam green of the cold soup, the gentle creamy yellows of the fish dishes against their white Ironside platters, the light from the votive candles flickering against the silverware. "Well, *almost*," she said, considering the aluminum-framed, plastic-webbed chairs around the table.

"Be careful, Dad," said Paul. "These wiggle a little. You OK? You want a pillow for your back? Ollie, you have something he can put behind him in this chair? His back's been bad. You got to stop working so hard, little buddy."

"Mashed potatoes! Who's the luckiest guy in the world?" yelled my father. As a paean to his favorite dish, I'd arranged layers of potato purée, roasted corn, and lobster meat in a shepherd's pie for my father.

"That's all he cares about," said my mother. "We drive six hundred miles and what he is concerned about is the mashed potatoes."

"Hey," yelled my father, "your grandmother O'Neill was a chef! Did you know that, honey?"

"Jesus, Chick!" said my mother. "Do you really think a *chef* cares about bohunk cuisine?"

"I guess she cares about her heredity, Boots," said my father.

"She inherited pastry," said Robert quickly. "Mom, I bet that comes from you."

"I used puff pastry to make you a napoleon of scallops and summer chanterelles," I said.

"Your grandma O'Neill made the best pastry," yelled my father.

"What are you talking about, Chick! Your mother's pastry had about as much finesse as a lead pipe. Look at this puff pastry! It's thin! It's almost as thin as my pie crust!"

"There's a butter champagne emulsion with chervil between the layers," I explained, "and the summer chanterelles are sweet. Some people think that they taste like lobster."

"I'm not really a lobster person," said my mother doubtfully, using her small fish fork to gently nudge the layers of her napoleon. "I like shrimp."

"Shrimp aren't local," I snapped.

"Well, I guess I just don't belong anywhere, then," sniffed my mother, her tone suddenly tearful. "You have no idea what's happening in Columbus, Molly." She nodded toward my father. "*He* is allowing his youngest son to play baseball. That's all they talk about. That's right. No college, no medical school. No! He's going to let Paul throw away his life on some ridiculous ball game! I am just sick! I am so upset, I can't even eat."

Turning to my youngest brother, my father rolled his eyes and, just below the table, used his hand like a shadow puppet to simulate a yapping mouth. He used his fork to stab the dish I'd made for Paul, tiny fresh crab-cake "burgers" on brioche buns under a "melt" of spicy hollandaise.

"Get out of there," said Paul, raising his fork as if to stab my father's hand while moving his torso to push against him. "We got enough trouble without you forgetting your manners here, Dad."

Seated in the shadow of the overgrown lilacs and forsythia, my parents looked older than I remembered. My father leaned back against his youngest son, affecting mock horror.

"I just want to help you guys, Mom," said Paul. "Ballplayers make a lot of money."

"There's something fishy about this," said my father, moving his first bite of lobster shepherd's pie around his mouth and staring contemplatively over my front gate. The usual crowd was returning from a tea dance. A group of four men dressed in sailor uniforms walked by in lockstep. They were followed by a group of men dressed like the construction workers that my father employed.

"Definitely something fishy," my father said. Two women passed, hand in hand. A Marilyn Monroe lookalike bounced by and blew kisses across the gate.

"*Jaaaayze!* Boots! Close your eyes!" yelled my father as two young men wearing gold lamé jockstraps and combat boots entered his sight line.

"Oh, shut up, Chick," said my mother, pushing her napoleon aside and reaching for one of the miniature crab melts. "We're the weirdos here."

My father once told me that hitting a baseball perfectly sends a vibration through the entire body, a quivering that seems to match that of the ball as it spins through the sky. For an instant, the entire world shares the same roaring pulse; the distinctions between the past, the present, and the future are revealed as false; and there is no doubt in anyone's mind that there is a God. Few batters experience a perfect hit. Those who do continue to play, often through humiliation and frequently through constant and excruciating physical pain, in order to once again experience that ringing of the marrow, that ecstatic sense of divine order.

My youngest brother had not yet experienced a perfect hit in the summer of 1979. He was about to enter his junior year of high school and didn't have the strength; nor had he yet faced pitchers with power enough to make a baseball quiver. He did, however, appreciate the sublimity of my crab cakes, where his past and future seemed to collide. As I walked Paul back to his hotel, many hours later, he said they reminded him of the crab melts of his childhood, and that he wanted to learn how to make them himself.

"So it's fresh lump crabmeat, not shredded, not canned," he said. "I don't know where I'll find that in Columbus."

"There must be a fish store there," I said.

"Nothing like here. Those things were so good. Did you see Dad's face? He loved them. So did Mom."

"You cook?"

"I do some of the stuff you used to do," said my brother. "They work hard, they're really tired when they get home."

"So you make dinner?"

"Not every night, but somebody's got to take care of them, Molly," said Paul earnestly as we walked along in the dark. "They're getting old, they don't have any money, and I'm the only one around. They let me go to Florida with my girlfriend Nevalee's family at spring break and I met all these baseball players. You should see how they live. Buying houses for their parents. Buying their wives whatever they want. Never worrying about money. Spending the winter with their kids. Going to restaurants every night."

Walking the wet, sandy rim of Provincetown Harbor late at night gives one the sense of having left a party. The glow and clatter of the restaurants, the *boom-boom-boom* of the discos, and the occasional moan or cry or giggle from the shadows all combine to make one feel separate. We were far too serious for such frivolity, my youngest brother and I, as we walked the tide flats that night.

"I don't know why Mom's so worked up about it," he said. "Baseball players aren't low-class these days. Lots of them go to college. Not that many even chew tobacco anymore."

Metamorphosis

I t was a dreary February afternoon at La Varenne, in Paris. Chef Fernand Chambrette pursed his lips and turned the back side of his knife to the carrot parings that had accumulated on the counter in front of him. An assistant instantly produced a tall copper pot and positioned it under the counter's edge, precisely where it needed to be in order for the chef to sweep the trimmings into the vessel without taking his eyes off his audience. He stared at us meaningfully through the lenses of his thick, black-rimmed glasses as he spoke. Another student stood at his elbow to translate.

"Rien n'est perdu, rien n'est créé," said the chef.

"Nothing is lost, nothing is created," repeated the assistant, pausing along with the chef so that these words might be recorded in the small, spiral-bound notebooks that each student held on his or her lap. Puckering his mouth to complete his thought, the round little Gallic despot continued.

"Tout est transformé," he said.

"Everything is transformed," said the translator.

Like the other thirty students, I tried to scribble down everything the chef said. Unlike my fellow students', however, my notebook did not also contain the telephone numbers of potential lovers, the addresses of dance clubs, or the train schedules for weekend jaunts to the Loire Valley or Burgundy. I had neither the money nor the time for such frivolity. I was twenty-six years old, my formal training in Paris was serious business, and I recorded every sight, every taste, and every word. "Everything is transformed," I wrote carefully in the same purple felt-tip marker that I'd formerly used to write poems.

The quote appears between a recipe for *filet de rouget aux concombres et paprika* and one for crème anglaise. This entry is preceded by pages describing each window of Fauchon, the gourmet grocery store, and it is followed by notes on the difference between the leaf gelatin favored by French chefs and the granular form used in the United States. As if to reassure myself of the epicurean butterfly that would, certainly, burst from the exacting and rigid confines of the culinary school, I underlined the phrase.

Metamorphosis was exactly what I'd hoped for as I rose through the ranks in Provincetown. I wanted to be transformed from a cook into the chef. After that, the distance between the chef and the star would be negligible. Just look at the heroic portraits in *Gourmet* magazine—Bocuse! Verge! Guérard! To be sure, they were all French, and they were all men. But I was hoping that a sojourn at an elite cooking school in Paris could mitigate my Midwestern roots. With luck, it might even compensate for my gender.

La Varenne was expensive. An eight-week course of study cost two-thirds of what I earned during my first year of cooking. I saved half of my salary and took in a roommate. By the time Café at the Mews closed for its winter hiatus in January 1978, I was, as my mother would say, "all set." Although no French culinary school would have been impressed by my training in either the Italian idiom or the feminist vegetarian idiom, La Varenne had nevertheless admitted me to its advanced course.

I was to be in Paris for ninety-two days and, after studying the Michelin guidebooks as well as *Europe on Five Dollars a Day,* I had determined that seven dollars a day would afford me the luxury of a few two- and three-star meals. Dining out, wine tasting, studying ingredients, and strolling through food markets were, I knew, all part of my education. I kept felt-tip markers and backup notebooks in my TWA flight bag, which I brought with me to Paris. Once there, I began recording my impressions. The temperature, the slant of the sun, the feel of the air, the headlines in *Le Monde,* the cost of cockles, the size of endive, the smell of Gruyère cheese melting in the buckwheat crepes on the sidewalks, the clanking of cases of empty wine bottles being picked up before dawn, the names of the dishes that appeared on the menus posted outside the restaurants that I passed on the hour-long amble from my room to school.

I'd arrived in January, a week before classes were scheduled to begin, and soon detected discrepancies between the guidebooks' projections and the actual cost of living in Paris. My means, I discovered, afforded me a cot-size garret at the Grand Hotel de France, a flophouse on Rue de Vaugirard. Nevertheless, it was important to immerse myself in French cuisine, and so in the days before my classes began I took myself to La Tour d'Argent and Taillevent. I filled pages with notes and all but emptied my wallet.

By the time classes began, I could only afford to supplement the tasting samples that were offered at school with a crepe or a croissant each weekday. I spent Saturdays searching for one good, cheap restaurant for dinner. On Sundays, when I walked the markets of Paris, I allowed myself one baguette and a small wedge of triple-cream cheese. By Sunday nights, I was dizzy and hollow. As I sat in my garret memorizing Escoffier, this feeling stoked my sense of destiny, my certainty of imminent fame.

I cooked and ate imaginary meals and was fortified by the hunger that remained. Wasn't I following in the footsteps of my heroes? Hadn't M.F.K. Fisher, Michael Fields, and Julia Child all come to Paris from America, young and hungry and poor? Hadn't Brillat-Savarin written that poverty sharpens tastes and deepens memory?

Like the long line of *cuisiniers* before him, Chef Chambrette had spent decades producing infallible renditions of traditional recipes before earning the right to vary the national culinary code and create a style uniquely his own. He'd succeeded. Long before it was fashionable, Chef Chambrette had eschewed stodgy, roux-thickened sauces and had lured everyone from Eisenhower to Rita Hayworth to his restaurant, Boule d'Or. His morning classes at La Varenne were composed of the eight advanced students; his afternoon demonstrations were also attended by beginning students—the chic and tidy wives and would-be wives who attended single lectures—and tourists. Unfortunately for us, the gradations of talent, experience, and commitment among his acolytes were lost on the chef. He thought we were all dilettantes and slobs.

"Pour mes péchés," he said often. "For my sins."

Chef Chambrette had retired from his restaurant with both fame and a considerable fortune, but in his leisure, he'd become addicted to art. His mania to collect had finally forced him to accept the appointment as head of the faculty at La Varenne, where he waged a daily war on anything that threatened his Cartesian view of cuisine. Recitation of Escoffier did not impress him. Like scales and arpeggios, he thought that the master's recipes had to live like an instinct, an infallible competency, in a cook's hands before they could be improved upon. He acknowleged precise renderings with a *mais-bien-sûr* nod, but disdained improvisation of any sort.

"Peut-être pour le chef du Mac-don-ALD's," he sneered, coldly eyeing the ketchup-red rouille sauce that I proudly produced the first day of class.

"Perhaps for the chef of McDonald's," the assistant added helpfully.

I'd assumed that, like any recipe I'd ever read, the mimeographed pages of instructions I'd been given for my first day's lessons were simply meant as a starting point. Eager to distinguish myself, I'd doubled the quantity of both red bell pepper and tomato that the recipe had required to achieve that bright color. I'd also been free with the cayenne pepper. The chef raised a spoon to his lips and allowed a drop of the sauce to touch his tongue.

"Du pain!" croaked the chef, gagging, and an assistant instantly produced a slice of bread.

"Bread!" called out the translator.

Learning to rein in my instinct to stray from recipes, however, came slowly. At first, I assumed that a mistake had been made: the chef just didn't understand that I was an advanced student and had therefore already transcended the literal interpretation of recipes. Ah, but soon he would see. Wasn't my free-form mosaic of duck livers and green peppercorns more interesting than the tidy layers that had been prescribed in the recipe I was given? And perhaps the other students did not read food magazines, maybe they did not know that overcooking vegetables was unhealthy and passé, but I did. For my vegetable garni, I steamed the haricots verts just long enough to soften them slightly and intensify their color, and then shocked them under cold running water. When I presented my healthy and nouvelle innovation, however, the chef was not favorably impressed.

"I am not a *cow*," spat the chef, who spoke heavily accented English under extreme circumstances. "I do not eat grass or raw vegetables."

"Mooo," lowed my fellow advanced students in sympathy later, as we hurried outside for a smoke.

"Mooooo," I replied, shaking my head.

We stood around the courtyard holding our Marlboros Continental-style and regarding one another as the chef often regarded us, with disgust. All of the eight members of that winter's advanced corps had liberal arts degrees. All of us had imagined that a future in the food service industry would be more creative and less corporate than practicing, say, dentistry or law. Most of us had spent a little time in American restaurants, where cigarettes, vodka, drugs, and sloppiness were de rigueur; more than any other aspects of Paris, the pomp and starch of the French kitchen was completely foreign.

My sense of superiority did not falter until my second week at school when we were making meringues. The chef moved in close to demonstrate whisking egg whites in a copper bowl. Looking down, I noticed that his well-polished little black clogs looked like Cinderella slippers next to my crusty, size-ten combat boots. His black-and-white-checked pants were well creased. His double-breasted jacket and white apron were spotless. His socks were black silk. The sheen and gloss and lightness of his meringue, I realized, were the logical consequences of the chef's fastidiousness.

The realization was acrid, like the vague memory that an infinitesimally charred veal bone can lend to a stock. "Zere eaze no beeg picture," hissed the chef, moving to stand slightly behind me and covering my forearm with his small, thick hand after giving me the wire balloon whisk. "Zere eaze only *details*," he whispered, scowling up at me.

"Woof," said my colleagues the next time we stole out to smoke. "*Details*!" they giggled.

"Woof," I replied halfheartedly. It had suddenly dawned on me that my transformation from chef to star rested entirely on my ability to follow instructions—something that I was constitutionally incapable of doing.

Sensing that my future lay in Chef Chambrette's mouth, I began to observe that orifice as closely and constantly as I would watch egg yolks and garlic while whisking in the oil to create an aioli sauce. The various degrees of pucker and purse dictated my confidence and mood.

After living in Provincetown, I understood fish better than I did meat; the chef noted this, and started giving me veal kidneys and sweetbreads to clean and prepare. He watched me butcher and dress chickens, and stared as I carved and cleaned a rack of lamb and shaped it into a crown roast. Tightening my lips, I would memorize the method described in the day's instructions and then, with the scowling mania of a builder following an architect's drawing, I would lift sinew or membrane here and bend a mound of flesh or crack a bone there to shape the meats according to instruction. No matter what I knew, I did what I was told. I began moving more and more slowly, halting frequently to double-check my instructions and, with increasing apprehension, to sneak peeks at the chef's mouth.

My excitement rose when, after first approving the appearance of a dish and then reassuring himself by taking a whiff of its aroma, he parted his lips and allowed his chubby pink tongue to emerge. Anxiety chased away my exultation as he then used a spoon to apply a minuscule quantity of the dish to his tongue and closed his mouth around it.

When he judged the appearance or aroma or taste of a dish lacking, revulsion curled his upper lip and frustration soured like spent adrenaline in the muscles of my forearms. Fear of error made my hands heavy and clumsy as I moved into lessons of charcuterie and set mounds of forcemeat first on parchment paper and then on the scale to measure in grams, again and again and—just to be sure—yet again. The effort of battling my own nature caused me to clench my jaw and squint. By the fourth week of classes, I was practically living on the premises.

"Qui est là?" he said, reentering the darkened kitchen late one evening to find me, alone, tongs in hand, crouched in front of one of the ovens. I was minding the beef bones that were roasting for the next day's demi-glace, turning each to promote even caramelizing and to discourage the slightest sliver of blackening.

"Quoi?" he said, coming upon me at dawn another morning as I used a paper towel to skim microscopic flecks of fat from a stock destined for aspic.

"Parfait," he purred softly a week later when presented with the nippled puff of the brioche I had made. Tenderly, he took the cushion of sweet bread in his palm. Bending toward it, he inhaled its yeasty scent. His lips parted. His eyes closed. He opened his mouth.

Pastry chefs tend to have cool hands. It is a tremendous asset when it comes to working cold butter into flour, a physiological advantage that promotes flaky pastry and slows the melting of butter cream in a pastry bag or chocolate ganache in the hand. When kneading dough, cool hands can actually slow the action of yeast; they also bespeak the precision and quiet reserve of the most accomplished bakers. More than any other branch of cooking, dessert-making is a science.

I did not have cool hands, I certainly didn't have a natural tendency toward precision, and I hadn't made desserts regularly for fifteen years. But at twenty-six years old, basking in the approval of a culinary star, none of that seemed to matter. The chef liked my brioche! The tingly fear left my forearms. My hands regained their certainty.

"Perhaps it is time for you to specialize," said the chef thoughtfully, and he began assigning me puff pastry and *sablés,* dacquoises, mousses, buttercreams, and tortes. Because I had no instinct for pastry, there were no inspired hunches to divert me from following the formulas I'd been given, and this had a remarkable effect: my desserts looked exactly like those displayed in pastry shops throughout Paris.

"Mais bien sûr," said the chef, who quickly became accustomed to the consistency of my efforts.

"Mais bien sûr," mimicked my fellow advanced students on the increasingly rare occasions that I joined them in the courtyard to smoke.

Bakers live in a world apart, a sweet and self-contained world that, due to the fine mist of flour and confectioner's sugar in the air, tends to feel like the inside of a snow globe. Restaurant cooks work as a team, side by side, like cogs in a machine. Bakers tend to be solitary. I was no longer one of the advanced students. I was the chef's pastry girl, and within six weeks of my arrival in Paris, on his recommendation, I found myself in the spun-sugar cocoon of a predawn apprenticeship at Lenôtre, then Paris's top patisserie. Three mornings a week, before my classes at La Varenne, I made mocha, chocolate, and vanilla buttercreams. The fourth day, I made puff pastry. The fifth day, I cut classes at La Varenne in order to assist the chefs at Lenôtre, who taught classes on sugar work, gelatin, creams, chocolate, and fondants.

My proficiency in cleaning sugar pots, copper bowls, barquette molds, ramekins, and charlotte pans was highly regarded. My creams and custards and mousses were consistent. My flamboyance, in fact, surfaced only when I picked up my pastry bag. Piped onto gâteaux and petits fours, my squiggles and flourishes tended to wobble and dance; my fleurs-de-lis and roses looked like Monet's waterlilies. But my speed, my efficiency, and my talent for buttercream left the men at Lenôtre unwilling to ridicule my efforts at decoration. Instead, they tried to divert me with sudden and urgent pleas for my assistance elsewhere.

"Mademoiselle, come quick!" one of the pâtissiers would shout in alarm whenever I reached for my pastry bag.

Sealed in my private pastry world, I failed to notice this pattern. The predictability of the recipes that I rendered—the tight little dance between chocolate melting or sugar caramelizing or a mixture of eggs, cream, and sugar warming on the stove while, on a nearby counter, various doughs rested and a custard cooled in a bowl set over ice—made me feel like a ballerina. Turning, turning, in a tiny, self-determined circle, I was going through time-honored motions—whisking, stirring, heating, kneading, cooling—and seeking nothing more than to perfect my form. I was also pleased to be part of a lifestyle in which flour, sugar, and butter were primary food groups.

"Merci," I said to Chef Chambrette. *"Merci beaucoup."*

The following winter I returned to Paris and took classes exclusively at Lenôtre. By the time I returned to Provincetown for the summer of 1980, my transformation was complete.

Ciro Cozzi asked me if I wanted to take over the Flagship, his stylish seafood restaurant in the east end of town.

"I'd rather create a bakeshop and make all of your desserts than run one of your kitchens," I informed him. Ciro was dumbfounded.

"I thought you wanted to be my chef," he said.

My friends and colleagues were equally baffled. Nobody goes from being a cook to being a pastry cook—even if they're commanded to do so by Chef Chambrette.

"I like working in the morning. It's quiet and cool in the kitchen," I explained to my friends and, when they appeared unconvinced, I added; "There aren't any waiters around."

"I have control," I told the cooks who continued to join me for breakfast and to discuss the food pages in the major newspapers on Wednesday mornings. "I set the menu, make each component myself, and assemble it," I said, serving the French toast that I now crafted from slices of stale brioche. "I don't have to depend on anyone else, I don't have to react to anyone else, there are no rushes or crises."

Pushing a pat of butter over his batter-fried sweet bread, my old mentor Alex said, "You may not be able to run the world, but at least you can control your cake, is that it?"

Well, that was part of it. Having once toasted the late morning with a tankard of coffee, I now rose before dawn and sipped a *café filtre* while my first tray of croissants baked in the basement of the Flagship restaurant. Any ragged remnants of midnight doubt were erased by the warm flake of a *petit pain au chocolat*. My sense of doing what I'd been born to do was renewed by the chocolate that melted and ran out of my morning pastry. The kitchen smelled like Paris.

But if I was buoyed by the satisfaction of realizing my vision—within weeks I'd created dessert lists for four restaurants and had more than doubled their dessert sales—I was also consumed by the careful orchestration required to keep it going on a daily basis, to supply the tortes and tarts and flourless chocolate cakes, the trays of mousse and zabaglione, the shortcakes, the berry pies and the fools, the ice creams, the sorbets, the granitas, the flans and crème brûlées and pots de crème to their various destinations.

By noon, after I'd finished my cooking, stocked my refrigerators, cleaned my bakery, and made a list of things to do the following day, I'd need a little pick-me-up. Sitting on the counter in the quiet kitchen, I'd lunch on a carefully chosen tasting menu of my own desserts. Reinvigorated, I'd then ride my bicycle to Race Point and take the bike trails along the back side of the cape tip or pedal to the Fine Arts Work Center to paint. At four p.m., I'd check in on each of the restaurants where my desserts were being featured.

The cooks usually clomped in while I was instructing the young cold-station workers—demonstrating the proper way to sprinkle confectioner's sugar on a chocolate hazelnut torte, or how to pipe whipped-cream bows on a strawberry tart, or how to use squeeze bottles to alternate drizzles of raspberry coulis and bittersweet chocolate syrup on profiteroles. My technique was, by then, so sure that I didn't require an apron. My range of motion had shrunk to minutely calibrated movements.

"Hey, Dessert Girl," a former colleague would say, slamming a knife down on the first joint of a chicken wing to remove it from the bird, "you ever going to do an honest day's work again?"

Smiling tolerantly, I would move closer to the dessert server and explain that one must dip a knife in boiling water in order to slice cleanly through the layers of buttercream, dacquoise, and ganache in a mocha torte.

"What're *you* doing here?" another would sneer as I demonstrated how to lift the muslin lining in a heart-shaped porcelain mold and turn a *coeur à la crème* onto a plate.

"Coming through," yet another would holler, pressing a roasting pan close to my back. "*Men* at work."

But by then my focus would be elsewhere. Arranging candied violets and rose petals on a frozen lemon soufflé with a pair of tweezers demanded all my concentration.

At first I reveled in my free and formless evenings. But almost everyone I knew worked at night, and soon this feeling of reprieve gave way to a restless sense of dislocation, of being an outsider, almost a tourist. Murray Moskovitz, who'd worked with me at the Mews, understood. He thought that I might be suffering kitchen withdrawal.

"Baking doesn't work for real restaurant junkies like us," he said. "It doesn't numb you enough, it doesn't exhaust you enough, it doesn't turn you into enough of an animal. And the sugar is murder on your teeth."

Murray, who was fifty-odd years old, had been an oral surgeon on Madison Avenue for most of his adult life. His practice was so successful that he and his family could afford to spend their summers in Provincetown. Once settled, however, despite his resolve to catch up on his reading or improve his tennis game, Murray would always take a job as a waiter. "I like being part of the heart of things," he said. "Otherwise I think too much."

Many mornings, after he picked up *The New York Times* at the market next door, Murray stopped by my bakery. Perched on the far end of my marble counter, he would gossip, taste my experiments, and offer me fatherly advice about my desserts, my teeth, and my love life.

"I am not sure where you are headed, but it feels right to me," he said.

Murray himself had some experience with metamorphosis. In 1975, after both of their children were enrolled in boarding school, Murray and his wife, Elizabeth, decided to pursue dreams of their own. Elizabeth, a flutist, wanted to play the bass; Murray, a cross-dresser, wanted to become a restaurant critic.

There was nothing impulsive about their decisions. For nearly forty years, Elizabeth had hauled her flute to lessons and Interlochen, auditions and rehearsals—and, eventually, even to Juilliard—all the while knowing that she'd been born to play bass. Murray's situation was slightly different. He had not spent his life feeling like a woman sentenced by physiology to impersonate a man; Murray was simply a man who liked to wear dresses once in a while. But in the early 1970s, Murray's fantasies gained a new precision and urgency. Amy Rosenzweig, his alter ego, became a foodie.

While Elizabeth studied the bass, Murray trimmed his oral surgery practice in order to begin Amy's culinary education. For the next decade, he spent the winter months doing teeth three days a week and devoting the balance of his time to cooking classes conducted by James Beard, Dionne Lucas, Lydie Marshall, Joyce Chen, Paula Wolfert, and Dianna Kennedy. He joined both the Dames d'Escoffier and the Chiens de Rotisserie in New York City and made regular pilgrimages to France—barging in Burgundy, driving from one three-star restaurant to the next, apprenticing in charcuterie shops and patisseries, and attending the Cordon Bleu.

In the summers, he waited tables. Sometimes he worked as Murray, other times as Amy Rosenzweig. But the closest he came to impersonating a restaurant critic was a skit he invented and performed at a drag show cabaret in Provincetown. His transformation was convincing. Fully aware of his doppelgänger, my brothers nevertheless had a difficult time believing that Amy Rosenzweig was, in fact, the wizard who had, gratis, tended to the tooth that Kevin chipped and Robert's impacted wisdom teeth.

"Dr. Mosko?" said Kevin. "You've got to be kidding me!"

The Moskovitzes and my brothers could not entirely assuage my anxiety and loneliness in my new life as a baker, but they did their best. On the evenings that Murray wasn't waiting tables or performing, he and Elizabeth often invited me to dinner. On Robert's day off, he and I played tennis late in the afternoon and then pedaled to Herring Cove for sunset. We would sit in the sand with notebooks on our laps, writing poems and stories until the light turned purple and we got cold. That summer, with the help of a friend who was a sommelier, I was also drinking a lot of wine: on Kevin's night off, he and I spent the evening on the wharf behind my house uncorking, sniffing, and sipping. It was the summer of Montrachet. My tasting notes were lengthy, detailed, and complete, but my stories never felt finished, and as the sun sank, my spirits plummeted as well.

At first it was nothing that a slice of *gâteau de framboise* or a few sips of Château Montrachet couldn't fix. But as the weeks passed, my fatigue became overwhelming. One minute I'd be sipping contemplatively, jotting notes, and bursting with a sense of my own good fortune. The next minute, the wineglass would suddenly be too heavy to hold and I'd feel as if I were serving a life sentence in a prison of disappointment.

"Are you on something?" Kevin asked, concerned.

I wasn't using drugs, but I was practically mainlining sucrose, and the highs and lows of this lifestyle were getting increasingly difficult to manage. I began making batches of candy in the mornings at work and keeping a supply of Valrhona chocolate stashed in my refrigerator at home. As the summer progressed, my desire to be energized and cheerful far outstripped my desire to wedge myself into Levi's with a thirty-two-inch waist. What had once been a single *pain au chocolat* became two, and soon I was chasing them down with at least one croissant smothered in beach plum jam before six a.m. Sensing a swoon coming on an hour or so later, I would stop working to nibble several cinnamon *palmiers*. Tastes of batters and mousse and buttercreams and meringues helped maintain my equilibrium until nearly eleven a.m., when I had a lunch composed only of dessert.

"Hey!" I would boom, bouncing into the café where Robert and Kevin bussed tables, with the enthusiasm of a motivational speaker working a crowd. An hour later, looking as gray and worn as a well-read newspaper, I would limp into Spiritus Pizza, barely able to summon the energy to order a double espresso Häagen-Dazs Coffee milkshake.

"What is the matter with you?" yelled Robert, storming into my apartment one evening in August after I failed to show up for our tennis date. Slouched in the club chair in the living room, I explained to him that I had ruined my life—I was writing "Happy Birthday" on carrot cakes instead of writing literature. What had I been thinking? The fans were never going to go wild for Pastry Girl! I started to cry.

"I'm calling Mom," said Robert. Instead, he pedaled through town to the Moskovitzes' house and returned with Murray.

"I have an idea," said Murray, kneeling in front of me to take my pulse and stare deeply into my eyes. Then he told Robert to get a glass of orange juice from the refrigerator. "Drink this," he ordered, watching me closely as I drained the glass. The effect was dramatic. Within moments, my energy and good humor were restored.

"It's the sugar," said Murray.

I thought he was nuts, and to prove that I was not hooked on sugar—that, indeed, sugar is not a drug—I immediately applied the discipline of baking to the discipline of eating: I foreswore all sweets but the licks and nibbles necessary to maintain the quality of my pastries. At Murray's suggestion, I tasted nothing casually. Instead, I measured a demitasse spoon of a given recipe to taste for its seasoning, put it on a small plate, touched my finger first to the sample and then to my tongue. In other words, I quit cold turkey, and I had a headache for a week.

One morning, alone in my hushed bakery, I pinched a dab of pastry from a large batch of dough, placed it alone on a baking sheet, and slid it into the oven. It was strictly routine. I needed to check the flavor, to make sure that I didn't need to add more salt or a touch of sugar before dividing the entire mass of dough into smaller discs and rolling each out to line my tart pans. A few minutes later, as I removed the baking tray from the oven and used a small metal spatula to lift the pinch of baked dough from the baking sheet, I thought of my mother. Had she felt like this when I was a tiny girl, watching her bake pies in our kitchen—alone and bored in the life she'd chosen? I held the pastry between my thumb and index finger. I observed its color and texture. I blew on it. And as I leaned forward to bite into it, raising my pinkie slightly, it suddenly hit me. I wasn't the chef. I wasn't on my way to becoming a star. I was turning into my mother.

Like flour on my hands, I brushed off the thought, but the solitude and silence of baking suddenly felt intolerable. A few weeks later—after Murray and Elizabeth had moved back to New York and Robert and Kevin had returned to Miami University in Oxford, Ohio—I accepted an offer to be the executive chef at an Italian restaurant in Boston.

"I'm working sixteen hours a day and the kitchen is so crazy I can't hear myself think," I wrote to Robert enthusiastically.

"The crew is fabulous, except for the pastry chef, who is a complete control freak. There but for the grace of God go I."

Art and Commerce

M y transformation from chef to chef-to-the-stars happened faster than I had anticipated. Within weeks I was meeting with the press regularly. I was cooking at Ciro's on Boylston Street in Boston; reporters tended to show up early in the evenings and ask me questions about everything from the state of cuisine to the restaurant's famous clientele. "Is Paul McCartney really a vegetarian?" one might ask. "What did Julia Child order? How about Ted Kennedy? Paul Newman?"

"Does Lillian Hellman really eat here every night?" another would ask. "I hear she sneaks out of Mass General and comes over here to smoke and drink."

Ciro Cozzi had wanted to create something fancier in Boston than his Neopolitan-American eatery at the tip of Cape Cod. He wanted a Northern Italian restaurant with a menu awash in cream and butter emulsion sauces, a dining room in which "red sauce" was a profanity. Having reached the age when many take stock of their lives, the man who'd started out as a bohemian painter wanted to justify the Mercedes-driving small-business owner he'd become. He wanted to make art. Banishing red-checkered tablecloths and Chianti-bottle lamps, Ciro built a sleek, Milano-chic restaurant in Back Bay.

To support his culinary vision, he hired a brilliant chef who'd graduated from Madeleine Kamman's cooking school, the Modern Gourmet, a man whose compulsion for perfection led him to practices such as discarding, rather than recycling, any ingredient not deployed within eight hours of its delivery. This purity had a positive effect on critics—Ciro's on Boylston Street was quickly heralded as one of the city's premier restaurants—but it was disastrous for the restaurant's bottom line. The chef was also a drinker, and soon after his glowing reviews, he and his sports car had a lethal encounter with a tractor trailer. In October 1979, I was hired to maintain Ciro's aesthetic standards while restoring the restaurant's commercial viability. I was to cut the staff—and the food costs—in half.

The press cheered my efforts, which immediately included a smaller menu and a simpler, cleaner, less confected style of cooking. Italian cooking was becoming the rage across the country, and since Boston was still a culinary backwater, the local food writers were loath to disparage an honest effort. They also liked the fact that I maintained Ciro's policy of letting them eat and drink for free. At five-thirty every afternoon, I had platters of sliced prosciutto, chunks of Parmesan, fried zucchini, bruschetta, and tortellini in pesto sauce set out on the bar at the front of the restaurant.

"Did Ted Williams really ask for your pesto recipe?" asked the gossip columnist for the *Boston Herald*. There were only a few other women running kitchens in Boston. There were even fewer cooking professionals who had a liberal arts education and could have become journalists themselves. I was good copy.

"In your opinion," asked a food writer from *The Boston Globe*, "will Italian cuisine topple nouvelle?" The restaurant critic from *Boston* magazine, on the other hand, was more interested in my position on the new American cuisine.

"Do you think we'll see a New England version?" he asked. "We've seen California, Cajun—can redefining chowder be far behind?"

My life as a chef was not, of course, only a press conference. I had thirty people working for me and they often asked for my attention.

"Eighty-six garlic," one would report. "Should I make the pesto anyway?" Another would sidle up to me with news of a leaking Frialator, a delivery of questionable chickens, a drunken dishwasher, a fight between two cooks. Some issues required immediate attention.

"Han Chen and Mario are stuck in the dumbwaiter," a porter informed me one evening. "The immigration guys came back."

Other issues—such as the pastry chef's reaction to my curtailing her menu and the presence of a labor-union organizer on my staff—were chronic. In fact, as the months passed, less and less about the restaurant caused my adrenaline level to spike. After nearly a decade in restaurant kitchens, I had cooked about 500,000 meals, and what had once been a life of bone-numbing terror had become a wearying routine punctuated only by the occasional challenge—the five hundred people who showed up for pasta the night before the Boston Marathon, the bar mitzvah that had been scheduled but not noted in our books, the sighting of Craig Claiborne, the New York restaurant critic, in the dining room. My accustomed sixteen-hour workday gave way to a leisurely ten hours, many of which were now spent in an office courting suppliers, policing food costs, counseling staff, and creating menus.

I was living across the river in Cambridge, and some blamed my diminishing presence in the kitchen on my commute. But it was less a matter of physical distance than a shift in my internal geography that had me eager to get back to my rented room. From the day that I moved to the Burlinghams' big house at the corner of Kirkland and Irving streets, I felt that I'd finally found the family that I'd been intended for—a family that recognized me as a writer.

Charlie Burlingham was a lawyer who collected stamps and the Bruins, the Red Sox, and the Patriots. His wife, Adair, called him "Stamps"; he called her "Doodles." She was the lunch chef at Peasant Stock, and also an aspiring writer. They had a Volvo wagon in the driveway, a baby grand, a Garland range, and many overstuffed bookcases as well as paintings by Charlie's grandfather, J. Alden Weir, all over their house. Their children—six girls and a boy from each of their first marriages—were grown, and the Burlinghams rented their empty rooms out to artists, writers, and musicians.

They were more interested in creating an artists' colony than they were in rental income. Charlie and Adair charged little or nothing and supplied their tenants with an unlimited supply of popcorn, white wine, and gumbo. Adair was originally from New Orleans. After spending an evening being interviewed in one of the ladderback chairs at that table, I couldn't imagine anything better than moving into the Burlinghams' empty nest. And Adair, arguing that cooking was an art form, made an exception to her rental policy—artists, musicians, and writers only—and offered me a room.

I'd been carrying a portable Smith-Corona typewriter around with me since college, but it had never fit anywhere as well as it did on Adair's youngest daughter's desk. The girl was still at Groton; I shelved my books next to hers in the bookcase. At the opposite end of the hallway, a playwright was typing, typing, typing. In a room between us, a violinist was practicing. Every morning, I sat in bed scribbling, and when the need for caffeine became critical, I typed up my efforts and carried the pages to the Coffee Connection. This was my Cambridge life, my writing life.

I was working on a short story titled "The Cuisine of Rosie the Riveter." I liked the title. But I wasn't sure what the story was, and therefore, every day, I wrote a new version of its beginning. Then, over a pot of Jamaican Blue Mountain coffee, I would edit these paragraphs before taking the train to work at eight a.m. Hadn't I always been a work/study student? Sitting at the wobbly wooden tables among the turtlenecks and chinos that packed the Coffee Connection, I felt as though I'd finally gotten to Harvard. Nevertheless, I couldn't get past the first few paragraphs of Rosie's story.

"It's so hard," agreed Adair, who was enthusiastic and resolute in her support. She herself had been working on a story for quite some time, and she empathized with me.

Adair's professional range occupied one wall of her kitchen. On the opposite wall was a small television, and between the two was a long farm table. In the evenings, Charlie sat on one side of the table with his stamps, a beer, a magnifying glass, and the Bruins playing on the television. Adair sat across from him with a glass of white wine and the notebook that contained her story. For the next few hours, a stream of friends, family members, lost souls, and scholars would drop by for some Cler Blanc, Orville Redenbacher, and good conversation.

Returning home from one of the workshops she taught, the playwright might be called into the kitchen to discuss the difference between romanticism and sentimentality with a retired and rather tipsy Shakespearean actor. The poet who lived on the third floor might drift in, followed by the violinist. If it was a Wednesday, Adair would be trying recipes from *The New York Times*. By the time I came home from work, the group might be shaping dough into discs to make Indian flatbread, or grinding up spices to make Paul Prudhomme's blackened fish, and the talk might have wound its way to politics. We debated the merits of socialized medicine, the role of public assistance, gun control, birth control, and the quality of coffee beans ground at home compared with those purchased already ground. We often talked about the effect of the White House on art and food—did we, in fact, have the Reagans to thank for the new American cuisine?

I could barely wait to leave the restaurant in Boston every day and join this tableaux.

"I thought you'd *never* get home," Adair would say, dropping her notebook, smoothing her chef's apron over her faded Marimekko dress, and pointing her tennis shoes toward the stove.

"You work too hard," said Charlie, who maintained an office downtown where he represented people he liked and took on pro-bono cases. "You work too hard, too, Doodles," he said to his wife.

"Don't be silly! Molly serves three hundred a day! I make lunch for twenty. Actually, today was only twelve, but this *estouffe*! You have to have some, Molly," Adair would say, pushing back the kerchief that she tied around her graying hair. Between the white wine and the hot stove, Adair's face was perpetually flushed, and it grew redder in her excitement for details of my day.

"Did the immigration agents come back? How's Rosie the Riveter? Did you see the article about you in the *Globe*? I clipped it. You have to start a scrapbook! Oh, wait till you read the new sentences I wrote today. Did Lillian Hellman come in for lunch?"

In the mornings, Charlie and Adair listened to *Morning Pro Musica* on WNPR. In the evenings, they listened to *All Things Considered, The News from Lake Woebegone,* and, with increasing familial pride, they listened to me.

"If you write stories one-tenth as well as you tell them, you'll get a story in *The Atlantic*," Adair would exclaim delightedly. Noticing my stricken look, she would add, "The muse will come. Rosie will speak to you. Here, have some wine."

On Kirkland Street, I often gazed up from my typewriter and out the window. I was searching for inspiration. I soon learned that I was staring at Julia Child's front door. She'd introduced French cooking to America—I couldn't believe that she was my neighbor! Locally, however, she was more famous for her driving.

"That's her Rabbit," Adair had told me, pointing to the Volkswagen as she and I walked up the block to Savenor's Market one day. "When the neighbors hear her gun it, everybody makes sure their children aren't playing in the front yard."

One day, when I was picking up chicken paillards for Adair, Jack Savenor, who owned the grocery store, introduced us. There was no mistaking the role model for some of the kitchen skits on *Saturday Night Live*. When she warbled her greeting—"Well, hello, dear. I've read so much about you. They say you are doing wonderful things in Back Bay, and I must get over there, even if it *is* Italian"—her voice was so familiar that I burst out laughing. The author of the book that had revolutionized my approach to Weight Watchers laughed back. Soon after, she made her first appearance at Ciro's. Pale and visibly shaken, Paul Bocuse followed her into the dining room.

"Have someone get him a scotch, dearie," she said, nodding toward Bocuse. Chauffeuring the chef from his hotel, it turned out, Julia had traveled some distance up on a sidewalk to avoid traffic and had also mistaken a police officer's "halt" for a go-ahead. "The French can be such scaredy-cats," she muttered to me.

Julia's presence at Ciro's was itself a generous gesture. She wasn't impressed by Italian food and considered the pasta revolution part of the dumbing down of America. Assuming that her companion shared her misgivings, she sought to reassure him.

"It's Northern Italian, almost French," she said. "In fact, the cook trained in France—didn't you, Molly?"

Regardless of our regional differences, however, Julia soon took me under her wing. "We have to stick together, dearie," she declared. We were, in her opinion, sisters in a big-and-tall sorority who shared the additional bond of a proficiency in matters béarnaise. I began standing up straighter and sometimes, instead of going to the Coffee Connection, I would stop by Julia's. Soon I was picking up the knives she set down midtask and finishing the jobs she abandoned in order to answer the telephone, make notes on a manuscript, or carry a cup of tea upstairs to Paul, her husband, who was quite ill. I instinctively cleaned in her wake—wiping counters, removing used pots and pans, emptying the sink of dishes.

I often found myself standing, measuring cup or whisk in hand, staring at the enormous Peg-Board on her kitchen wall where each utensil was outlined.

"Upper-left-hand corner, dearie," she said, coming up behind me one morning as I searched for the egg-beater shape. My brow was knitted: I was beginning to bring the same earnestness to our time together that I brought to most things that I cared about.

"I spend a great deal of my life trying to save myself from myself," Julia continued. "Now, you can probably remember exactly where you put everything, so you don't need these kinds of visual aids. But what could we do to remind you to smile a little more often?"

At her urging, I gave Julia a copy of the beginning of my story "The Cuisine of Rosie the Riveter," along with the recipes that I intended to include. When we met at Legal Seafood to discuss my efforts, Julia did not, as I hoped, volunteer to introduce me to her publisher. She did, however, have an alternate plan. She was thinking of writing a dessert book.

"Wouldn't that be fun to do together?" she asked.

That wasn't the sort of writing I had in mind. "I'm not a baker," I said coolly.

"Well, neither am I, dear. But does that terribly matter? I was never so much a cook as a ham," she said. "Any humorless home economist can teach people to cook. It takes someone who isn't afraid to make a fool of herself to make them *want* to cook, or *love* to cook."

Pursing my lips, I nodded.

"Besides, dear," she said, "you've written only three pages! Remember, all that matters in the end is getting the meal on the table."

Lillian Hellman would, I decided, be a better mentor. The playwright was, during the fall and early winter of 1981, at the Phillips Brooks House at Massachusetts General Hospital and did, in fact, often sneak out for dinner at Ciro's. She drank a lot and smoked a lot and had gotten into the habit of calling me in the kitchen early in the day to plan her meal. We'd gotten friendly, and when she and her friend Peter Feibleman decided to write a culinary memoir, Lillian asked me to test the recipes. Assuming that such a project would bring me closer to literature, I eagerly accepted. Lillian was, however, far less poetic than I'd imagined.

Rising, a gnarled and raging phoenix from her hospital bed, she would not declare, "I must make art." No, she would rasp, "I gotta make a goddamned living." Even more startling, she shared Julia's view of deadlines. Rather than staring out the window, making notes in a fine journal, and then waiting for inspiration to strike, the ailing and irascible playwright faced the empty page the way I faced a stove: as work that had a beginning, a middle, and an end. She was prone to outbursts and scathing tirades, and she scared me as much as fifty meals ordered all at once. I quickly lost the dreamy reverence I'd always had for words and began to see them as ingredients. By the time *The Boston Globe* called and asked me to write a story about pancakes, the boundaries between art and commerce seemed more porous.

"Sure!" I said.

"We want your name and your recipes," the editor replied. "You can dictate the story and I'll write it for you."

"Oh, I can write," I quickly assured her. Then, with a mania that would define the next twenty years of my professional life, I proceeded to research the science, history, economy, sociology, and folklore of pancakes from the Stone Age forward. I studied recipes from history books, cooking pamphlets, and modern-day cookbooks, which, in turn, led to a study of various flours, fats, skillets, and griddles—and, of course, maple syrup. I also found it necessary to research various stirring techniques—whisk, fork, mechanical beater, electric mixer—and to make at least fifty different pancake batters. One night, after closing, I filled every one of the twenty-four burners on the restaurant's stove with skillets containing different pancake renditions and required my staff to participate in a blind tasting. My father's recipe won.

"Do you want to put his name on the recipe?" I asked the editor. She'd assigned me a three-hundred-word story and had been surprised to find that my three-thousand-word pancake opus was actually readable.

"We want your name," she said.

I tend to date men who see the parts of me that my family can't recognize, intellectuals whose lack of interest in baseball limits the likelihood of filial bonding. My brothers were an impenetrable fraternity; I've never dated a man who would have wanted to join. Instead, I've always been careful to go out with men who view the O'Neills of Columbus as a diorama in a living-history museum—men who treat me as one might comfort and champion someone who'd managed to escape from a cult.

My preferences were established early on, and so was my brothers' response to any male seeking my attention. In seventh grade, when my first date called to take me to a dance, Mike accosted him on the walkway that led to our front door.

"You better not go in there," said my oldest brother. He towered over the frail comedian from my Latin class, who wore glasses and always had a note from his doctor excusing him from gym. The other members of the O'Neill fraternal order stood behind Mike, holding the usual items—aluminum baseball bats, wooden baseball bats, and big, fat Wiffle-ball bats.

"My mom just cleaned the living room carpet," Mike continued. "And if you track dirt on it, she'll kill you."

When seeking to address one of my companions, my father would always begin with the name of the boy who was banished to preserve the clean carpet and then proceed through several decades of my romantic interests.

"Freddy, er, Bill, no, ah, Greg, Charlie, ah, ah," he'd say. A confusion that was as much about the world in which he found himself as it was about the identity of his daughter's unlikely companion rose in his voice. By the time I moved to Boston in 1980, even my father could see that waterbeds and bongs had rendered his nation a postbaseball society. As his dream of spawning an infield languished, he spent more and more hours on the back porch of the house on East Cooke Road, watching the Canada geese, finches, cardinals, robins, and bluejays over the pond behind the abandoned O'NeillDome.

"Jean Carlos, ah, ah, Aedan, no," he would say. Finally, as if calling a winning bingo number, he would yell, "Stanley!"

"Well," my mother would reply, rolling her eyes, "I'm glad we got *that* out of the way."

In general, there wasn't much more to say. My mother had hoped that her daughter would take off her apron, marry well, and *hire* a cook. Luckily, she was too occupied by her work at the hospital to spend much time dwelling on her disappointment. But on the subject of saving me from restaurant kitchens, my family and Stanley were in complete accord.

"You're a writer," said Stanley. Ten years my senior, Stanley had cooked in restaurants to support the novels that he wanted to write. By the time we met, he'd begun to write about food and wine for *Boston* magazine. Having studied constitutional law, he brought a thoroughness similar to mine to any reporting job. Not having worked for Lillian Hellman, he weighed and measured each word for hours. Stanley, who'd grown up in the South, was sure that the right cadence would eventually launch him from columns on Beaujolais Nouveau to novels along the lines of *Light in August*. He was willing to sacrifice comfort and security for his art, and he hoped that I would be, too. I moved into his studio on Beacon Hill and we were married in 1981. Charlie and Adair insisted on giving our rehearsal dinner.

"Look at her *arms,*" said my mother as we sat around at the Burlinghams' table the night before our wedding. "Those burns are going to scar. And what happened to her hair? It looks like she burned it, too!"

"Medallions of pork flambéed with calvados," drawled Stanley. "You would have enjoyed that dish, Virginia. She did a sage spaetzle and spiced cabbage. But don't worry, your daughter's making a real name for herself. Soon she can stop cooking professionally and write full-time."

"Well, let's hope that happens before she flambées her brains out," my mother replied.

Increasingly, I was hoping the same thing. I had a few assignments— *Gourmet* had asked me to write a story about Provincetown; *The Boston Globe,* several neighborhood weeklies, and a wine quarterly continued to call; but I couldn't afford to stop cooking.

A year after we were married, Stanley took a job at *Food & Wine* magazine, and we moved to New York. Shortly after we arrived, Donald Forst, the editor of *Boston* magazine, called me. He'd noticed my byline in the *Globe*.

"You can keep doing what you are doing and eventually you're going to be just another ordinary food writer, simpering on about airy soufflés and satiny hollandaise," he said. Mr. Forst was a newspaper editor from New York City who had come to Boston to save its tabloid newspaper and had remained, briefly, to run its city magazine. He'd been married to a restaurant critic in New York City, and his voice had the flat, nasal finality of a criminal court judge in Brooklyn. "Or," he said, "you can come work for me, learn how to be a reporter, and make a name for yourself."

I began commuting back to Boston the next day. And, over the next three years, for the princely sum of three hundred dollars a month, I wrote a column about food and another column about wine for the city magazine. In order to learn how to report other sorts of stories, I followed more experienced journalists from crime scenes to news stories. Believing that a good food writer had to be able to write about anything, my editor also assigned me business stories, fashion shows, flower shows, dog shows, and high teas.

"Do you want your *byline* on this piece of shit?" he would ask gently, using a red pencil to slash through the clever and carefully wrought phrases of which I was so proud. "If you know the story, you can tell it," he'd say. "If you don't know it, then get out of my office and find out what it is, because you've got to stop the fucking *writing* and start just *telling*." I could tell he was pleased with my progress.

Several years later, when he agreed to oversee the start-up of *New York Newsday,* my editor called to say that he had the perfect job for me. "You're going to be my restaurant critic," he said. "Nobody has any idea who you are, and you're going to go out there and kick ass and make a name for yourself."

Do You Know My Name?

Restaurant critic! In those years, before the Zagat guides appeared and peer reviews abounded on the Internet, restaurant reviews still determined which dining rooms thrived and which languished. Imagining the power of my pen and tongue kept me chewing sugarless gum and sucking Pepto-Bismol throughout the winter of 1984 as I prepared to assume this weighty mantle.

I spent hours at the New York Public Library, reading restaurant reviews on microfilm. I walked from restaurant to restaurant across Manhattan and studied all the published guidebooks. I traveled back to France to accompany a Michelin guide inspector on his rounds. I went to Italy and San Francisco. No matter where I was, I woke up in a panic every morning at four o'clock.

"What?" said my husband, who tirelessly provided a solace that was unheard of among the O'Neills. We lived in a rent-stabilized two-room apartment in a former welfare hotel at the corner of West Fifty-fifth Street and Broadway, along with a considerable number of hookers, gamblers, drug addicts, folk artists, actors, and thieves.

"I just can't." I rolled off our futon, tiptoed to the bathroom, stood in front of the mirror, and stuck out my tongue. In the kitchen, I had never suffered misgivings about the acuity or authority of my palate, but I shuddered as I imagined the potential consequences of a single mistake: folding businesses, ruined lives.

Sitting up in bed, Stanley reached for his glasses and attempted to place restaurant criticism in its proper perspective.

"Let's say you mistake the gray sole for Dover sole," he said. "Could the misidentification of a flatfish prolong the Cold War? Cause dangerous fluctuations of the world financial markets? Instigate nuclear warfare?"

"I would never mistake gray sole for Dover," I hissed. I feared personal retribution, not global catastrophe: my terror was of annihilation, the only reasonable response to my good fortune. And as an O'Neill, I also knew that the only antidote was backbreaking effort and personal perfection.

I'd already established relationships with the real estate brokers and restaurant designers who could tell me what was opening and when. I regularly entertained several financial consultants who, by analyzing a restaurant's funding and spending, could predict its stability. I spent hours on the telephone with food purveyors and liquor distributors, finding out which restaurants were ordering high-quality goods and which were ordering institutional canned goods, meat, fish, and produce. I talked to chefs, cooking teachers, and food experts, went to every food and wine tasting possible, and spent hours hanging around the test kitchen of *Food & Wine,* where I'd taken on a monthly column parsing ingredients and sampling recipes.

All this background work helped to ease my anxiety, but I still needed a look. The chef's costume that I'd worn for a decade was clearly out of the question. The ensemble that I sported when not in the kitchen—black jeans, a T-shirt, a long tuxedo jacket, and short, black lizard-skin cowboy boots—was equally ill-suited to my new and terribly important position. I needed a wardrobe that would allow me to blend in among the well-cut ensembles that were seated, shoulder pad to shoulder pad, along the velvet banquettes in Manhattan's finest dining rooms.

As the golden era of the young urban professional took shape in New York City, dining out was becoming a form of theater, and the most interesting reviewers were becoming its divas, a new sort of social critic. In order to avoid being snookered by preferred seating, free champagne, or dishes prepared with more than the usual alacrity, however, reviewers had begun donning wigs and gigantic hats.

It offended my sense of substance.

"This is serious business, not a big game of dress-up," I argued as my husband sighed and pulled himself up from the futon, slouched to the former closet that housed our tiny stove, and began spooning espresso into an aluminum pot.

"Considering some of your likely dining companions," he said as the espresso gurgled from the bottom to the top of the little pot on the stove, "I'm not sure you'll need to worry about disguises."

He was right. I had my brothers, and I had my friends from Provincetown, like Murray Moskovitz. Maybe it was time for a trip to the dentist.

Dr. Moskovitz was wearing a strap around his forehead on which a small light was mounted. It looked like a miner's helmet.

"Hmmmm," he said, peering into my open mouth.

"Yes," he said, prodding my gums with a cold metal pick, "I see what you mean."

"Jus a phoo aw-fits," I said through the cotton logs that lined my mouth.

"A look," said Murray thoughtfully. Turning off his headlamp, he pushed his rolling stool back a few inches to observe my face.

"You can close now," he said, lifting a strand of hair that had escaped my ponytail and pushing it up to create a wave that blew back off my forehead. "Your mouth is fine but the hair . . . I think we are going to want to get you into Frederic." Snapping off his latex gloves, he picked up the telephone and called his secretary.

"Carol, get Frederic on the phone and see if he can take Ms. O'Neill today." Hanging up again, he turned back to me. "Get the look and everything else follows." Then, straddling his rolling stool, Murray returned my chair to the upright position, instructed me to rinse, and scooted around to face me.

"Molly, I have a proposition for you," he said intensely, with barely contained excitement. "I will be your social secretary. You need to meet people and I know everybody." In addition, he went on, his staff would make all my restaurant reservations, invite and confirm my dinner guests, keep my calendar, and prepare my expense account. This, Murray pointed out, would free me up for more important things—not only to taste and observe, but also to think strategically about what to review and when to review it, so that I could quickly distinguish myself among the other critics.

In exchange for all this, Murray had only one request: that I let him come along as Amy Rosenzweig and pretend to be the critic. Suddenly the fear and foreboding that had haunted me for months gave way to a feeling of hilarity, and I started to giggle as Murray removed the blue bib that was still clipped around my neck. I told him that it was an offer I couldn't refuse.

"Oh my dear, you have given me the opportunity of a lifetime," Murray said, beaming. "You know how long I've wanted to be a restaurant critic! This is going to be a great adventure."

Then he rolled his stool back to the telephone and dialed James Beard's number.

"Jim," said Murray, "I have someone I want you to meet. The answer to my prayers."

Before our first restaurant visit, Murray and I had each worked out our strategies.

Aping the *New York Times* policy, I planned to visit each restaurant three times and sample each dish twice before writing about it. Like most of my self-styled enterprises, this required the sort of mind-numbing diligence that only the ambition-crazed—or the terrified—could endure. I carried soft-sided notebooks that I'd found at a Korean bookstore in midtown because they were small enough to fit in the palm of my hand and could be slipped, unnoticed, between the folds of a napkin in my lap. I scribbled constantly throughout the meal, noting each presentation, each flavor, the look and feel of the dining room, the gait of the waiters, the conversations that floated around me. Every night, no matter what time I arrived home, I transcribed these notes. In the mornings, I synthesized them into the beginnings of a review and then read the newspapers and trade journals and plied the telephones for restaurant news. I published three columns a week. Between lunch and dinner, I studied the menus I stole and wrote the final reviews.

Murray concentrated on the social aspect of our adventure. We had agreed to dine together Tuesday, Wednesday, and Thursday evenings. We were frequently joined by Elizabeth and Stanley, but in order for me to taste each item on the menu, it was best to invite at least four other guests. As if our evenings out comprised one long debutante season, Murray selected our companions with an eye to weaving me into the social fabric of New York. He also made an effort to recruit the appropriate experts. So, as Italian chic upset the city's long-held bias for French fare, Murray delivered Marcella Hazan and Michael Fields to discuss the change and sample the results. As bows to Asia became trendy and tapas became a way of life, Murray called Barbara Tropp and Jimmy Chin and Penelope Casas to the table.

In addition, while other restaurant critics relied on hats and scarves, Murray created three distinct personae for his critic to assume. After a day performing root canal therapy in midtown, he would jog home and begin the long, arduous process of becoming Amy Rosenzweig, restaurant critic, in disguise.

To test-drive the theme-park restaurants that were designed for tourists, Amy became Debbi Chandler, a busty blonde from Indianapolis who lived in Great Neck and whose cadence had the cantering quality of a PTA member calling to raise funds for the marching band.

For visits to restaurants that were designed to beckon expense accounts, on the other hand, Murray became Dr. Lambert-Schwartz, a lean and erect cardiologist with salt-and-pepper hair who had graduated from the University of Pennsylvania. Dr. El, as she was called at the table, was the guru of the occluded-artery set and well suited to those less artful and more service-oriented restaurants where the tastes of the diners always trump the inspiration of the chef.

But the most exciting restaurants—those whose kitchens were run by a wildly talented chef and whose dining rooms were designed to be a scene—were set aside for Murray's favorite persona, Naomi Levine. Naomi had studied anthropology at Berkeley and had worked for Alice Waters. She was a producer at *Sesame Street,* favored vintage Chanel suits, and wore Victorian lockets on black velvet choker ribbons around her neck. Naomi loved sushi, Thai, French, and anything reminiscent of Chez Panisse. With her town house on Perry Street and her smoky, come-hither voice, Naomi was cooler than any trend.

"I want to make your picture," Andy Warhol told Naomi one night as we sat at the River Café sampling Larry Forgione's new American cuisine and trying not to show how dazzled we were by Manhattan, twinkling like Oz across the black river. Warhol and his crew were regulars in the parties that Murray arranged; so were Perry Ellis, the fashion designer, and Ed Koch, who was then the mayor. Murray knew everybody. He did their teeth. He had a talent for matching personalities with the spirit of a restaurant. I had a talent for evaluating cooking and dining rooms.

Within moments of walking in the front door, I usually knew how many stars a place merited. I could tell by the smell of the place, the expression on the waiters' faces, the posture of the other diners, the emotional valence of the dining room. It comes down to a lack of dissonance: How well does a restaurant deliver on what it promises?

I reserved the highest rating—four stars—for the perfect confluence of business and art. Otherwise, my ratings reflected how frequently or rarely something happened that intruded on that promise. In theory, then, a dive that claimed to be nothing more than a dive but was, from its moist and skunky bathrooms to its rude waitresses and thick crockery, a perfect dive, could—if its cooking was shockingly perfect—earn three stars. And a plush and expensive place aiming to redefine cuisine that fell short of the mark in dozens of tiny ways might earn only one star. I made the subsequent visits, but I was rarely surprised.

There was always a hush about a four-star dining room. If the service and the setting and the wine list supported the artist in the kitchen, the diners felt cosseted even as they were catapulted into a new realm of taste. Their inevitable anxieties—"Uh-oh, look at all these fabulous people . . . am I rich enough, thin enough, savvy enough . . . will I be revealed as an imposter?"— would never be allowed to coalesce into a frown, a nervous casting about, or, worst of all, a raised and beckoning finger.

For the first year or so, it was thrilling to discover New York through its restaurants—and to learn that world well enough to be able to predict its next moves. It was also exciting to figure out the words and rhythms that could create or quell a reader's appetite. I loved the glittering evenings, loved to exhale in the backseat of Murray's car after dinner and deconstruct the dishes and dinner guests as the city slid by outside the car. But as the job became more routine, I began to find Murray's larger-than-life gatherings wearying. In particular, I developed a strong aversion to Naomi, and I began to dread our evenings together.

In the heady food world of the late 1980s, California had come to New York, which meant Naomi's West Coast perspective was useful when assessing the trembling towers of grilled ingredients and flourless chocolate cakes that were suddenly on every menu. But I came to resent her easy opinions and the deference with which she was treated wherever we dined. I really hated her theatrical practice of bending low over her plate and moving her hands to direct the food's aroma to her bobbed and slightly upturned nose—while I was forced to take notes unobtrusively under my napkin. Of course, with the electricity and intrigue typically generated by the parties that Murray arranged, I could probably have set my computer up at the table, run a telephone wire to the maître d' stand, and written and filed my review without risking detection. Perhaps I was beginning to make a name for myself, but not in the places that I cared about most.

"Naomi!" squealed the maître d' at the Gotham Bar and Grill.

"Mademoiselle Levine," purred Maguy Le Coze at Le Bernardin.

"Ciao, bella," whispered Pino Luongo at Le Madri.

The fact that Naomi didn't exist did nothing to assuage my jealousy.

The parties Rosenzweig were always immediately escorted to a table in the center of the dining room. Centerpieces were plumped, maître d's watched, waiters hovered, corks popped giddily out of bottles of Billecart salmon rosé. Other guests stole sideways glances, and chefs, who'd not yet developed the habit of bounding from kitchen to dining room, would peer through the diamond-shaped windows in the swinging kitchen door in order to catch a glimpse of the Very Cool Party. I didn't need a hat. Murray had arranged for his friends Perry and Calvin to dress me, and in my tailored suits and blousy shirts I was just another thirty-something career girl hanging on to the beautiful people. I was invisible.

Luckily, I also had another, even more foolproof method of protecting my anonymity: my brothers.

In 1982, Robert moved to the city to attend the master's program in creative writing at New York University. He was in his bohemian phase and he purchased the essential lifestyle supplies—along with musk-scented candles, black jeans, and T-shirts—from blankets laid out by people selling their belongings on Astor Place. Upon entering stylish restaurants in midtown, he sometimes made the mistake of inquiring about parking.

"I drove my pickup," Robert would explain earnestly to the maître d'. He'd been the beneficiary of one of my father's battered vehicles and, shortly after receiving his first tuition bill, had used the pickup truck to found O'Neill Brothers' Moving Company. He enjoyed flaunting his claim as a working-class hero. As if embodying first one and then the other of our parents' hopes for their progeny, Robert had begun to swing between two visions of his future. In one, he was a moving mogul. In the other, he was an imperious epicurean and the author of the much-heralded novel *Mover's Memoirs*. He would meet me near the front door of the evening's restaurant, unbuckle the thick leather corset that he wore over his T-shirt, and accept a sport coat from the maître d' without breaking character.

"Parking! I can't afford more tickets. One of my guys lost an armoire in the Park Avenue tunnel, another one got busted on one of the parkways where trucks are prohibited. You know I spend a day a week at traffic court?" Then, turning to the maître d': "Let me give you some cards. If one of your customers ever needs a mover, give us a call. I personally guarantee that every guy on the job has at least two years of postgraduate education." When changing homes, Robert claimed, New Yorkers cared more about the quality of the personnel than the appearance of the vehicle.

"I'll give you a ten percent finder's fee," Robert would promise the maître d', coughing as he retied the laces of his high-top sneakers. "O'Neill," he'd wheeze up from the floor near the front door of the restaurant as a line formed behind him, "O'Neill Brothers' Moving: The Civilized Movers."

Kevin was the other O'Neill brother mover. He'd also come to the city with visions of making it. With an undergraduate degree in political science, an interest in gardening, and five summers of professional salad-making experience, Kevin was not sure exactly what he wanted to make it *doing*. In the section of his résumé dedicated to his professional goals, Kevin had stated simply: "Opportunity for advancement." In the meantime, he was managing La Tulipe, a wonderful French restaurant downtown, and helping Robert move households. Kevin had also found that being a mover was an excellent way of meeting available women, another opportunity for advancement that interested him greatly.

"We don't know him," Kevin would say, glancing around to make sure that no models, actresses, or aerobics teachers were noting Robert's discourse or his getup.

"I'm *supposed* to be anonymous," I whispered.

"Yeah," said Kevin, glancing over my head into the restaurant to nod and smile at first one and then another beautiful diner. "Tell me about it."

But Robert had a certain downtown charm. He would regale us with tales of New Yorkers on the move—the man with the glass piano, the couple with the iguana on a leash, the woman with a dozen parrots, the boyfriend with a gun, the wife who could afford only to be moved from the apartment where she'd lived for forty-seven years to the sidewalk in front of the building—that were by turns hilarious and poignant. In this, as well as his constant effort to maintain, adapt, and expand the family myth, Robert managed to remain the glue between us all.

"That's where Dad would have pitched if he hadn't hurt his back," he said one day, slowing the moving van as we drove through Brooklyn in search of wood-oven pizza. "That was Ebbets Field. Now it's a housing project. Where's the religion?"

"This is where it all began," he said excitedly another night as a taxi, ferrying us to a Turkish restaurant, turned onto East Twenty-ninth Street, and the Church of the Transfiguration came into view. "The Little Church Around the Corner. This is where they eloped to after Mom's aunt died. This is where the dynasty began."

No matter what misgivings we had about one another, the O'Neills of New York invariably rediscovered a deep, common bond when the O'Neills of Columbus came to town.

"Jaaaayz," Pat would bellow, when viewing a line of wineglasses set in front of him on a restaurant table, adding, as Kevin quickly surveyed the surrounding room, "you guys got any beer?"

Pat now had a set of twins, and he'd left waterbed sales in order to reestablish himself as an entrepreneur. He offered landscaping services in the summer, wood delivery in the winter, and carting services anytime, and he taught his offspring to answer the telephone as we ourselves had as children: "O'Neills!"

"This place is loose!" he would holler, after driving a truckload of wood or a household to New York City. "Hey, Rob, hey, Kev, we got to go to Yankee Stadium. Hey, Molly, why don't you let me take you to the Cheyenne Diner? I got paid! You just save your money, honey. It'll be more fun than eating frog legs."

"The Cheyenne Diner," Kevin would purr in relief, sliding on his Ray-Bans.

"Nineteen-forties Paramount style, Ninth Avenue," Robert would say, nervously assessing the time of day and the density of the traffic. "The food sucks. You're going to have a heart attack if you don't watch out, Pat. I'll drive."

Mike, on the other hand, would have no part of greasy spoons or out-of-the-way eateries. Since joining my father in the excavating business, he'd replaced the broken-down equipment with gleaming new backhoes and had increased revenues. Much to my father's astonishment, his firstborn son was always current in all payments and taxes. Mike credited his marketing skills for this success. Shortly after joining my father, he'd minted a new corporate identity and had had it printed on the invoices, the business cards, and the doors of the trucks. "O'NEILL EXCAVATING," it read. "WE DIG COLUMBUS!" When visiting New York, Mike, whose starter marriage had ended in divorce, intended to meet beautiful women and rub shoulders with captains of other industries.

"I'm Mike O'Neill," he would announce, sticking out his hand and hovering a little too close to anyone he met. If greeting a man and seeking to reveal something even more impressive than his tall, dark good looks, he would add, "My sister's the restaurant critic."

When extending his hand to a woman, however, Mike would growl softly and, turning to Kevin, say under his breath, "Hurt me."

Robert, Kevin, and I were not unhappy when our visitors headed back west through the Lincoln Tunnel and we could return to our accustomed routine. We dined together three nights a week. I liked to make first visits with a party composed of Kevin, Robert, and two or three low-key members of the food cognoscenti. It was important to experience a restaurant as a tourist or an outer-borough diner would. My brothers guaranteed this experience. In addition, Robert possessed a food memory even more capacious than my own, Kevin had a fine eye for the business of restaurants, and both had acute and well-developed palates.

I ate in twelve restaurants each week and published my opinion of fewer than half of the ones I visited. The readers were, I felt, better served by being told where to go than they were by being told where not to go. With the exception of overrated, highly touted places, I didn't write about restaurants that were tedious or foolish, the ones that were badly imagined or poorly executed. I also ignored those fated to fail by dint of filth, lousy food, shaky financing, poor management, or a calamitous location.

My brothers liked participating in the early elimination round. The surest sign of a troubled restaurant was a fidgeting among us, the barely contained urge to jump from the table and attend to the slouching waiter with the stained apron, the party waving for a check, the stumbling customer in need of an escort, the chef who'd read too much and cooked too little, the gritty salad, the tagliatelle on the far side of al dente, or the sad, dry tuna steak.

"Go home," said Kevin, sounding like a coach releasing a player as he watched a mouse scurry across the floor of a venerable French restaurant near the United Nations.

"Sit down," snarled Robert, after tasting a dish composed of sautéed sweet breads in a raspberry sauce that was served in a hollowed kiwi and was, in his estimation, a strikeout.

Notepad in lap, I noted the misses, the collisions, and the rare, seamless moments of synchronicity. I was at the center of a certain world at a time when that world mattered a lot. For a while there was no place else I wanted to be. Regardless of how they embarrassed me, there were no companions I wanted more than my brothers. Next to Naomi I was a drudge and a rube, but with my brothers, I was the stylish guide, the eternal sophisticate, the chosen—at least I thought I was.

"Follow me," the maître d' would say, once we'd all arrived and Robert had finished distributing his business cards and tying his sneaker. Our host would then lead us to a small table near the bathroom or the kitchen.

In the summer of 1985, Amy Rosenzweig suffered a massive coronary while talking to a group of writers at the Fine Arts Work Center in Provincetown. For the next few years, Murray's personae aged dramatically, although gracefully, without benefit of cosmetic surgery or hair color, and spent more and more time on the Cape.

My husband, who had nothing against Murray personally, was initially relieved by this turn of events. The restaurant critic's life—twelve meals a week in restaurants, most of them group activities—was not what Stanley had had in mind when he dreamed of a marriage between writers.

"There has to be some limit," said Stanley. "This thing is devouring you, you are becoming it, there is nothing left, we have no time alone." He established a one-restaurant-a-week policy for himself and otherwise remained home at the Hotel Woodward, reading or writing. I agreed to take weekends off, but visions of quiet romance quickly gave way to panic.

Not long after I had struck this bargain with my husband, Kevin picked me up for dinner and informed me of a change of plans. We were not spending the evening surveying the clam shacks of Coney Island, he said; we were going to New Britain, Connecticut, to watch our youngest brother play in a double-A baseball game.

"I can't miss a night of work," I cried. "I have a *deadline!*" The O'Neill Brothers' Moving Company had upgraded from a pickup to a panel truck by then. Passersby might have suspected an abduction as Kevin steered toward the West Side Highway.

"Let me out!" I screamed, grabbing for the handle of the door. "What will I do?" I wailed. "Put my name on a white space in the paper? Write a note saying, 'Sorry, but I had to go to a ball game!' I can't waste a night at some ballpark! Are you out of your *mind?*"

Riding high above most traffic in midtown, I saw my life reversing itself. In a sickening *whoosh* I was sucked from restaurants and spit out into a smoky press box in a baseball stadium.

"Noooooooooo!" I screamed, kicking the floor of the vehicle. "Stop the truck! Let me out! Help! Help!"

Kevin was undeterred. "We'll do a double-header the next couple nights," he said. "We'll get to the restaurants, but we have to go watch Paul. Not one of us has gone to watch him play. It's not right." He turned up the collar of his Polo shirt and slid his Ray-Bans onto his nose.

In 1981, the Cincinnati Reds had selected Paul in the fourth round of the major league draft. The telephone on the wall of my parents' kitchen rang with the news. It was one of the few times our mother had seen our father cry. He was sixty-one years old and had waited most of his life for this call.

Paul reported to a minor league team in Billings, Montana, several days after his high school graduation, and throughout that summer and the next he played in Cedar Rapids. But we only saw him when the season ended and he came home to Ohio. In his first few years, my parents could afford only one trip to see their youngest son; the rest of us were busy. We were also bored by baseball and found it difficult to take our little brother's career seriously.

The night that Kevin abducted me to New Britain, my outrage quickly turned to dread of yet another Little League game, and my brother shared the sentiment.

"Pitiful," Kevin yawned as we sat together through several rain delays that night and, after play resumed, the team slipped and slid on the wet outfield and tripped on the baselines.

"*Go, Paul!*" I cheered when he stepped to the plate, adding, under my breath, "Knock in all the runs and get us out of here."

And then, an instant after the pitcher released his first throw, when its destiny became clear, we understood the seriousness of the game Paul was playing. The ball grazed his batting helmet. In the stands along the first-base line, Kevin and I leaped to our feet. Paul threw his bat and, slowly, stormed toward the mound.

"What's he doing?" I panicked.

"Killing the pitcher," said Kevin calmly.

"But he's never had a fight in his life!" I said.

"The pitcher doesn't know that," said Kevin as the dugout cleared and the confrontation turned into an infield fracas. "Wouldn't it scare you to see Paul charging? Look at him. He's getting huge. He's growing up."

The sun was rising when we got close enough to see Manhattan's skyline. With rain delays and extra innings, the game had lasted five hours. Paul was five-for-five and had scored the winning run. After the game, we took him out to eat. The only place open was a Friendly's. I didn't take notes on the meal; instead, Paul borrowed my pen and practiced signing his autograph on the back of the paper place mats and then on a stack of paper napkins. "Paul O'Neill," he wrote. "Paul O'Neill. Paul O'Neill. Paul O'Neill." By the time we left, the table was littered with pieces of paper covered with his signature.

"Don't worry, I picked all of them up," said Kevin, as a view of the city opened like a promise against a pink and orange sky through the windshield of his truck. "Who's working to protect your name in haute and humble eateries nationwide?"

Getting There

By 1990, I'd left *New York Newsday* to begin writing features for *The New York Times,* and I still could not believe my good fortune. While reporting for the paper, I was also looking for stories and recipes for my first book, *The New York Cookbook,* and every taste I pursued took me into a wider world. Courting a street vendor's falafel recipe, I followed him from Manhattan's Diamond District to the outer reaches of Brooklyn and ended up spending weeks immersed in Afghan culture; stalking a superb matzo ball took me inside a Hassidic sect. Investigating the secret of pad thai led me to a group of women who'd earned their freedom from the brothels in Bangkok to which they'd been sold as children. While searching for the perfect fried chicken, I'd been pulled from a church supper in Harlem to a string of African-American churches across the South—and through a brief history of the civil rights movement. Day after day, I walked the city looking for recipes and the stories that went with them. And in the evenings, I cooked.

Sadly, this career change hadn't come about soon enough to save my marriage: Stanley and I had parted ways, wistfully but amicably, in 1987. Still, after such a public life, it was almost a relief to be alone in the large, bright loft into which I'd moved. And after nearly five years of being cooked for, it was exhilarating to be mistress of my own dinner again. My neighborhood was a little dicey, but in my big new kitchen I could cook and serve dinner for twenty, and I often did. When I neglected to invite company, I cooked for twelve, anyway. Then I would wander the halls of my building, knocking on doors and announcing, "Dinner!" If this failed to produce a family-size crowd, I would carry food to the police precinct next door or distribute it to the crack-addicted transvestites who lived on the corner of Thirty-sixth Street and Ninth Avenue.

"Is there something like a little wine around here?" Julia chirped, raising a cleaver above the thigh joint of a rabbit. She and I were cooking dinner in my kitchen with Roger Vergé and Paul Bocuse—who suddenly materialized at the counter beside her and relieved her of the cleaver. Bocuse had huge farmer's hands; unlike Julia's, however, his fingers moved with great finesse once they held a knife. *Thwack, thwack, thwack.* In five strokes, he'd cut through the animal's major joints. At the stove, Vergé was already rendering bacon in a heavy-bottomed stew pot. In the time that it took for me to coax the cork from a bottle of Bordeaux, the two chefs had located the white flour, poured some into a shallow dish, seasoned it with salt and pepper, and dredged the rabbit joints.

The smell of caramelizing apples and toasting crust told me that it was almost time to remove the tarte tatin, which I was baking in a skillet, from the oven. As I got out my Provençal place mats and began setting the table, Julia turned her attention to a vinaigrette. The rest of our dinner guests were due in less than an hour.

When Julia was in town she often came by for dinner, frequently with chefs and other stars in tow. My soirees were becoming famous. My loft belonged to the architect Scott Bromley, who'd also designed Studio 54 and whom I'd met a decade earlier in Provincetown. Scott lived upstairs, and night after night his friends and mine—journalists, artists, designers, chefs, politicians, athletes, and pretty people—gathered at the big, round French country table that I'd installed in the center of my spare, wire-shelved, and white-Formicaed home.

"I'll cover you from the terrace with my Uzi," I promised at midnight, when my guests began peering from my wraparound windows at the huddles of crack dealers and bands of gang members who roved the blocks ten stories below. An occasional rhinestone glint from one of the transvestite hookers who worked the trucks on West Thirty-sixth Street was often the only light.

"Ah ha hah ha!" Julia warbled delightedly. "Oh, what fun, dearie! You're coming along just fine!"

Indeed, at thirty-seven years of age, I was almost the daughter my mother had always wanted. My brothers were still scrambling to find their footing in the world, but I was a postfeminist, postmodern, almost-Gwinn. I could feel the tug of war relaxing at a mitochondrial level. I had arrived!

I'd barely had time to savor this triumph, however, when my brothers began leaving town.

"Where will you get your material?" I said one evening later that month when Robert and I were in his moving van. We'd turned onto Central Park South from Fifth Avenue, narrowly missing several police barriers, and my brother was furious at the street conditions.

"Jesus," he said, "it's like Calcutta."

Robert had finished graduate school and was engaged to a young woman from the Midwest whom he'd met on a moving job. They were preparing to move back to Ohio, where, he said, the streets were wider, less congested, and in better repair. He was going to teach at a small college and he hoped to supplement his stipend by finishing *Mover's Memoirs*.

"You're not going to find glass pianos or pet iguanas in Ohio," I warned him as he edged his truck forward and clicked his tongue at the close-packed traffic. Kevin had already married and moved to Jacksonville, Florida, where he and his wife had opened a futon store. It didn't seem fair. Manhattan was finally my oyster and now my brothers were reverting to suburban fare. The truck stumbled and crashed into a pothole.

"Dammit!" hissed Robert. "I'm so sick of this place. That wasn't a pothole, man, it was a crater! I could've cracked an axle."

"You love your friends here!" I said. "You love hanging out with other writers!" But Robert continued as if he hadn't heard.

"Holes in the street, homeless people everywhere, but let's not talk about it. We are too cool for that."

"There's no La Luncheonette in Ohio," I said.

"We're not raising a family here," said Robert firmly, adding, "If I get an irrepressible urge for french fries at two a.m., I'll go to a McDonald's drive-through."

"You can't go to the drive-through," I reminded my brother. "You don't have a minivan, you're too thin, and your IQ is above the legal limit. Besides, if you go back to Ohio, you'll never finish your book! I thought we came here together! Why are you leaving just when it's getting really fun?"

"Why do you want to live *here*?" asked Robert as his front wheels plunked into another pothole. "Do you want to become just another desperate career woman in a town full of limp guys with fear-of-commitment disorder? Come back to Ohio! You don't want to date some loser who's, like, too short to play so he becomes Mr. Rotisserie Baseball, do you? Mr. I-don't-have-the-grit-to-stand-by-a-narrative-so-I'll-just-live-in-sound-bites. Mr. *Ironic Detachment*. Have you *considered* what a cop-out that is? This place is morally reprehensible and the roads suck. You can't raise a family here!"

I was, in fact, beginning to worry about finding a father for the children I meant to raise. But this frisson of fear only fortified my determination to defend my city of choice.

"You know, Robert, there's still nothing to eat in Ohio!"

"I can cook, Molly," said my brother. "Remember? You taught me how to cook?"

For a year or two, Paul was the only sibling who visited me in New York. This had little to do with any affinity he had for the life I led or the city I lived in. I was wide-eyed and open to adventure, and Paul was a natural conservative; he feared variety and change. By the time he was twenty-two years old, he'd married Nevalee, his childhood sweetheart, undergone a religious conversion, and settled in Cincinnati, less than two hours by car from where we'd grown up. By 1990, however, Paul was playing in the major leagues, and his team, Cincinnati, came into town to challenge the Mets a few times each season.

I did my best to drop everything when Paul came to New York. With Kevin and Robert no longer in residence, I placed a high premium on brothers, especially brothers in need. And, as Paul struggled to distinguish himself in baseball, he certainly appeared to fit in that category.

By major league standards, my brother's salary was still modest and so was his sense of self. I recognized his terror and burn to achieve when I watched him from the family section at Shea Stadium. Just as I sat down to the dark screen of my computer every morning, sure that I'd forgotten how to connect one word to the next, Paul arrived at the ballpark convinced that he would be revealed as an imposter.

Holding the bat in the on-deck circle, my brother would first stare at his hands and then, as he practiced cutting the wood slowly through the air, he would stare down the barrel and move his lips like my father did when he read. I imagined that my brother was trying to persuade himself that he deserved a hit, reminding himself of all the hits that had gone before. The sight made me feel tender and protective of him, the way I had when we were kids.

"Will you pick me up?" Paul said when he called from his room at the Grand Hyatt Hotel in May 1990. He was in town for a two-game series against the Mets and, as usual, he wanted to go out to lunch. "You still have an expense account, right? My meal allowance doesn't buy much more than the greasy spoon."

I was standing on the terrace of my loft, cradling the portable phone as I deadheaded my petunias, and, as usual, I tried to convince him to come to my loft for lunch instead. "You can bring your friends, if you want," I added. "I've got plenty of food in the house."

Since Paul had moved up to the major leagues, I often arranged my out-of-town writing assignments to coincide with his game schedule, and had therefore squired many of his teammates to restaurants in Atlanta, San Francisco, Los Angeles, and Houston. Like them, my brother had initially preferred steakhouses and hotel dining rooms, but he quickly discovered that he needed carbohydrates to maintain his weight and stamina. He also had a taste for good food.

"They want to go to the Palm," he said. "I want to go to Union Square Café. They still have that sushi tuna, right? And pasta? I have to have pasta, too."

In addition to my brother's wariness in New York—he viewed both its littered and graffitied topography and its wild and varied demography with narrowed eyes—I found his ability to inhale platters of *troffiette al pesto* and *fusilli col buco alla carbonara* and still lose weight extremely irritating. I kept reminding myself that, for him, it was a curse. Despite the fact that he ate like a human Hoover and drank high-calorie protein concoctions between meals, his weight was dropping, and he worried about losing strength in the later innings of a game. He alternated between grim resolve and despair. Even his voice sounded thin when he called from hotels on the road after night games.

"Hey, Ollie, it's Oh-Fer," he would say, sounding as hopeless as a country-western song. "Oh-for-five tonight. Isn't that cute? Aren't you proud to be my sister, huh?"

Sometimes, when his game was televised and I watched him struggle, I tried to call him first afterward, and make him laugh. I was famous throughout the family for my superb imitation of our mother. "It's your mother, Paul," I said so convincingly that I could hear him inhale sharply on the other end of the line. "What in the name of God is the matter with you? They're not paying you the big bucks to go oh-fer, buddy boy."

I knew that when his game lagged, Paul's faith and his family were what kept him going, and so I sometimes tried to reframe my insights so that they would square with his worldview. Once when he called me, despairing, I asked my brother what he heard when he was standing in the batter's box.

"Every negative voice in the stadium, everything that I've ever regretted, every time I've stunk it up in my whole life," he replied.

"That's the voice of the devil, Paul," I argued. "Just say, 'Get thee behind me, Satan.'"

The effect of this advice was dramatic—a long, hot hitting streak—but when my mother heard the story, she accused me of betraying the religious skepticism that she and I shared. "Next, you'll pretend that you voted Republican along with your father and brothers," she sniffed. To me, however, it was only a matter of semantics: self-hatred, the devil, the cosmic no, one's inner Inchy—weren't they all essentially the same thing?

"Why me?" Paul said when his timing was off or he couldn't see the ball. I sometimes wondered, though, which was more frightening: failure or success. "Why me?" he added one day over lunch in New York, after confiding his embarrassment that, even at a rookie's salary, he now earned more in a month than his father had ever earned in a year.

I asked myself the same question—"Why me, why am I so lucky?"—most mornings when, arriving at *The New York Times* hours before most of the editorial department, I got into an elevator with the printers. I described them to Paul—bowed and muscular men with large hands. They reminded me of our father, I said, and the mixture of respect and contempt with which they looked me up and down made me painfully conscious of my designer suits.

Two years earlier, having suffered the same sort of massive heart attack that had killed four of his five brothers, my father had had quadruple-bypass surgery—or, as my mother called it, "open heart." He was now seventy years old, but he still couldn't afford to stop working.

"No," we said, when the waiter offered dessert. "Just the check," I added.

"Want to walk a little?" I always asked when we emerged from one of these meals. I never stopped hoping that my youngest brother might come to share my affection for the streets of New York. Only when he said that he couldn't, that he had to get back to the hotel and focus before he got on the bus to go to the stadium, would I remember that I, too, had work to do.

"But you're coming tonight? Right?" Paul asked. "I should have them leave you a ticket at will-call? Hey, thanks for lunch. So will you drop me off? At the hotel?"

Paul and Nevalee had, by then, a seven-month-old son, so it was more difficult for her to join him on the road. Without his family, Paul felt disoriented and bereft.

"Yeah," I said. "I'll be there."

I would go out to Shea early on the 7 train and, swinging my knees over the seat in front of me during batting practice, I would edit my day's work and read the transcripts of the interviews I'd had with chefs and other food experts. As the stadium began to fill, I would read the social histories and anthropology books that I lugged to the games along with food magazines and newspapers in a heavy leather bag on my shoulder. Sometimes, in the long, slow ballet of the game, my ideas coalesced into stories. I also kept a small notebook in my lap; restaurant reviewing had left me capable of making notes without taking my eye off the ball.

I didn't think to ask my friends or colleagues to accompany me to these games, and I was surprised when they began to invite themselves. Why would anyone who did not have a family obligation choose to sit in a beer-drenched stadium and watch a game better seen on television? It did not occur to me that the smell of grass and sweat, of leather, liniment, and wood, might slake the inchoate pastoral yearnings of urban sophisticates. It did not occur to me that my younger brother might be making a name for himself. In fact, I was startled whenever I stood next to him, surprised by his height, his power, the thick cut of his muscles under his increasingly well-made suits.

That May morning, though, as I weeded the window boxes on my terrace and talked to him on the telephone, I knew that Paul was more than able to make his own way down to the Union Square Café. If I could get out to Shea Stadium, the least he could do was save me from an unnecessary cab ride all the way across town to pick him up at the Hyatt.

"I'll wait at the side door," he insisted. "You can just swing by and pick me up and we'll go from there."

"Oh, OK," I capitulated. "I guess it's easier to come to the side door than to get a taxi to stop on Forty-second Street."

"I dunno about that," said Paul. "All I know is that they keep the fans away from that side door."

My parents, too, now started visiting New York City once a year when the Reds were in town. Inveterate bargain hunters, they couldn't resist a two-for-the-price-of-one vacation: for the cost of airfare, they could see two of their children at once. In addition, each of them could, for a few days, inhabit the lives they'd dreamed of when they had taken the train from Columbus to New York City to get married.

Through Paul, my father got to imagine what it might have felt like if he himself had ever made it to the major leagues. In fact, ever since his first day as a professional ballplayer, my youngest brother had been less himself and more an incarnation of my father's big-league ambitions. My mother, on the other hand, had a different agenda, which I—at the opposite end of the birth order and the only daughter—was in charge of executing. When we spoke about an upcoming trip on the phone, she would sound breathless and girlish.

"I'm not coming to New York City to sit in some ballpark, Molly. I'm coming for the restaurants and the theater and the shopping! What are we going to *do*?" she asked eagerly. "I need to get my frocks organized."

I planned our time together assiduously, scrimping for theater tickets, calling in favors so that we could get into the Metropolitan Museum before it opened to the public, rearranging my work schedule so that expense account visits to the best restaurants would be necessary during the few days that my parents joined my brother at the Hyatt. Staying with me proved to be out of the question: both of them were appalled by my neighborhood. "I've *got* to be in a hotel," my mother said firmly, and Paul conferred with his team's traveling secretary to get them a room near his.

When they visited in the early summer of 1991, Paul stayed at the hotel with Dad after breakfast while I took my mother to the Met uptown. By late morning, the two of us were strolling down Fifth Avenue like high school girls on a class trip. "Oh, there's the Plaza, now *that's* where I meant to live! Do they still serve tea in the afternoon?"

Then we stood, side by side—my mother dressed entirely in white, and I in black—in front of the windows at Bergdorf Goodman. "Look, Molly," my mother said, enchanted. Our reflections were superimposed on a grouping of mannequins in Chanel suits. "God, how I envy your life," she continued, as I glanced at my watch. "So many choices, no responsibilities, you're free, you can make a real contribution to society!"

If we hurried, I calculated, we'd still make our lunch reservation: I aimed us toward the hotel and set a snappy pace. "Jesus, Molly, what is this, the New York Marathon?"

Despite my father's frailty, he, too, now loved to be on the move. When the Reds were playing at home, he drove from Columbus to Cincinnati with the regularity of a UPS truck. Long uninterested in travel, he suddenly became enthralled with airplanes, hotels, and National League cities. He was in high spirits when we picked him and Paul up at the hotel: nothing made him happier than spending time with his youngest son.

We took a yellow cab to Le Cirque. Paul sat up front with the driver. "By God, I think O'Neill Excavating could get some roadwork in this town!"

Dad said gleefully from his spot between my mother and me in the back. My mother, extremely distrustful of taxi hygiene, was less sanguine. In an effort to protect her white pantsuit as well as her safety, she was clinging to the strap above the window, trying to maintain minimal contact with the seat as the taxi lurched up Park Avenue.

My father leaned forward into the small opening in the sheet of bullet-proof plastic that separated the front of the cab from the back and peered into the Styrofoam box that was open on the seat next to the driver.

"Black beans!" he hollered to the driver. "I used to have those at a Cuban joint in Tampa when I played ball down there.

"You Cuban, Jose?" asked my father. "What else you got down there? Rice? Pork? Fried banana? What's your name, anyway?"

"Jesus," gasped my mother. She rolled her eyes and stared out the window in an effort to convince anyone who might be looking that her fellow pas-senger was not, in fact, her husband of forty-odd years but instead some stranger with whom she was sharing a ride.

"Think you can give that black bean recipe to my daughter?" hollered my father as the taxi raced to make light after light up Park Avenue. "Maybe she can put it in the newspaper for you."

"I don't think she needs black beans, Chick. She writes for *The New York Times,* not the *Podunk Express,*" said my mother. "Jesus! Paul, tell him to slow down! If we hit another bump like that, it's going to split the grafts on your father's heart wide open!"

"Take it easy!" Paul said sharply to the driver. "You OK back there, little buddy?" he asked.

"Thank God!" my mother said, when a man in a footman's uniform opened her door. "*This* is more like it." She released the hand strap to accept the white-gloved hand offered to her. "This is what I was born for. Now, did you ever for a minute think, Molly, that you'd be the one to follow the Gwinn tradition? You know they had an interest in the Columbus paper."

After pushing out of the taxi behind my mother and winking conspira-torially at the footman, my father countered, "Ah, Boots, the Gwinns got nothing to do with this. Her great-uncle Mark Twain wrote for newspapers and her great-granddad O'Neill was a newspaper man, too."

Taking the two five-dollar bills that I'd passed through the plastic window to him, my youngest brother said, "Since when? I thought he was a ballplayer," and handed the money to the driver.

*   *   *

I remember exactly what I was doing at two p.m. on November 3, 1992. I was preparing to run out of the office and vote for Bill Clinton. Standing next to my desk at *The New York Times,* I had just buttoned up my black cashmere coat when the phone rang; I picked up the receiver on the second ring.

"Your life has just gotten a whole lot better," cried a jubilant voice that, in the pause following this announcement, identified itself as one of my dining partners from my restaurant critic days, a minority owner of the New York Yankees.

"We're bringing one of your brothers back to town!" he hollered. "We traded for Paul!" My desk was on the aisle that ran between "women's sports" (the newspaper's style section) and men's sports (the section of the newspaper dedicated to athletics). Instinctively, I sat down, lowered my head, and covered my face with my hand.

"Isn't that great?" yelled my caller. "Aren't you excited? We're bringing him in for a press conference tomorrow. You gotta come up to the stadium and be there for him. OK? Hello? Hey, you still there?"

In fact, I was not fully present. I was already trying to imagine the immediate consequences of this news. How would my parents feel about losing Paul to New York? How would Paul and Nevalee feel about leaving the house they'd just built in Cincinnati? Where, within driving distance of Yankee Stadium, would they feel safe and comfortable? I was suddenly and fiercely nauseated.

My first book, *The New York Cookbook,* was scheduled to be published the following month. The cover was pinned to the bulletin board on my desk, the book-club orders had been strong, and the initial reviews had been terrific. And yet, I realized, as the other line on my telephone began to flash and the sports editor came up behind me and started *tap-tap-tapping* my shoulder, even this success had failed to move me out of the ballpark and set me in a world of my own.

"They're saying he's not great with the press," repeated my friend on the telephone. "You got to come help him out up here tomorrow."

"OK," I said.

"Also, we haven't reached him. We had to leave a message on his answering machine. Do you know where he is?"

"He's, ah, either playing tennis with my brother Robert or out voting for Bush," I said. Then I put down the phone, ran to the ladies' room, and threw up.

"Paul's going to lose it," said Robert when I reached him by telephone.

"Dad's going to lose it," said Mike.

"Ah, don't be a rube," said my father. "There's no place like New York. That short right-field fence, the history. It's a great move for your brother. He'll do great there. I'm not worried, no, sirree, Bob, I'm not worried about your brother at all," he said before passing the telephone to my mother.

"So," she said, "where are you taking me to lunch?"

My brother and his wife were shocked by the cost of real estate in the city, and the day after he was traded to the New York Yankees, they bought a two-bedroom condo on a golf course in Westchester. I was dumbfounded.

"It doesn't even smell like New York," I said.

"It reminds me of home," said my sister-in-law.

"But you won't all fit in there," I said.

"We don't really live here," said Nev. "We *live* in Cincinnati, we just spend the summer here." In addition to its golf course, their condo complex had a swimming pool, tennis courts, security, valet service, and a nearby playground as well as parking lots where children could throw balls and ride bicycles safely. It also had a very large limo for hire. It was shiny and white and it bore a close resemblance to the cocktail lounge of the Hyatt. When he first went to the Yankees, Paul dispatched the car whenever he felt that those near and dear to him needed protection.

The telephone would ring in my loft in Hell's Kitchen and Paul would say, "Mom and Nev are coming into the city for lunch. I'm putting them in the limo, they'll pick you up." Or, "Dad wants to drive to the park with me. He shouldn't sit there alone for four hours before the game starts. If I send the limo, will you come up and sit with him?"

My father, who had been shrinking since his open-heart surgery, seemed more and more frail. He'd always sailed through his days unburdened by memory and oblivious to time. But after he turned seventy-five years old, this tendency became more pronounced and his doctors began to ask him if he knew the date and the name of the president. When it came to game time, however, my father was punctilious. Six hours before the first pitch was scheduled to be thrown, he would begin dressing for the event, choosing the newest and most expensive sports clothes from his closet, checking them for wrinkles, and matching the ensemble with one of the Tam o' Shanters he'd begun to wear. Finally, he would slide carefully into one of the silk Yankees warm-up jackets that Paul had given him.

"Huh?" he would ask, modeling his ensemble. "OK?" Arriving at the park for batting practice, my father would sit behind home plate, chatting up the ushers as they wiped down the seats, exchanging dining tips with the vendors, and leaning over the rail onto the field to exchange life stories with the groundskeepers.

"Hey ya, Whatsy," he'd say, nodding his head toward Paul and offering his hand to the ticket seller, the young player's wife, the reporter, the security guard, the people in the seats two rows away. "Chick O'Neill, Paul's dad. Grah ha ha!"

In the family section of major league ballparks, my father was not a ditchdigger. He was royalty, and he was beneficent. Over and over again he told the story of the O'Neills. He recited it like a parable of infinite possibility, opening his eyes wide, shaking his head in wonder, and allowing the Polish beer vendor, the Puerto Rican selling coffee, and the Jamaican security guard to imagine that their own great-great-grandson might one day swat for the majors.

The bobbing pompom on the top of my father's hat did terrible things to my youngest brother's heart when he glanced up to the family section from the field. Our father's determination to sit in the stadium while the players stretched and took batting and fielding practice and the grounds crew prepped the field also wreaked havoc on my work schedule.

"I'll send the limo," Paul would wheedle, as if the promise of a Hyatt-on-wheels would, of course, trump my deadlines at the newspaper. My father was unaware of the burden that his pregame activities placed on me. In fact, in his excitement to catch up with people he'd never met, my father barely registered my arrival when I trudged toward him at the stadium.

"Hey ya, honey! Meet ole Whatsy here. Grah ha ha," he'd say, glancing up from a conversation. "Ole Whatsy's son wants to play ball, too, honey!"

As his heart disease progressed and the oxygen levels in his blood began to dwindle, my father's voice got weaker. By 1996, it was so soft and so halting that, on a windy day or when the music was pounding at the stadium, I often had to repeat what he said to his new best friends.

"He asked how many children you have," I said and then, after my father elbowed me and repeated what he had, in fact, said, I issued a correction.

"Actually, he asked how many children you thought I could have if I wait much longer to start having them," I said, adding, "My father wants you to know that I am over forty years old."

Promptness, my father felt, was as important to procreation as it was to baseball games. By then I was the only one of his children who had failed to reproduce. My father was deeply concerned and, after five years of single life in Manhattan, so was I. I was not, however, eager to discuss this situation in the family section of Yankee Stadium and tried to steer these conversations away from marriage and babies and toward cooking. Always eager to keep any dialogue cantering along, my father would cheerfully follow suit.

"He said that if your mother came from the Old Country she probably has a recipe for colcannon and kolache," I said, explaining, "My father thinks I need those recipes to put in my next cookbook."

"You tell 'em, honey," my father wheezed as he gazed at the cool green grass and the tawny diamond below. "You be good."

My mother didn't share my father's concerns, per se.

"Oh, he just thinks that if you haven't procreated you haven't lived, Molly, and that's ridiculous," she said. "If I had it to do over again, I'm not sure I would."

She did, however, have her own questions about the choices I had made. "Where is this newspaper stuff going to *lead,* Molly?" she asked. "Out all the time, eating all the time. When does it get easier? When can you relax? When do you start to make some money?" My brother's salary had, by then, set a new standard for success in our family.

"It just doesn't seem right to me that with no education, some ballplayer can go out there and get paid more for an at-bat than you, with all your education and work, get paid in a year," she said. "Does that seem fair to you? Everybody I know that reads that paper says they read it because of you. Now, I ask you, Molly, shouldn't they pay you more?"

This inequity was only one reason that my family had contempt for the Media. The O'Neills of Ohio held the Media generally responsible for bad news, bad taste, and shattered secrets. The Media—in the form of the sportswriters who occasionally criticized his performance and misquoted him—were also the bane of my brother's career. They hung around his locker, pestered him with stupid questions, and then they misspelled his name.

"Here's your typical Media," my father said once, handing me a sports page in which an African-American player named Eric Davis was identified as Paul O'Neill. Gradually, during the years when Paul played for the New York Yankees and I wrote for *The New York Times,* my family began to view me less as a food writer and more as a member of the Media.

"*Why* do they have to show that?" my mother asked one night as we sat in Paul's condo. My sister-in-law had taken my father to the stadium that evening; my mother and I were baby-sitting and watching my brother on television. He'd taken a third strike and the camera closed in on his face as a life-and-death anguish seized his features and then, in the blink of an eye, deepened into an Old Testament sort of rage.

"My God," she said, as the camera shifted from her son's face to show the dugout, where his teammates, their laughter barely suppressed, were shifting down the bench and away from the watercooler toward which the furious dark cloud of my brother was headed. When my brother decked the five-gallon watercooler, my mother said to me, "Jesus. What is the *matter* with these people? Molly, why can't you talk to them? Do you think this is a good thing for children to see? Their hero destroying somebody else's property? Why can't they respect your brother's privacy?"

For his first five seasons in New York City, Paul's natural elegance, along with the deadly aim of his arm in the field and the long, steady sweep of his bat, had been somewhat eclipsed by his legendary tirades, his implacable perfectionism, the disappointment and rage that he perpetrated on himself and the team's watercooler. His statistics were strong. In 1993, he batted .311. The following year, there was a baseball strike, but he still led the league with .359 and twenty-one home runs. Fans created signs that read, "ONeill," turning the first letter into a target. They waved the signs along the right-field line in 1995, when he hit .300, in 1996, when he hit .302, and in 1997 when he hit .324.

My brother, however, could not stop personalizing the fact that a perfect 1,000 is unknown in baseball, that the game requires one to fail at least twice as often as one succeeds. He blamed himself, and his resulting misery and outrage were, for a time, followed as avidly as his contributions to two all-star teams and the Yankees 1996 World Series championship.

That changed in game five of the 1997 American League championship series in Cleveland. Then, with the Indians needing only one more game to clinch and the Yankees down by a run, Paul came to bat in the ninth inning. With two outs, he hit a ball off the outfield wall. He hit it so hard that the ball ricocheted back to create a play and yet, defying all probability, Paul made it to the base safely. Then, running against all odds, he launched into second base headfirst. I was in New York, watching the game on television, and on the screen it looked like he were flying. "As if," I wrote several days later in *The New York Times,* "by sheer will a man can defy gravity and fate."

That possibility didn't linger. The next batter flied out, stranding Paul and ending the game. The stunned denial on my brother's face as he bent to remove the shin guard he'd worn into the batter's box reflected my own shock. For the first time in my life, I understood the limit of human effort.

His soar to second base, on the other hand, changed the way Paul was seen in New York. The eloquence of his fierce hope—he'd been playing hurt and, caught midflight by a camera, his face was a study in agony—lingered in the public mind. George Steinbrenner, the team's owner, began calling him "the Warrior," in a tone that implied something noble—a knight, perhaps, or a samurai.

"I don't know what he's talking about," said my brother. But the honorific stuck and "The Warrior" joined the repertoire played at Yankee Stadium— "Keep the Faith" by Bon Jovi; "Baba O'Riley" by The Who; "Spirit in the Sky" by Norman Greenbaum; "All Right Now" by Free; "Crumblin' Down" by John Mellencamp; and "Tall Cool One" by Robert Plant—whenever Paul approached the batter's box.

But the warrior's life is not an easy one. By 1998, my father was dwindling dramatically and Paul was haunted by the idea that his game, and only his game, could keep our father alive. His misery was boundless.

"Have you talked to Cheerful?" Robert asked one afternoon when he called me at work.

"Yeah, he called me from the car a few minutes ago from the George Washington Bridge," I said.

"Jayze," said Robert, "he's not going to jump, is he?"

Other than the relief he found in his wife and children, Paul's principal refuge had been the big black Suburban that he drove from Westchester to the stadium. It was the only time he was alone, and the car became his meditation room—the place where he could inhale and exhale deeply, the place where he could visualize winning and pull himself into focus. But by 1997, he was recognized even through the windows of his car and pursued by fans. On a night off, he might park half a block away from a restaurant and in the walk to its front door be asked to sign a dozen autographs. He needed the tinted-windowed anonymity of the big white limo more and more.

"We're going to an Italian restaurant!" my mother announced as I stooped into the open door of the white limo in the spring of 1998. She and my father had driven in from Westchester, where they were staying with Paul.

"We're going to an Italian restaurant," my father repeated mockingly. He flapped his hand like a yapping mouth. My mother pretended not to see and continued.

"I think I like Italian better than French," she said, as I crawled toward the girls' end of the limo. "Except for the wine. I don't like Pinot Grigio."

My brother, who was holding the remote control, muttered, "I don't know why you even bother ordering white wine in an Italian restaurant," and stared at a replay of the Yankees game on the television screen. He now selected our restaurants and paid for our meals. "No way," he'd say, shaking his head violently and waving off any attempt to share the cost. "Jesus," he said now in the limo, shifting uncomfortably and trying to stretch his legs.

"I don't fit," I said, wedging myself between my mother and my sister-in-law. My body was puffy and painful and soft. I'd remarried by this time, and I'd been taking fertility drugs. Except for the month of rest that followed each of my four miscarriages, I had been pregnant for three years. Exhaling, I blew my breath upward over my face. I was always hot.

"Its like a damned submarine in here," said my father, squinting from his spot on the limo's wraparound leather banquette. It was clear to the rest of us that he was simply teasing my brother; like my mother, he was thrilled to be sliding through Manhattan in the big white car. Pressed against his youngest son, my father looked a little like a ventriloquist's dummy in the cocktail-lounge darkness of the car's cabin; his white patent-leather shoes and matching belt glowed, and his one-liners seemed designed both to flatter and provoke his buttoned-down straight man.

"Got that right," said Paul. He glanced out one of the limo's dark windows and then back up at the replay on the bright television screen.

"Can you open a window and let some air into this hearse?" cried my father. Then he began fiddling with the buttons and levers on the car door, knowing that the threat of being exposed would cause the muscles around my brother's jaw to twitch.

"Chick!" my mother said. "He does not *want* people staring and carrying on. And neither do I!"

Heat blasted over me and I jerked around, angry and accusing. After thirty-six months, I still thought that oven doors were opening. I still thought that something I ate was making me sick. I still thought that my clothing was causing my stomach to cramp and my breasts and ankles to ache. I still couldn't believe that the discomfort came from inside me.

"I think you better stop this stuff," said my mother, glancing at my flushed face with concern. "It's not healthy. You've got a stepdaughter and, believe me, Molly, at your age, you don't want to get into an infant." My second husband had come with a sheepdog and a two-year-old daughter from a previous marriage. "Where is Arthur tonight, anyway?" she asked. I explained that he was at home baby-sitting.

"It was nice of him to give you a daughter, honey, I'll give him that," shouted my father. "She looks like you used to, and she's smart like you, too. What'd you say his name was?"

Nevalee started laughing. "Chuckie," she said, fanning my face with the playbill from that afternoon's matinee, "you know your son-in-law's name."

My body was not the only thing that was betraying me. I'd also lost my passion, and sometimes I thought, my talent, for my work. Thinking about food caused my stomach to clench and my esophagus to quiver. I needed several naps a day and frequently excused myself from interviews in order to cry. I thought that I should leave the paper. "Then what?" my mother had asked. Closing my eyes, I leaned back in the seat. The smoky glass that separated the cabin from the driver's seat was hard and cold against the back of my head.

"Don't throw up," I told myself.

"Are these windows sealed shut?" asked my father.

"Are we almost there?" Nevalee asked.

It was rush hour. The sidewalks were crowded with people released from work, people running and striding and signaling taxis. Little gusts of early summer wind tousled skirts and ponytails here, flattened T-shirts and seersucker jackets there. Inside the limo we were breathing stale air.

"The heck with this," cried Paul, suddenly. Leaning forward, his head brushed the ceiling. "Hey," he called up to the driver, "how do you open the windows back here?"

Thin Air

"Give 'em hell, Molly!" rasped my father from the gurney in the back of the ambulance as it zoomed across the George Washington Bridge.

My father believed that all modern medicine men were gougers, fops, and finks. His disgust for the idea of "extreme measures" was complete, and when his health first began to dwindle, he was less interested in his therapeutic options than he was in signing a "do not resuscitate" order. Nevertheless, in September 1999, when he was seventy-nine years old and had run out of other options, he agreed to be flown by ambulance jet from Columbus to New York for an experimental surgery that might open the clogged vessels leading to his heart.

I'd met his plane at the Teterboro airport, and while two attendants rode with my father in the back, monitoring the tubes and machines to which he was connected, I sat in the front of the ambulance. The driver let me work the siren. This gave my father a sense of control over his destiny.

"Let 'er rip, honey," he croaked. His voice was, by then, always weak and hoarse. He was failing rapidly. His oxygen levels were precariously low, he was frequently in pain.

"I wish you'd figured out another way to get here for the play-offs, Dad," I yelled.

"Just you worry about that siren, Sister Sue," he said.

It was rush hour, and I gave my father a running commentary on the traffic, the litter, and all the crimes and acts of indecency that were certainly taking place around us. It was twilight. I told my father that the lights from Yankee Stadium lit up the sky. I told him I thought I saw my brother waving at us and asked the driver if we could turn on WFAN radio station and listen to the pregame show.

"Screw the radio," my father replied. "Just blast yer siren, honey. Give 'em all hell! Floor this sucker!"

That's when I realized that my father—who had an instinctual sense of both the heroic and the inevitable—had come to New York City to die.

"That's it, honey," he rasped from the rear of the ambulance. "The hell with 'em all, let's fly."

My mother had taken a commercial flight from Columbus. The year of constant caring for my father had left her exhausted, nearly as fragile as he was, and, uncharacteristically, afraid. When she walked into my father's room at Lenox Hill Hospital, I was screaming at the pay-for-view administrator on the telephone.

"It *cannot* take an hour to process a payment," I insisted, raising my eyes toward my mother and my free hand toward heaven. "Do you have any *idea* how long an hour is in baseball?" In his bed, my father made a dismissive, airy sound and shook his head wearily, but I would not take no for an answer.

"My father's *got* to watch the game," I reiterated, stamping my brown suede loafer. Rummaging in my knapsack I found a bottle of water and chugged it. Waving the empty bottle, I declared, "It's a matter of life and death!"

"Jesus," said my mother, rolling her eyes. Looking around the room, which was smaller and older than the ones at her hospital in Columbus, she winced and bit her lip. "You better watch out, Molly. This place looks like *One Flew Over the Cuckoo's Nest*," she said. "If you aren't careful, they'll lock you up and then what will I do for dinner?"

"You have got to be kidding me," I screamed.

"Well, of course I am, Molly," said my mother. Closing her eyes and swallowing hard, she added, "It *is* way past my dinnertime, though."

My father was operated on the following afternoon. A small device was inserted into his chest and radioactive particles were shot through the occluded blood vessels around his heart. When he was wheeled back into his room after the procedure, which was a success, my father appeared to be almost comatose, lost in the sort of dreamy netherworld that can claim a young child for hours and hours. The O'Neills of Columbus are not given to displays of affection, but his groggy state suggested that it was safe to say something. Leaning over him to adjust his covers, I told my father that I loved him.

"REALLY?" he yelled, suddenly in full voice, his eyes flying open. "I thought you didn't!"

Stunned, I realized that although we hadn't been close for forty years, I'd never stopped loving him. "I just wish we knew each other better," I said.

"Well, honey," said my father, "now we can get acquainted."

That was one of the last coherent things my father said to me. Somewhere between Ohio and New York, it turned out, he had picked up a staph infection and he spent the last month of his life in Lenox Hill's intensive care unit, drifting in and out of consciousness.

My mother kept her visits short. "I think I'm better at working in hospitals than visiting them," she admitted. Paul was in the bone-crunching home stretch of the baseball season. While he played, I stayed with my father. After his games, Paul drove into the city and sat in intensive care for most of the night. Other brothers flew in and out of New York, but their families and the distances they had to travel meant that I was often alone with my father during the last month of his life. It was the most time we'd spent in each other's company in quite a while.

Events had conspired to return us to the way we'd been best together: one of us vulnerable and nonverbal, the other tender, cheerful, and in charge. For the first time in decades, I forgot about all the other things that I had to do. We spent hours watching the play-offs, my father tethered to life support, me tethered to him. There is a phrase that the Irish use to describe a time and a place in which the boundaries between heaven and earth become porous. They say that "the air is thin." That was how it felt in my father's hospital room, and between us, too, the air was thin. Time collapsed, and my life seemed like an outfit that I'd tried on for only a moment. Any second, my father would come take me out for ice cream.

I remembered how my father taught me to fish in the front yard—the whirring sound of the reel, the feel of his legs behind my back, the smell of Old Spice, the sound of his voice in my ear as he told me to keep my eye on the target and cast my line long. Nothing in my life had ever been as real as that moment. So much of what I'd become since then was because of my father's lesson. Soon after this lesson, however, my father's attention was distracted by the arrival of my brothers. And perhaps that loss explains why I became someone he could never recognize or know.

At this point, in fact, my father seemed only to know Paul. After hours sitting next to his silent form, I was surprised and hurt when my brother walked into the room and my father became—suddenly and in defiance of the most astute medical diagnosis—animated and aware. But as the days passed, his awareness came to matter less than my own. I finally admitted to myself how much we had in common—our easy cheer, our energy, our bullheaded determination, our indiscriminate curiosity, our need to be liked, our ability to unwrap people like presents. Baseball was my father's foil, the thing he used to draw people close and keep them away. Food was mine. My father never really saw me—at least not as an adult. But the things he'd told me when I was a child, the things about who he was and who I was and what mattered in life, were, as it turned out, mostly true. I'd always been my father's daughter.

My stepdaughter, Ariana, was eight years old by the time my father was lapsing in and out of life behind the glass wall of an isolation room in the intensive care unit. Some days he was intubated. Other days, he was breathing on his own. I would put on the requisite gown and mask and mittens and boots and enter his room. The day she visited, Ariana stood outside the glass, making faces, practicing her pliés and twirls, throwing kisses and waving.

"Hi, honey!" my father said, waving back.

"That's my little doll," he confided, pulling my arm so that I bent down low and close to listen. "That's my little girl. By God, you better believe you'll be hearing from her one of these days."

Even after my father seemed reduced to nothing more than biological function, we kept the television in his room tuned to baseball. The machines registered his response to games one and two of the World Series. Shortly after the Yankees won game three, my father died.

On the other side of town, I'd jumped from bed and run to the telephone before the first ring of the hospital's call sounded. At home in Westchester, Paul was still awake. His hand was already on the receiver when the hospital called him.

Paul played the next night. Pat and Mike went to the stadium, but I stayed home. I'd planned to run up to Westchester to sit with my mother, but several newspapers had asked for obituaries, and I was still writing and answering reporters' calls by the time the first pitch was thrown. I watched the game on television. On the screen Paul was gaunt and pale, and suddenly no longer young. Was this really my little brother? The baby I'd carried on my hip into the backyard and watched toddle toward first base? I'd only turned away for a moment, it seemed, and he was gone. It was all gone.

The Yankees won that night; our family agreed that Dad wouldn't have died had he not been convinced that the victory was assured. After the final out, when the team ran onto the mound for the champions' hug, my youngest brother suddenly appeared on the television screen. He was locked in an embrace with Joe Torre. His face was pressed into the manager's shoulder, and he was sobbing. Paul still cringes and leaves the room when the clip is replayed. I still think it was his finest moment.

Small Ball

Lots of New Yorkers were anxious about game five of the 2001 World Series.

After the World Trade Center was leveled, concerns about both the propriety and the safety of large public gatherings had prompted Major League Baseball to suspend play for a week. Baseball justice—for millions of fans the highest moral arbiter—demanded that the Yankees return from this hiatus and win the 2001 play-offs. And they had. The same justice demanded a World Series victory, as well. But as the postseason ran into November, the Yankees' triumph over the Arizona Diamondbacks seemed less than assured. A new sense of vulnerability had entered the national consciousness. The venerable, the iconic, and the righteous all seemed at risk. Fans and players alike felt threatened by the unexpected.

Arizona was young and erratic and unlikely. The players made silly mistakes and the more experienced Yankees easily parlayed these into important outs and runs. But again and again, with the deadliness that comes from not yet knowing the cost of dreams, the younger team had erupted into grandstand-pleasing feats and victories. Facing game five of the 2001 World

Series, Arizona was leading three games to one. The Yankees had to win the game—the final home game of the series—to stay alive.

My brothers and I shared the predictable postseason excitement as well as the post-9/11 misgivings with thousands of others. But we also had a private source of anxiety. Our youngest brother had decided to retire. Game five would be his last game at Yankee Stadium.

For twenty years, Paul's career had been our family's organizing principle. His game had kept us connected to something greater than ourselves as well as to one another. What would we talk about if not Paul's hot streaks and slumps, his glory, his torment, the arms he threw up to heaven, the dirt he kicked on his way back to the dugout, the batting helmets he hurled? Whom would we make fun of? Where would we get together if not to watch Paul play? Who would we be without baseball?

Kevin was the only immediate family member who'd decided not to attend the game; pointing out that he had a wife and daughter to think about, he'd refused to come up from Florida. The rest of my family was passionately preoccupied with logistics. What time should we convene at Paul's condo in Westchester to proceed to the stadium? What route—and what form of transportation—would be most advisable?

"Subway, just like everybody else," said Pat. His truck, which resembled the beaters that my father had driven, had not been able to make the trip and, unwilling to fly, he'd convinced a childhood friend to drive him to New York.

"No way," said Robert. In addition to teaching, Robert also ran Paul's Web site and memorabilia business. At card shows and public appearances, he positioned himself as Paul's bodyguard. "That's what they'd blow up first," Robert declared. "I have two kids at home. I can't take that risk."

"Well, I think you're nuts to go at all," said my mother. "Why in the name of God would you want to go sit in the freezing cold? I'm staying at Paul's and having a nice dinner and watching it on the big screen with the children."

"We can't *not* go, Mom," said Mike, adding, with a straight face, "Is the limo bulletproof?"

"There's twelve of us, we can't all fit into the limo," said Nevalee. "I'm going to rent a Comfort Coach."

"No way!" snorted Pat. "If I go down, I don't want my grandchildren saying, 'He got blown up in a Comfort Coach.' I don't! I want them saying, 'My granddaddy was blown up with thousands of other Americans who loved the game too much to stay home!'"

"I'm not sure we should go," said Nevalee. "What would happen to all the kids if we got blown up?"

"Well," said my mother, "don't look at me!"

But just as I was rarely involved in my brothers' sporting disagreements, I stood separate from this battle. I was, however, in the cool, fallen-leaf nights, already missing my brother the baseball player. I was missing the phone calls, the stadium, the dinners, and even the limo rides; all the bridges we'd built between our different temperaments and different worlds. Paul was going back to Ohio; I'd be the only O'Neill left in New York.

But the loss that I dreaded most was something less obvious. For nine years, Paul and I had, without realizing it, continued our parents' contest. Our other siblings had gotten on with their lives, leaving the two of us in New York City dueling to dominate the family story. As my brother discussed retirement, I realized that I was playing tug-of-war with someone who was about to let go of the rope.

The windows of the Comfort Coach were tinted; the seats were as large as La-Z-Boy recliners. There was also a large conference table behind the driver set with mountains of sushi, steamed shrimp, and antipasto, along with buckets of iced Kendall-Jackson Chardonnay and, for Nevalee and me, twenty-ounce bottles of Diet Coke: we were doing Weight Watchers.

"Did you see the news?" asked Nev as I slid into the seat next to her and reached for a shrimp.

"They're saying the stadium is the number-one target. My parents are going crazy, the kids are begging me to stay home with them. I decided not to go, but then Paul called and said I had to. If it's going to get bombed, I want us to go together, but I want my kids there, too, and Paul said no way."

"Well, who does *he* think he is, Shirley Temple?" I asked, using my mother's voice. The bus was suddenly quiet: our mother was supposed to be at Paul's house with all the children.

"Oh my God," said Nevalee, "you should have heard her this morning at the mall. I found this black Armani sweater—the perfect butt wrap—and she says, 'If you don't want people noticing it, what the hell are you *wrapping* it for?' Then, when I started to tie it around my waist, just to make sure it covered, she starts in about the cost."

I nodded. "My Gawd, Nevalee, how can you waste your money like that? Why don't you just wear an apron backwards? Jesus, I'll knit you a butt wrap for half that price."

"That's exactly what she said," cried my sister-in-law. "She cracks me up. Gosh, I think I'm going to have to use my carb points on wine. I'm so nervous."

"I'll show you carb points," Mike said, standing up in the aisle of the Comfort Coach, sucking in his abdomen and flexing his biceps. "Like a rock," he said, driving the heel of his fist into his stomach. "Two-ten, cholesterol one-fifty, eleven percent body fat. Working out every day."

"Looking good!" said Nevalee, who had never lost her cheerleader's cadence. "Maybe we should talk about some Grecian Formula," she added.

"Maybe we should talk about paying retail," Mike said, reaching down to pick up the pullover that was folded neatly on the lap of Sandy, his wife.

"Missoni," he said, waving the garment. "One-fifty, down from fifteen hundred, sixty-five-percent cashmere."

"Sweee-eet," cheered Nev.

"Kmart," bellowed Pat, tugging at the baby blue polo shirt he was wearing. "Three for ten dollars, down from eleven ninety-five, mostly polyester." Then, pulling at the sleeve of the Yankees warm-up jacket that he was sitting on, he yelled, "Paul's closet, grah ha ha!"

Across the aisle, Robert rolled his eyes and continued talking to one of Paul's high school friends.

"You can't make a living writing," said Robert. "I'm thinking of getting into documentary films. Maybe doing a late-night cable show on poetry, like Letterman, you know, but with poets. What do you think?"

From the other end of the Comfort Coach, Mike yelled, "I think the remuneration may not be at the Letterman level, Rob." Since finishing his business degree and saving the excavating company, Mike moved through the world like a highly profitable year-end report. His success had, ultimately, allowed my father to retire.

"Everybody better take their own tickets," said Nevalee. Pushing up from her seat, she took a wedge of cardboard strips from her purse, fanned them out, and began distributing them. "In case we get separated."

"We appreciate you guys!" Pat paused in front of each officer and offered his hand as we stop-started in the teeming crowd from the subway toward the press gate. "You guys are doing a darned wonderful job! Thank you!" Pat's accent, his booming voice, the wallet sticking out of the back pocket of his jeans, identified him as a foreigner. Still, my brother felt that he should clarify his status.

"We're not even from New York, we're from Ohio!" he hollered at the cops. "Hey, I was down at Ground Zero this morning and I'm tellin' you, you're all heroes, you know that? Thank you. We appreciate it."

Pat worked the security force like a politician visiting a battlefield. The cops smiled tolerantly and most shook his hand. Mike, Robert, Nevalee, and the rest of the crew from the Comfort Coach had managed to lose us in the crowd.

"Just doing your job! No problem-o," yelled Pat when a guy who looked like airport security pulled him over just outside the press gate. "Bet you hear a lot of Spanish around here, huh?" he added, as he turned his pockets inside out at the guard's request. His wallet thudded to the ground, followed by a cascade of loose change and then a flurry of Dentyne wrappers, empty wintergreen Life-Saver rolls, and several plastic coffee-stirring sticks.

"Hey, you get any suicide bombers yet? Any suspicious characters?"

"Jesus, Pat," I hissed, "shut up."

The security officer regarded him as he might a convicted felon until a voice called out to us. From the opposite side of the gate, the Yankees' traveling secretary had recognized me. "It's OK, they're family!" he shouted. "Let 'em in!"

Without taking his eyes off Pat, the guard nevertheless nodded to a colleague—"Arms out!" she barked—who swept us with an electric wand. Then he put my bag on the belt of an X-ray machine.

By this time, the secretary had pushed his way back through the crowd. Crouching to pick up the contents of Pat's pockets, he shooed us toward the turnstile.

"Sorry," he whispered. "It's just crazy; sixty thousand fans and all we need is one nut. Sorry."

As Pat and I were shepherded ahead of the crowd and toward the turnstile, dozens of fans politely stood aside to let us pass; they smiled, they nodded, they shushed their children.

"It's OK, Mr. O'Neill," said the traveling secretary quietly. "Just go through the gate, Mr. O'Neill, enjoy the game."

Like a zombie, my brother finally moved into the stadium ahead of me. Just inside the gate, he leaned against a concrete column and crouched to tie one of his sneakers. When he stood up, I could see that he was pale.

"I was just frisked coming into a ballpark," he said quietly. "Do you realize we were frisked and metal-detected to get into a ballpark? A *ballpark*! It's all over, honey. That's all she wrote for our world."

Pat took a deep breath and exhaled. Then he stuck his hands deep into the pockets of his jeans, pulling them lower on his hips. "OK," he said, "let's go."

Behind us, a little voice from the line outside the gate screeched, "Whose family?" Sitting on his father's shoulders, wearing a blue satin yarmulke that bore the New York Yankees insignia, a little boy was pointing over the crowd toward Pat and me. His voice ripped the air like locked brakes on a car careening our way. "Daaad?" he shrieked. "Daaaaad? Whose family?"

Turning to face the little boy, my brother Pat clenched his fists, raised both his arms to embrace the crowd, threw back his head, and bellowed into the greasy concrete tier overhead: "WE ARE THE O'NEILLS!"

Turning to display the big white letters that spelled "Yankees" across the back of his borrowed jacket, Pat spread his arms wide and did a little shimmy. Then he looked over his shoulder, waved to the crowd, and yelled: "THANK YOU ALL FOR JOINING US TONIGHT. THANK YOU! THANK YOU! THANK YOU, NEW YORK!"

"They gotta play small ball tonight," said Pat, shivering next to me in the stands in left field. A row behind us, Robert expanded on this theme.

"The accumulation of doing little things right," he said, "the interdependency. Forget swinging for the fences, forget stardom, just get the next out, just move the runner ahead. That's what you learn as you age in this sport, and that's how they're going to win tonight."

"Is that so, Charlie?" asked Mike, referring to our father's habit of predicting a game hours before the first pitch was thrown. In fact, it was not until the ninth inning, when they were trailing by two and had two outs, that the Yankees rallied and tied the score. Three innings later, at midnight, they won the game. But for most of the evening, the situation looked grim. Paul was 0-for-3.

It was far too cold for baseball that night. "Football weather," said Mike indignantly.

"You'd think the richest franchise in baseball could shell out for a few space heaters," growled Robert from deep under the collar of his bomber jacket. "I mean, what about the players? Do you know how injury escalates in the cold?"

I ran up to the press box several times just to get warm. I was there once when my brother stood in the on-deck circle, kick-kick-kicking his leg and swinging the bat slowly, staring down its barrel. "Twenty years in the major leagues, his last at-bat, and he's still trying to get it right," hooted one of the reporters. My brother grounded out.

I was willing to blame the weather. So were Mike and Pat and Robert. "Hot chocolate!" they said whenever I rose from my seat.

"Coffee! Tea! Anything warm," they said from beneath mufflers and collars, reaching for their wallets and adding, "Here, you want some money?"

"I should have brought a thermos of broth," I fretted.

"Yes, you should have," said Mike.

"I'm going to call Kevin," I said, and an inning later, "I better call Mom."

After several hours, I could no longer leave my seat. We were all hunched into ourselves, our chins pulled low beneath our collars. We'd wrapped cashmere scarves around our heads. We'd crossed our arms over our chests and tucked our hands up the opposite sleeves of our coats, giving us the appearance of being in straitjackets.

By the bottom of the ninth, the Yankees were still trailing—2–0—when New York took the field. Beneath the collar of my jacket, I was blowing loudly into my sweater to create patches of warmth, so the roar barely registered at first. But then the wave of sound that had started up in the right-field stands swept around the stadium and finally reached us and suddenly, we were all on our feet, chanting with the crowd almost before we'd registered what we were saying.

Paul Oh-ne-Uhl, Paul Oh-ne-Uhl, Paul Oh-ne-Uhl.

Paul had had a bad game and their team was losing, but it didn't matter; 56,018 Yankees fans had risen from their seats to recognize my brother as he trotted out one final time to the position that he had occupied for nine years. Play was stopped. The stadium seemed to shake. There was no doubt about it: the fans were going wild. And in that moment, as we pushed to our feet and opened our lungs and began to roar, my brothers and I were finally just like everybody else.

Epilogue: American Cuisine

In the final scenes of a video tribute made in honor of his retirement, Paul's three children congratulate their father on his career. The oldest, Andy, who most resembles Paul, says matter-of-factly, "Way to go, Dad." The youngest, Allie, says, "I love you, Daddy." The middle child, Aaron, who was eight years old at the time, says, "Congratulations, Dad," pauses for a moment, and then, staring into the camera, he adds, "Boy, am I glad it's over."

"It cracks me up every time," said Paul as he unpacked the container of giant prawns that a restaurateur friend had flown in from Italy to Cincinnati and prepared for our family's summer gathering at Pat's house. Lifting each steamed and chilled pink body as carefully and tenderly as if it were an infant, Paul arranged the prawns on a platter.

"Sometimes I watch the end over and over, you know, Molly, the way you used to listen to some records," he continued. "I can't believe how young they look. Four years is a long time in a kid's life."

Looking up from the stove where he was sweating leeks and proscuitto and potatoes for his famous mussel and saffron chowder, Robert said, "Forty *minutes* is a long time in an entrée's life, Paul."

Like batters vying for the better spots in the lineup, the two had competed for the main-course position in the meal. Robert had capitulated, finally, and agreed to make the appetizer. But, just as he had fumed at Little League teammates whose play did not match his pitching, Robert resented Paul's tardiness.

"I don't know why you *have* to do the entrée when you *know* you are going to get the prawns and you *know* it's going to make you late," he said.

"He can't do the prawns ahead," said Paul. "They dry out."

"We don't *need* the prawns, Paul," said Robert. "*I'm* making the appetizer, you're making the entrée. Why do you have to bring prawns? There's already too much food."

Since Paul's retirement, discussions over the merits of a slider versus a sinker have given way to debates over the efficacy of hickory chips as opposed to vine cuttings on the grill, the exact definition of al dente, and the better choice for baked halibut—wasabi butter? a mixture of olive oil, garlic, olives, and red pepper? a marinade of lime and mango with a touch of Thai chili paste? My brothers ridicule one another for everything they don't know. They ridicule one another for pretending to know everything.

"What did *you* make, Mike?" asked Robert when Mike and Sandy walked in. She was carrying a platter of mint-chocolate brownies.

"I made her make brownies," replied his older brother, adding quickly, "But I can grill. You want me to grill something? I got a top-of-the-line gas model with the built-in cutting board in my backyard."

When they discuss the meals they've had and the meals they are planning to prepare, my brothers remind me of the young cooks who worked in my test kitchen ten or fifteen years ago. Most of the recipes also sound familiar to me, like the names of people in my high school graduating class. While my brothers have gone gourmet, I've become more interested in everyday cooking. I've been traveling around the country collecting family recipes and their stories. After decades of chronicling the ways that food can be used to distinguish a person or a group of people from others, I've become fascinated by how cooking holds people together, how it knits generations and communities. I organize fund-raising potlucks to fight hunger and I gather heirloom recipes; I feel lucky that neither meat loaf nor macaroni vanished while I was looking the other way.

"You can't write the history of American food without the recipe for my hickory-smoked steak," Pat shouted over from the oil-drum smoker he was tending across the yard. In the kitchen, Robert was still huffing about Paul's late arrival.

"The meat's going to be ready and the fish isn't even started," he said, stirring heavy cream into his chowder. *Tsk-tsk-tsking,* Robert began to remove the mussels he'd previously steamed from their shells.

"Leave those out of mine! I can't stand mussels," said my mother, walking into the kitchen carrying a large pan of cherry crisp. "Can somebody take this for me? Oh, Paul, you got the shrimp!"

In the breezeway connecting the kitchen and the backyard, Kevin and I were pulling the husks away from ears of corn and removing the silk. We planned to rub half the corn itself with lime butter and the other half with ancho pepper butter, pull the husks back up, tie them with butcher twine, spritz them with water, and give them to Pat to cook in his grill. Kevin, who was visiting with his family from Florida, only buys organic and he only buys wholesale. We were facing a bushel of corn, as well as looks of incredulity from my sisters-in-law, who were holding small plastic glasses of wine and perched on white plastic chairs nearby.

"Too much work," said my mother, walking from the kitchen into the breezeway, where beverages were already iced down in large tubs. "I can't stand cooking anymore. Where's the Chardonnay? Isn't it party time?"

Paul, who had renovated the room that once housed his baseball memorabilia in order to create space for a wine cellar in the basement of his home in Cincinnati, said, "We've got something we want you to taste, Mom. Nev, did you open that Pinot?"

And then, having finished arranging the shrimp, he positioned a bulb of garlic on the counter under the heel of his hand and leaned into it, breaking the mass into dozens of purple cloves. With the seriousness of purpose he once applied to hitting, he then peeled the cloves one by one, sliced them into translucent wafers, and began pressing them into the halibut steaks that he'd arranged, on olive oil, in a baking pan. Carefully then, practicing the rocking motion he'd observed on Food TV, he began to julienne red bell peppers.

"Can somebody help me pit these olives?" he asked. "Preheat the oven, will you, Rob?"

From outside, Pat yelled, "Is somebody making mashed potatoes?"

"We have potatoes in the chowder," yelled Robert, bending over the counter to tear the basil leaves that, along with saffron threads, he would add to his chowder just before serving. "We're not going to have them *again.*"

"Yeah, we are," said Pat, who, like our father, believes that there is no such thing as too many potatoes. "You can't have hickory steak without mashed potatoes. Molly, will you make them and don't, like, add fish eggs or anything, OK?"

Signaling silence from those of us facing her, Nevalee walked out of the kitchen and into the breezeway, stuffing one of Sandy's mint-chocolate brownies into her mouth as she did so.

"Don't tell Paul," Nevalee whispered.

"Give me a bite," whispered my mother.

"Go ahead," yelled Paul from the kitchen. "Just don't talk about it all night long like it's a mortal sin."

"Rob, can you put a pot of water on for potatoes?" I called.

"No," sniffed Robert, who was by then using a steak knife to cut the oil-cured black olives and remove their pits.

"You know I tried a lot of wood before I chose hickory," said Pat. "I mean, I've been chopping firewood and cooking on it for twenty years. I am willing to bet that I put as much thought into the effect of hickory on prime, aged strip steaks as the forefathers put into figuring out that ash makes the best bat for a hide-covered ball. You know my steaks, Molly. You want the recipe. It's *original,* unlike those of others I know, not to mention any names, who get their recipes from *TV.*"

The smoke was, by then, clouding over the kitchen window, making it difficult to see the field that lay behind the house. Pat lives in a farming town outside Columbus. His ranch-style home is the most modest of all of ours, and yet it is where we meet most often. Settled in the middle of three flat acres, it bears a striking resemblance to the house on Cooke Road where we grew up. After the backyard and second garage, there is a baseball diamond. In the last picture taken of him, my father was walking with Pat, away from the camera, toward that field.

My fourteen nieces and nephews had been taking batting practice as we cooked that Sunday in late July. The sound of bat against ball and impassioned debates over scoring decisions rose, from time to time, above the clatter of pots and pans and various points of contention in the kitchen.

As Robert turned his attention to a vinaigrette and Kevin carried the corn out to Pat's barbecue, Paul placed his halibut in the oven. Dinner was almost ready when my nieces and nephews trotted from the ball field into the backyard.

"When are you coming?" one called. "Dad? You said."

"You promised!" another cried. "Nine innings, kids against adults."

"Come on," said another.

"I want you to eat first," said Pat.

"It's time for a clubhouse break," Robert called.

"Dinner first, then ball," said Paul.

"Finally," said my mother, holding her wineglass high as my sisters-in-law bit their lips and avoided one another's eyes. "My Gawd, Molly, maybe it was all worthwhile."

Author's Note

The characters in this book are real, but I have altered some descriptions and used pseudonyms in order to protect the privacy of those who preferred not to be identified. This is a work of nonfiction; however, memory is at best self-serving. I have deliberately omitted or streamlined certain chapters of my life, so as not to exhaust the reader; I have also, for obvious reasons, reconstructed a great deal of dialogue. Whenever the narrative strays from the literal, however, I have tried to remain faithful to the emotional truth of the characters and their story.

Acknowledgments

For encouraging me to write this book, I am grateful to the late Mark Rosenberg and Mary Frances Fisher, as well as Isabel Allende, Guillaume Betbeder, and Stanley Dry. For insisting that I write this book, I thank Andrew Wylie.

Alice Truax, friend and editor, helped me imagine and shape this book, and for this, as well as for her unflagging commitment to words and her ability to supply the courage to write them, I am deeply grateful. I am also indebted to Nan Graham and Alexis Gargagliano for their faith in this work, their excellent structural suggestions, and their wise editing. For giving me the space and succor it takes to find one's voice, I thank the Corporation of Yaddo.

My mother, Virginia O'Neill, spent nearly a year collating family documents and writing her memories of our life, and this helped stir my own. My brother Pat O'Neill recalls every play of every Little League game in which any family member ever played, and this was almost as invaluable as his unfailing good humor and his gigantic heart. I also relied on my brother Robert, whose mind for dates and dialogue and baseball history is almost matched by his ability to parse and correct everything from facts to syntax in a text. It is not easy to be written about, and I am also grateful to each of my brothers for being large enough to suspend their own versions of our lives long enough to improve mine.

Kae Dineno energetically conducted valuable cultural and historical research for me. I also thank the Ohio Historical Society and, for his excellent social history of Columbus, Professor Henry L. Hunker. In Nebraska, I am grateful to the Ravenna Genealogical and Historical Society and to the historian and author Winona Snell for her tireless pursuit of the facts of the O'Neill family. In the final months of his life, my late uncle Jack O'Neill was extremely forthright in discussing my father's childhood, an act of courage in a family bound by secrets. My aunt Peg was also very helpful. She wishes to note, however, that whenever an O'Neill mouth is flapping the lies are flowing.

I want to thank Charlene Jendry at the Columbus Zoo for sharing her memories of the young Colo and also for arranging a face-to-face with the gorilla, who is now fifty years old.

In recalling Northampton, I am grateful to the historical work of Kaymarion Raymond, the staff of Off Our Backs, and Diane Damelio, Oceana O'Connelly, and Marjorie Posner. In recalling Provincetown, I am grateful to Mary Jo Avelar as well as Billy Mavis, the late Howard Mitchum, Lincoln Sharpless, and Clem Silva.

To those who read various drafts of this manuscript and improved it with their generous comments—Noel Brennan, Ed Breslin, Peter Davis, Nancy Hechinger, Suzannah Lessard, Judith Nichols, Mike Sokolov, Helen Tworkov, and Vincent Virga—I am indebted.

List of Illustrations

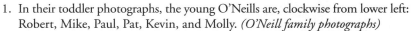

About the Author

For a decade, Molly O'Neill was the food columnist for the *New York Times Magazine* and the host of the PBS series *Great Food*. Her work has appeared in many national magazines, and she is the author of three cookbooks, including the award-winning *The New York Cookbook*. She lives in New York City.